CATS ARE BETTER THAN MEN

Cats Are Better than Men

Beverly Guhl

Hodder & Stoughton

LONDON SYDNEY AUCKLAND

First published in the United States of America in 1994
by Doubleday, a division of Bantam Doubleday Dell Publishing Group, Inc.

First published in Great Britain in 1994
by Hodder and Stoughton, a division of Hodder Headline PLC

British Library Cataloguing in Publication Data
Guhl, Beverly
  Cats are Better Than Men
  I. Title
  818. 5402
ISBN 0–340–62477–9

Printed and bound in Great Britain by
Mackays of Chatham PLC, Chatham, Kent

Hodder and Stoughton Ltd
A Division of Hodder Headline PLC
338 Euston Road
London NW1 3BH

To cats and men everywhere,
without whom this book could not have been written

Beverly Guhl has designed and marketed everything from greeting cards and stationery to decorative magnets, record albums, and mugs. She has also written and illustrated two previous books: *Purrfect Parenting* and *Teenage Years—A Parent's Survival Guide*. The mother of two college-age children and one cat, she lives in Austin, Texas, where she is Director of Graphics for the Texas Department of Protective and Regulatory Services. Although a staunch supporter of human rights and gender equality, she says she would probably vote for a cat if one ran for office.

CATS ARE BETTER THAN MEN

They never complain about your weight.

They never accuse you of being
too emotional.

Is dis my itty bitty Kitty? Es it is! It IS my itty bitty Kitty!! Oooooh, Mummy wuvs her itty bitty...

They can show their emotions.

They take an interest in your work.

They never leave the seat up.

They don't care how much money you spend.

They don't use up all the hot water.

🐾

They don't need to see a shrink.

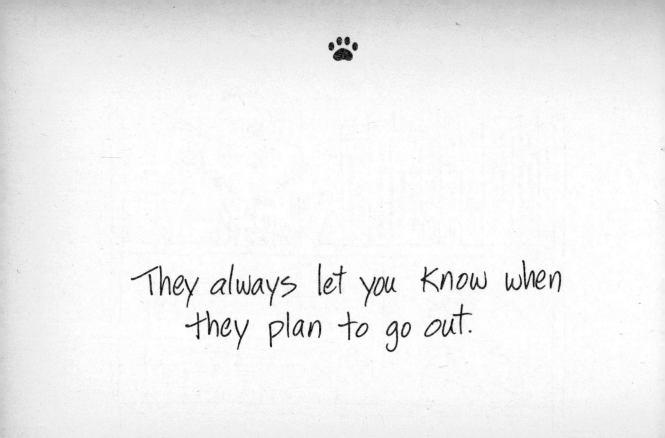

They always let you know when they plan to go out.

They're eager to please you.

They never have other plans.

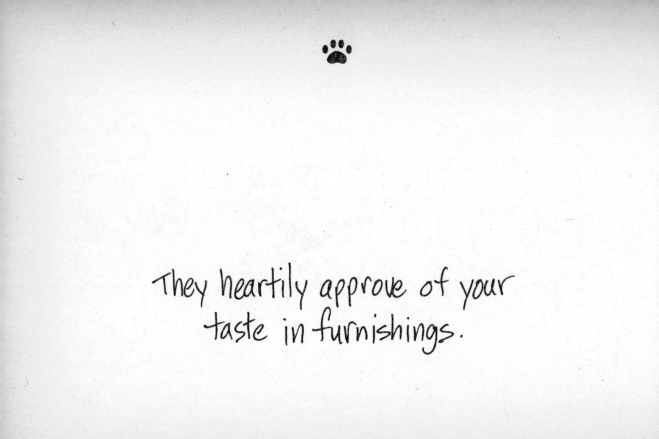

They heartily approve of your
taste in furnishings.

They don't complain about work
or their boss.

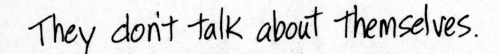

They don't talk about themselves.

They're kissable, and there's
no beard burn.

They don't require closet space.

They don't cheat on you.

They listen to your problems.

They never try to make you
feel guilty.

They don't care what you wear to bed.

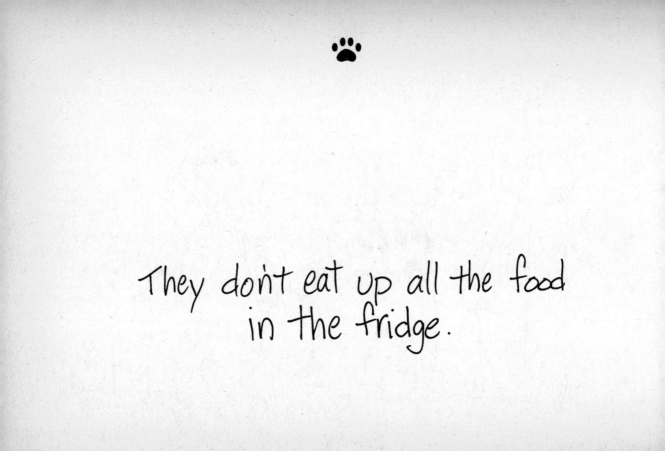

They don't eat up all the food
in the fridge.

They never say they'll call
then never call.

They LOVE yard work.

They like to snuggle all night long.

They never break dates at
the last minute.

They're never late for dinner.

Their grooming habits are
never in question.

They never complain about your cooking.

...or your friends...

...or your new hairdo.

They don't work weekends.

They never ask to borrow money.

They _LOVE_ leftovers.

They think you look wonderful
in the morning.

They can take care of themselves
when you go out.

They don't leave smelly socks
all over the house.

They never make you feel stupid.

They're always bringing you gifts.

They don't hide behind a newspaper.

They love your fuzzy terry bathrobe as much as you do.

They don't care if you don't shave
your legs for days or weeks.

They _LOVE_ your mother.

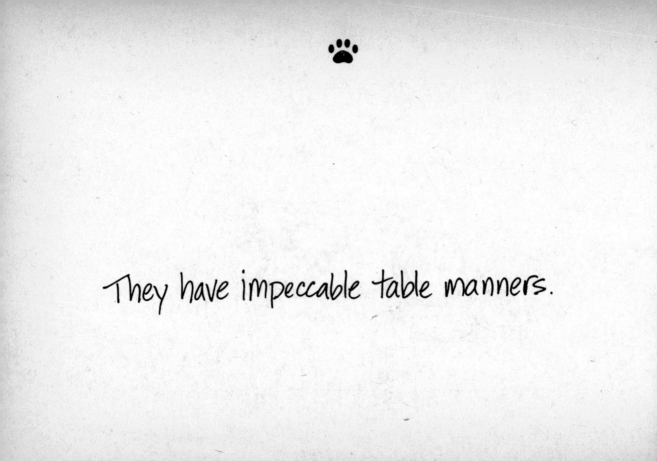

They have impeccable table manners.

They're never on the phone.

🐾

They like romance novels, too.

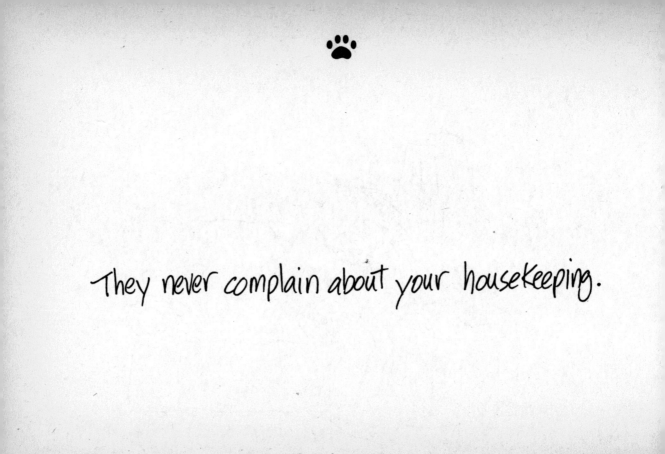

They never complain about your housekeeping.

They don't watch sports on TV.

They love dinner parties.

They don't hog the covers or snore.

PURE

ANDREW MILLER

SCEPTRE

First published in Great Britain in 2011 by Sceptre
An imprint of Hodder & Stoughton
An Hachette UK company

3

Copyright © Andrew Miller 2011

A CIP catalogue record for this title is available from the British Library

Hardback ISBN 978 1 444 72425 7
Trade Paperback ISBN 978 1 444 72426 4

Typeset in Janson Text by Hewer Text UK Ltd, Edinburgh

Printed and bound by Clays Ltd, St Ives plc, Bungay, Suffolk

Hodder & Stoughton policy is to use papers that are natural, renewable
and recyclable products and made from wood grown in sustainable
forests. The logging and manufacturing processes are expected to
conform to the environmental regulations of the country of origin.

Hodder & Stoughton Ltd
338 Euston Road
London NW1 3BH

www.hodder.co.uk

ANDREW MILLER

was born in Bristol in 1960. He has lived in Spain, Japan,
Ireland and France, and currently lives in Somerset.
His first novel, *Ingenious Pain*, was published by Sceptre
in 1997 and won the James Tait Black Memorial Prize
for Fiction, the International IMPAC Dublin Literary
Award and the Grinzane Cavour prize in Italy. He
has since written four novels: *Casanova*, *Oxygen*, which
was shortlisted for the Whitbread Novel Award and
the Booker Prize in 2001, *The Optimists*,
and *One Morning Like a Bird*.

In memory of my father, Dr Keith Miller,
and of my friends, Patrick Warren
and George Lachlan Brown.

FIRST

The time will come when the sun will shine only on free men who have no master but their reason.

Marquis de Condorcet

1

A young man, young but not *very* young, sits in an anteroom somewhere, some wing or other, in the Palace of Versailles. He is waiting. He has been waiting a long time.

There is no fire in the room, though it is the third week in October and cold as Candlemas. His legs and back are stiffening from it – the cold and three days of travelling through it, first with Cousin André from Bellême to Nogent, then the coach, overfull with raw-faced people in winter coats, baskets on their laps, parcels under their feet, some travelling with dogs, one old man with a cockerel under his coat. Thirty hours to Paris and the rue aux Ours, where they climbed down onto cobbles and horse-shit, and shifted about outside the haulier's office as if unsure of their legs. Then this morning, coming from the lodgings he had taken on the rue – the rue what? – an early start on a hired nag to reach Versailles and this, a day that may be the most important of his life, or may be nothing.

He is not alone in the room. A man of about forty is sitting opposite him in a narrow armchair, his surtout buttoned to his chin, his eyes shut, his hands crossed in his lap, a large and rather antique-looking ring on one finger. Now and then he sighs, but is otherwise perfectly silent.

Behind this sleeper, and to either side of him, there are mirrors rising from the parquet to the cobwebbed mouldings of the ceiling. The palace is full of mirrors. Living here, it must be impossible not to meet yourself a hundred times a day, every corridor a source of vanity and doubt. The mirrors ahead of him, their surfaces hazed with dust (some idle finger has sketched a man's bulbous cock and next to it a flower that may be a rose), give out a greenish light as if the whole building were sunk, drowned. And there, part of the wreck, his own brown-garbed form, his face in the mottled glass insufficiently carried to be descriptive or particular. A pale oval on a folded body, a body in a brown suit, the suit a gift from his father, its cloth cut by Gontaut, who people like to say is the best tailor in Bellême but who, in truth, is the only tailor, Bellême being the sort of place where a good suit is passed down among a man's valuables along with the brass bed-warmer, the plough and harrow, the riding tack. It's a little tight across his shoulders, a little full in the skirts, a little heavy at the cuffs, but all of it honestly done and after its fashion perfectly correct.

He presses his thighs, presses the bones of his knees, then reaches down to rub something off the ankle of his left stocking. He has been careful to keep them as clean as possible, but leaving in the dark, moving through streets he did not know, no lamps burning at such an hour, who can say what he might have stepped in? He scrapes at it with the edge of his thumb. Mud? Hopefully. He does not sniff his thumb to enquire.

A small dog makes its entrance. Its claws skitter on the floor. It looks at him, briefly, through large occluded eyes, then goes to the vase, the tall, gilded amphora displayed or abandoned in one of the room's mirrored angles. It sniffs, cocks its leg. A voice – elderly, female – coos to it from the corridor. A shadow passes the open door; the sound of silk hems brushing over the floor is like the onset of rain. The dog bustles after her, its water snaking from the vase towards the crossed heels of the sleeping man. The younger man watches it, the way it navigates across the uneven surface of the parquet, the way even a dog's piss is subject to unalterable physical laws . . .

He is still watching it (on this day that may be the most important of his life, or nothing at all) when the door of the minister's office opens with a snap like the breaking of those seals they put on the doors of infected houses. A figure, a servant or secretary, angular, yellow-eyed, signals to him with a slight raising of his chin. He gets to his feet. The older man has opened his eyes. They have not spoken, do not know each other's names, have merely shared three cold hours of an October morning. The older man smiles. It is the most resigned, most elegant expression in the world; a smile that appears like the flower of vast, profitless learning. The younger man nods to him, then slips, quickly, through the half-open door of the office for fear it might shut on him again, suddenly and for ever.

2

'St Augustine,' says the minister, holding between two fingers a part-devoured macaroon, 'informs us that the honours due to the dead were intended, principally, to console the living. Only prayer was effective. Where the corpse was buried was irrelevant.' He returns to the macaroon, dips it in a glass of white wine, sucks at it. Some crumbs fall onto the papers piled on his immense desk. The servant, standing behind his master's chair, looks at the crumbs with a kind of professional sorrow but makes no attempt to remove them.

'He was an African,' says the minister. 'St Augustine. He must have seen lions, elephants. Have you seen an elephant?'

'No, my lord.'

'There is one here. Somewhere. A great, melancholy beast that lives on Burgundy wine. A gift from the king of Siam. When it arrived in the time of His Majesty's grandfather, every dog in the palace hid for a month. Then they grew used to it, began to bark at it, to bait it. Had it not been hidden away, perhaps they would have killed it. Fifty of them might have managed.' He glances across the desk at the young man, pauses a moment as though the elephant and the dogs might also be figures in a parable. 'Where was I?' he asks.

'St Augustine?' says the young man.

The minister nods. 'It was the medieval Church that began the practice of burying inside churches, in order, of course, to be near the relics of the saints. When a church was full, they buried them in the ground about. Honorius of Autun calls the cemetery a holy dormitory, the bosom of the Church, the *ecclesiae gremium*. At what point do you think they started to outnumber us?'

'Who, my lord?'

'The dead.'

'I don't know, my lord.'

'Early, I think. Early.' The minister finishes his macaroon. The servant passes him a cloth. The minister wipes his fingers, puts on a pair of round-rimmed spectacles and reads the sheet of manuscript on the top of the pile in front of him. The room is warmer than the anteroom, but only by a very little. A small fire crackles and occasionally leans a feather of smoke into the room. Other than the desk there is not much in the way of furniture. A small portrait of the king. Another painting that seems to depict the last moments of a boar hunt. A table with a decanter and glasses on it. A heavy porcelain chamber pot by the fireplace. An umbrella of oiled silk propped under the window. Through the window itself, nothing but the ruffled grey belly of the sky.

'Lestingois,' says the minister, reading from the paper. 'You are Jean-Marie Lestingois.'

'No, my lord.'

'No?' The minister looks back at the pile, draws out a second sheet of paper. 'Baratte, then. Jean-Baptiste Baratte?'

'Yes, my lord.'

'An old family?'

'My father's family have been in the town, in Bellême, for several generations.'

'And your father is a glover.'

'A master glover, my lord. And we have some land. A little over four hectares.'

'Four?' The minister allows himself a smile. Some powder from his wig has whitened the silk on his shoulders. His face, thinks Jean-Baptiste, if it were continued outwards a little, would come to an edge, like the blade of an axe. 'The Comte de S— says you are hard-working, diligent, of clean habits. Also that your mother is a Protestant.'

'Just my mother, my lord. My father . . .'

The minister waves him to silence. 'How your parents say their prayers is of no interest. You are not being considered for the post of royal chaplain.' He looks down at the paper again. 'Schooled by the brothers of the Oratorian Order in Nogent, after which, thanks to the generosity of the comte, you were able to enter the Ecole Royale des Ponts et Chaussées.'

'In time, my lord, yes. I had the honour of being instructed there by Maître Perronet.'

'Who?'

'The great Perronet, my lord.'

'You know geometry, algebra. Hydraulics. It says here that you have built a bridge.'

'A small bridge, my lord, on the comte's estate.'

'A decoration?'

'There was . . . It had some aspect of that, my lord.'

'And you possess some experience of mining?'

'I was for almost two years at the mines by Valenciennes. The comte has an interest in the mines.'

'He has many interests, Baratte. One does not dress one's wife in diamonds without having interests.' The minister has perhaps made a joke and something witty though respectful should be said in return, but Jean-Baptiste is not thinking of the comte's wife and her jewels, nor of his mistress and her jewels, but of the miners at Valenciennes. A special kind of poverty, unrelieved, under those palls of smoke, by any grace of nature.

'You yourself are one of his interests, are you not?'

'Yes, my lord.'

'Your father made gloves for the comte?'

'Yes, my lord.'

'I might have him make some for me.'

'My father is dead, my lord.'

'Oh?'

'Some years past.'

'Dead of what?'

'An affliction, my lord. A slow affliction.'

'Then no doubt you wish to honour his memory.'

'I do, my lord.'

'You are ready to serve?'

'I am.'

'I have something for you, Baratte. An enterprise that handled with the necessary flair, the necessary discretion, will ensure this progress of yours does not falter. It will give you a name.'

'I am grateful for your lordship's trust.'

'Let us not speak of trust just yet. You are familiar with the cemetery of les Innocents?'

'A cemetery?'

'By the market of les Halles.'

'I have heard of it, my lord.'

'It has been swallowing the corpses of Paris for longer than anyone can remember. Since the days of antiquity even, when the city barely extended beyond the islands. It must have been quite tolerable then. A patch of ground with little or nothing around it. But the city grew. The city embraced it. A church was built. Walls built around the burying ground. And around the walls, houses, shops, taverns. All of life. The cemetery became famous, celebrated, a place of pilgrimage. Mother Church made a fortune from burial fees. So much to go inside the church. A little less to go in the galleries outside. The pits of course were free. One cannot ask a man to pay to have his remains piled on top of others like a slice of bacon.

'They tell me that during a single outbreak of the plague fifty thousand corpses were buried at les Innocents in less than a month. And so it continued, corpse upon corpse, the death-carts queuing along the rue Saint-Denis. There were even burials at night, by torchlight. Corpse upon corpse. A number beyond any computation. Vast legions packed into a smudge of earth no bigger than a potato field. Yet no one seemed troubled by it. There were no protests, no expressions of disgust. It may even have seemed normal. And then, perhaps it was a generation ago, we began to receive complaints. Some of those who lived beside the cemetery had started to find the proximity an unpleasant one. Food would not keep. Candles were extinguished as if by the pinch of unseen fingers. People descending their stairs in the morning fell into a swoon. And there were moral disturbances, particularly among the young. Young men and women of hitherto blemishless existences . . .

'A commission was established to investigate the matter. A great many expert gentlemen wrote a great many words on the subject. Recommendations were made, plans drawn for new, hygienic cemeteries that would once again be outside the city limits. But recommendations were ignored; plans were rolled and put away. The dead continued to arrive at the doors of les Innocents. Somehow room was found for them. And so it would have continued, Baratte. We need not doubt it. Continued until the Last Trump, had it not been for a spring of unusually heavy rainfall, five years past now. A subterranean wall separating the cemetery from the cellar of a house on one of the streets over-looking it collapsed. Into the cellar tumbled the contents of a common pit. You may, perhaps, imagine the disquiet felt by those who lived above that cellar, by their neighbours, their neighbours' neighbours, by all those who, on going to their beds at night, must lie down with the thought of the cemetery press-ing like the esurient sea against the walls of their homes. It could no longer hold on to its dead. One might bury one's father there and not in a month's time know where he was. The king himself was disturbed. The order was given for les Innocents to be shut. Church and cemetery. Shut without delay, the doors locked. And so, despite the petitioning of His Grace the Bishop, it has remained ever since. Shut, empty, silent. What is your opinion?'

'Of what, my lord?'

'Could such a place simply be left?'

'It is hard to say, my lord. Perhaps not.'

'It stinks.'

'Yes, my lord.'

'Some days I believe I can smell it from here.'

'Yes, my lord.'

'It is poisoning the city. Left long enough, it may poison not just local shopkeepers but the king himself. The king and his ministers.'

'Yes, my lord.'

'It is to be removed.'

'Removed?'

'Destroyed. Church and cemetery. The place is to be made sweet again. Use fire, use brimstone. Use whatever you need to get rid of it.'

'And the . . . the occupants, my lord?'

'What occupants?'

'The dead?'

'Disposed of. Every last knucklebone. It will require a man unafraid of a little unpleasantness. Someone not intimidated by the barking of priests. Not given to superstitions.'

'Superstitions, my lord?'

'You cannot imagine a place like les Innocents does not have its legends? It is even claimed there is a creature in the charnels, something sired by a wolf in those days – nights we should say – when wolves still came into the city in winter. Would you be scared of such a creature, Baratte?'

'Only if I believed in it, my lord.'

'You are a sceptic, no doubt. A disciple of Voltaire. I understand he particularly appeals to young men of your class.'

'I am . . . I have heard, of course . . .'

'Yes, of course. And he is read here too. More widely than you might guess. When it comes to wit, we are perfect democrats. And a man who had as much money as Voltaire cannot have been entirely bad.'

'No, my lord.'

'So you do not jump at shadows?'

'No, my lord.'

'The work will be both delicate and gross. You will have the authority of this office. You will have money. You will report to me through my agent, Monsieur Lafosse.' The minister glances over Jean-Baptiste's shoulder. Jean-Baptiste turns. On a stool behind the door a man is sitting. There is time only to notice the long, white fingers, the long limbs dressed in black. The eyes also, of course. Two black nails hammered into a skull.

'You will tell Lafosse everything. He has offices in Paris. He will visit you at your work.'

'Yes, my lord.'

'And you will keep the nature of your business to yourself for as long as is practicably possible. The people's affections are unpredictable. They may hold dear even a place like les Innocents.'

'My lord, when am I to begin this work?'

But the minister is suddenly deaf. The minister has lost interest in him. He is turning over papers and reaching for his little glass, which the servant, moving around the desk, guides into his outstretched fingers.

Lafosse rises from his stool. From the depths of his coat, he takes a sheet of folded and sealed paper, then a purse. He gives both to Jean-Baptiste. Jean-Baptiste bows to him, bows more deeply to the minister, steps backwards towards the door, turns and exits. The man who was waiting with him has gone. Was he an engineer too? That Jean-Marie Lestingois the minister mentioned? And if the yellow-eyed servant had looked at him first, would he be the one now charged with the destruction of a cemetery?

He gathers up his riding coat from where he left it draped across the chair. On the floor, the dog's urine, having exhausted its momentum, is slowly seeping into the wood.

3

For a corridor or two, a wing, he is sure he is retracing his steps. He passes windows big enough to ride a horse through, even, perhaps, an elephant. He descends flights of curving steps past enormous allegorical tapestries that shiver in the autumn draughts and must have exhausted the sight of scores of women, every detail detailed, stitch-perfect, the flowers at the foot of Parnassus, French country flowers – poppies, cornflowers, larkspur, chamomile . . .

The palace is a game, but he is growing tired of playing it. Some corridors are dark as evening; others are lit by branches of dripping candles. In these he finds jostling knots of servants, though when he asks for directions they ignore him or point in four different directions. One calls after him, 'Follow your nose!' but his nose tells him only that the dung of the mighty is much like the dung of the poor.

And everywhere, on every corridor, there are doors. Should he go through one? Is that how you escape the Palace of Versailles?

Yet doors in such a place are as much subject to the laws of etiquette as everything else. Some you knock upon; others must be scratched with a fingernail. Cousin André explained this to him on the ride to Nogent, Cousin André the lawyer who, though three years younger, is already possessed of a sly worldliness, an enviable knowledge of things.

He stops in front of a door that seems to him somehow more promising than its neighbours. And can he not feel an eddy of cool air under its foot? He looks for scratch marks on the wood, sees none and gently knocks. No one answers. He turns the handle and goes in. There are two men sitting at a small, round table playing cards. They have large, blue eyes and silver coats. They tell him they are Polish, that they have been in the palace for months and hardly remember why they first came. 'You know Madame de M—?' asks one.

'I am afraid not.'

They sigh; each turns over a card. At the back of the room, a pair of cats are testing their claws on the silk upholstery of a divan. Jean-Baptiste bows, excuses himself. But won't he stay to play a while? Piquet passes the time as well as anything. He tells them he is trying to find his way out.

Out? They look at him and laugh.

In the corridor once more, he stops to watch a woman with heaped purple hair being carried horizontally through a doorway. Her head turns; her black eyes study him. She is not the sort of person you ask directions of. He descends to the floor below on a narrow stone screw of service stairs. Here, soldiers lounge on benches, while boys in blue uniforms drowse curled on tables, under tables, on window seats, anywhere there is space for them. Towards him come a dozen girls running half blind behind their bundles of dirty linen. To avoid being trampled, he steps (neither knocking nor scratching) through the nearest door and arrives in a space, a large, spreading room where little trees, perhaps a hundred of them, are stood in great terracotta pots. Though he is a northerner, a true northerner, he knows from his time waiting on the Comte de S— that these are lemon trees. They have been lagged with straw and sacking against the coming winter. The air is scented, softly green, the light slanting through rows of arched windows. One of these he forces open, and climbing onto a water-barrel, he jumps down into the outside world.

Behind him, in the palace, countless clocks sing the hour. He takes out his own watch. It is, like the suit, a gift, this one from Maître Perronet upon the occasion of his graduation. The lid is painted with the masonic all-seeing eye, though he is not a mason and does not know if Maître Perronet is one. As the hands touch the hour of two, the watch gently vibrates on his palm. He shuts its case, pockets it.

Ahead of him, a path of pale gravel leads between walls of clipped hedge too tall to see over. He follows the path; there is nothing else to guide him. He passes a fountain, its basin waterless and already full of autumn leaves. He is cold, suddenly tired. He pulls on his riding coat. The path divides. Which way now? Between the paths is a little arbour with a semicircular bench and above the bench a stone cupid mottled with lichens, his arrow aimed at whoever sits below him. Jean-Baptiste sits. He unseals the paper Lafosse gave to him. It contains the address of a house where he is to take up his lodging. He opens the mouth of the purse, pours some of the heavy coins into his hand. A hundred livres? Perhaps a little more. He is glad of it – relieved – for he has been living on his meagre savings for months, owes money to his mother, to Cousin André. At the same time he can see that the amount is not intended to flatter him. It feels closely calculated. The going rate for whatever he is now, a contractor, a state hireling, a destroyer of cemeteries . . .

A *cemetery*! Still he cannot quite take it in. A cemetery in the centre of Paris! A notorious boneyard! God knows, whatever it was he had expected on his journey here, whatever project he imagined might be offered to him – perhaps some work on the palace itself – this he had never dreamt of. Could he have refused it? The possibility had not occurred to him, had not, in all likelihood, existed. As to whether digging up bones was compatible with his status, his *dignity* as a graduate of the Ecole Royale des Ponts et Chaussées, he must try to find some way of thinking of it more . . . abstractly. He is, after all, a young man of ideas, of ideals. It cannot be impossible to conceive of this work as something worthy, serious. Something for the greater good. Something the authors of the Encyclopedie would approve of.

In front of the bench, a dozen sparrows have gathered, their feathers puffed against the cold. He watches them, their ragged hopping over the stones. In one of the pockets of his coat – a pocket deep enough to put all the sparrows inside – he has some bread from the breakfast he took in darkness, on horseback. He bites into it, chews, then pulls off a corner of the bread and crumbles it between thumb and finger. In their feeding, the little birds appear to dance between his feet.

4

On the rue de la Lingerie, her chair positioned at the right-hand side of the window in the drawing room on the first floor, Emilie Monnard – known to everyone as Ziguette – is gently sucking her lower lip and watching the day close over the rue Saint-Denis, the rue aux Fers, the market of les Halles. The market, of course, has long since been packed away, its edible litter carried off by those who live on it. What remains, that trash of soiled straw, fish guts, blood-dark feathers, the green trimmings of flowers brought up from the south, all this will blow away in the night or be scattered by brooms and flung water in tomorrow's dawn. She has watched it all her life and has never wearied of it, the market and – more directly in her view – the old church of les Innocents with its cemetery, though in the cemetery nothing has happened for years, just the sexton and his granddaughter crossing to one of the gates, or more rarely, the old priest in his blue spectacles, who seems simply to have been forgotten about. How she misses it all. The shuffling processions winding from the church doors, the mourners tilted against each other's shoulders, the tolling of the bell, the swaying coffins, then the muttering of the office and finally – the climax of it all – the moment the dead man or woman or child was lowered into the ground as though being fed to it. And when the others had left and the place was quiet again, *she* was still there, her face close to the window, keeping watch like a sister or an angel.

She sighs, looks back to the street, to the rue aux Fers, sees Madame Desproux, the baker's wife, coming past the Italian fountain and pausing to talk to the widow Aries. And there, up by the market cross, is Merda the drunk. And that is Boubon the basket-maker, who lives alone behind his shop on the rue Saint-Denis . . . And *there*, coming from the end of the rue de la Fromagerie, is that woman in her red cloak. Did Merda just call something to her? It must relieve him to insult a creature lower even than himself, but the woman does not pause or turn. She is too used to the likes of Merda. How tall she is! And how absurdly straight she holds herself! Now someone, some man, is talking to her, though he keeps himself at a distance. Who is he? Surely not Armand (or should one say, it is all too likely to be Armand)? But now they part and each is soon lost to view. When darkness falls, some among those men who, in the light, tease her or insult her, will pursue her, make an arrangement, a rendezvous in a room somewhere. Is that how it works? And once they are in the room . . . Ah, she has imagined it, pictured it in great detail, has even, in the privacy and firelight of her bedroom, made herself blush furiously with such thoughts, sins of the mind she should confess to Père Poupart at Saint-Eustache, and perhaps would if Père Poupart did not look so like a scalded pig. Why are there no handsome priests in Paris? One has no inclination to confess anything to an ugly man.

'Anyone interesting in the street, my dear?' asks her mother, coming into the room behind her, a candle in her dimpled hand.

'Not really.'

'No?'

Madame Monnard stands behind her daughter, strokes the girl's hair, absently winds a finger in its beloved thickness. On the rue aux Fers, a lamp-lighter is propping his ladder against the lamp opposite the church. In silence they watch him, his neat ascent, his reaching into the glass head with his taper, the blossoming of yellow light, his swift descent. When Madame and Monsieur Monnard first came to the house, there were no lamps at all on the rue aux Fers and hardly any on the rue Saint-Denis. Paris was darker then, though everyone was accustomed to it, inured.

'I am afraid,' says Madame, 'that our new lodger has become lost. As he is from the country, I very much doubt he will be able to find his way among so many streets.'

'He can ask people,' says Ziguette. 'I suppose he can speak French.'

'Of course he can speak French,' says Madame, uncertainly.

'I think,' says Ziguette, 'he is going to be very small and very hairy.'

Her mother laughs, covers her mouth, her little brown teeth, with her hand. 'What silly notions you have,' she says.

'And he eats,' continues Ziguette, who since earliest girlhood has been given to flights of this kind, sometimes amusing, sometimes alarming, 'only apples and pig's feet. And he wipes his fingers on his beard. Like this.'

She is miming it, clawing her fingers through the air beneath her shapely pink chin, when, with a clatter of wooden sabots, the servant girl comes in.

'You have not seen anyone, have you, Marie?' asks Madame.

'No,' says Marie, stopping in the gloom by the door, her young and sturdy figure braced as if for some accusation.

'Your father assured me he would be home early,' says Madame to her daughter. 'It would be most unfortunate if we had to receive him ourselves. Marie, Monsieur Monnard has not sent some message, has he?'

The girl shakes her head. She has been the servant there for eighteen months. Her own father was a tanner in the faubourg Saint-Antoine, dead of the typhoid when she was too young to remember him. Like everyone else in the house, she suffers from dreams.

Dusk gives way to the first of the night. Madame Monnard lights more candles. She pokes the fire, carefully. They burn wood, and wood is expensive. A little log no longer or thicker than a man's arm costs twelve sous and one needs twenty such to keep a fire burning all day. She sits, picks up the edition of the *Journal des Dames Modernes* she and Ziguette were so entertained by yesterday and turns again to the illustration of the savages, noble savages – great lords in their own savage kingdoms – whose faces were fantastically printed from chin to eyes with blue tattoos, swirls and spirals like plans for formal gardens. Just imagine if their lodger should arrive with such a face! What a coup! Better even than the pianoforte (and what a triumph that had been, the instrument raised up on a pulley like a cow being rescued from a quarry, then swung through the window, half the neighbourhood looking on). A pity it cannot be kept in tune. It drove Ziguette's poor tutor almost to tears, though it must be admitted Signor Bancolari was the sort of gentleman never far from tears.

On the floor below, the street door thuds. A draught, finding its way up the stairs, ripples the candle flames in the drawing room and a few moments later Monsieur Monnard appears. He is still wearing his leather apron from the shop, the leather dark with use, with age, though why it should be necessary for him to wear an apron at all given that he has no fewer than three perfectly competent apprentices to do all the polishing and sharpening is quite beyond Madame Monnard's understanding, quite beyond. Her husband, however, must be master in his own house.

They greet each other. He greets his daughter, who is now at the piano stool picking out notes that may or may not be part of some melody she knows. He takes off his wig and scratches hard at his scalp.

'Still no sign of our guest?' he asks.

'Ziguette,' says Madame Monnard, 'has been saying the most ridiculous things about him. She thinks that because he is from Normandy, he will not speak French.'

'In Brittany,' says Monsieur Monnard, 'they speak something quite impenetrable. It's thought they learnt it from the gulls.'

'Why is he coming, anyway?' asks Ziguette. 'Wasn't he content at home?'

'I assume,' says her father, 'that he intends to make his fortune. Isn't it why anyone comes to Paris?'

Marie asks if she should bring in the soup. Monsieur wishes to know what kind of soup they have today.

'Bones,' says Marie.

'She means from Tuesday's veal,' says Madame Monnard. 'To which we have added any number of pleasant things.'

'Like pig's feet,' says Ziguette, which sends her mother into trills of delighted laughter.

5

He arrives between the soup and the serving of a little stew, also made with the remains of Tuesday's veal. He had not intended to arrive so late, nor in darkness. His luggage, a large, ribbed trunk (one rib cracked when it was unloaded from the top of the coach), is carried between himself and an enormous mute boy, some relation of the people he lodged with last night by the coaching offices.

'We were afraid you had become lost!' calls Monsieur Monnard, affably, from the top of the first flight of stairs. 'Lost entirely.'

'I was at Versailles, monsieur, and then the horse was lame . . .'

'Versailles!' echoes Monsieur Monnard, watching the young man ascend towards him, then ushering him into the half-warmth of the upstairs room. 'Monsieur Babette has been at Versailles today.'

'Baratte, monsieur.'

'Eh?'

'I am Baratte. My name, monsieur. Baratte.'

He is given a place opposite Ziguette. There is some debate as to whether the stew should go back to the kitchen while the new arrival has his soup. Will the soup be hot enough? Does Monsieur Baratte *care* for soup?

'And how was Versailles today?' asks Monsieur Monnard, as if Versailles were a place he frequented.

Jean-Baptiste takes a spoonful of the tepid soup and discovers in himself a violent hunger. Had he been alone, he might have drunk it straight from the bowl and immediately found somewhere to fall asleep. Still, he must make some effort to ingratiate himself. These people will constitute his most intimate society, at least for a while. He does not want them to think he is dull or rude, a boorish provincial. Does not want them to think he is any of the things that in moments of weakness he believes himself to be. He looks up from his bowl. What a large, red mouth that girl has! It must be the grease from the soup that makes her lips shine so. 'Versailles,' he says, turning to her father, 'is the strangest place I've ever seen.'

'A very good answer,' says Madame Monnard with a decisive nod of her head. She tells Marie to pour their guest some wine. 'And another stick on the fire, Marie. I've never known it this cold in October.'

He learns that the Monnards like to talk – a quite different sort of talking to the more deliberate rhythms he grew up with in Bellême. They also like to eat – soup, stew, fried dabs, beetroot salad, cheese, a little cake. Everything, as far as he can tell, properly cooked, but everything having at the back of it some odd taint, a flavour he does not think should live in food.

After dinner, they sit by the fire. In the cold seasons the room is both drawing room and dining room and serves well enough, though the presence of the pianoforte means that when crossing the room, one must always make a little detour. Monsieur Monnard relieves some tension in his face with a series of grimaces. The female Monnards pretend to sew. There's a scratching at the door. A cat is admitted, a cat quite as big as the dog Jean-Baptiste watched piss on the floor outside the minister's office, a black tom with a ragged half-moon missing from one of its ears. It is called Ragoût. No one can remember why or agree on who named it. It comes straight towards Jean-Baptiste, sniffs at the soles of his shoes.

'What have you been up to, you naughty fellow?' says Madame Monnard, scooping the animal with some effort into her lap. 'I won't answer for his morals,' she says, laughing gaily, then adds, 'Ragoût and Ziguette are inseparable.'

Jean-Baptiste glances at the girl. It seems to him she looks at the cat with some distaste.

'The little gentlemen who like cheese,' says Monsieur Monnard, 'do not last long in this house.'

'What Ragoût don't get,' says Madame Monnard, 'my husband traps with his little machines.'

'Machines?' asks Jean-Baptiste, for whom the word has always produced a certain thrill.

'I make 'em and sell them at the shop,' begins Monsieur Monnard. 'A cage, a spring, a little door . . .' He makes a movement with his hand. 'The creature is imprisoned. Then you need only drop the trap into a pail of water.'

'Marie cuts their throats,' says Ziguette.

'I'm sure she does no such thing,' says her mother. To her guest she says, 'My husband has an establishment on the rue des Trois Mores.'

'Selling traps, monsieur?' asks Jean-Baptiste.

'Blades, monsieur, from plain to fancy. We finish and sharpen and polish. We are quite favoured by the Quality. Père Poupart of Saint-Eustache cuts his meat with one of my knives.'

'When it gets cold,' says Ziguette, 'rats come inside. Into the house.'

'It was the same at home,' says Jean-Baptiste, 'on the coldest nights.'

'In Normandy?' asks Madame Monnard, as though amazed to hear rats had discovered so remote a spot.

'You must miss it,' says Ziguette.

'Home?' For a moment, in his weariness, he sees crows, black rags, lifting off a field at dusk, sees the lonely spire of a country church. 'I suppose I am content to be where my work takes me.'

'Very manly,' says Madame Monnard, probing the cat's fur.

'And what is your work here?' asks Ziguette. She looks so pretty when she asks this, so pert in her creamy gown, he is tempted to tell her exactly what he has come to do. He wonders what Lafosse has said, what story, if any, he has told them.

'I am here,' he says, aware that all three are suddenly listening to him intently, 'to make a survey of les Innocents.'

'Les Innocents?' repeats Madame Monnard, after a pause during which nothing could be heard except the purring of the cat, the crackle of the fire.

'I am an engineer,' he says. 'You were not told?'

'Who would tell us?' asks Monsieur Monnard.

'The same as made the arrangement for my lodging here.'

'We were informed of nothing but that a gentleman from Normandy would have need of a room.'

'With meals,' adds his wife.

'Indeed,' confirms Monsieur Monnard. 'A morning and an evening meal.'

Ziguette says, 'We had a musician stay with us once.'

'A rather particular gentleman,' says Monsieur Monnard.

'With red hair,' says Madame.

Ziguette opens her mouth as though to add something; then, after a beat, a quarter-note of hesitation, she closes it again.

'Yours,' says Madame, smiling complacently, 'is a very practical vocation. One must congratulate you.'

'My teacher,' says Jean-Baptiste, 'at the Ecole des Ponts, was Maître Perronet. He is the greatest engineer in France.'

Above the cat's head, Madame Monnard applauds him with her fingertips.

'And did you ever build a bridge?' asks Ziguette.

'One. In Normandy.'

'And what did it cross?'

'The corner of a lake.'

'One does not think of lakes having corners,' says Ziguette.

'You had better tell Marie, monsieur,' says Madame Monnard, 'if you prefer coffee in the morning or chocolate.'

'The musician liked chocolate,' says Ziguette.

'Marie will bring it to your room if you wish it,' says Madame. 'And water for your toilette. You have only to name the hour.'

'He has not seen his room yet,' says Ziguette.

'No, indeed,' says her mother. 'I believe he has not.'

'Then I shall help you up the stairs with your trunk,' says Monsieur Monnard, rising. 'It will be too heavy, even for Marie.'

The room is at the back of the house, the floor below the attic. The two men, puffing a little, carry the trunk up the four flights of stairs from the hallway. Marie goes ahead of them with a candle.

'I think you'll have everything you need up here,' says Monsieur Monnard.

'Yes,' says Jean-Baptiste, looking from the narrow bed to the table and chair, the tripod stand with its glazed tin bowl, the narrow fireplace, the shuttered window above the bed.

'Ziguette has her room across the corridor. Madame Monnard and I sleep in the room below. Marie, of course, is in the attic. Your predecessor was in the habit of asking her to remove her sabots when she was above him. An acute sensitivity to noise.'

'You wish me, monsieur, to pay the rent in advance?'

'Very businesslike of you. I admire that in a young fellow. Now then, let us see. Six livres a week, I think. Candles and firewood not included.'

Jean-Baptiste, turning his back a little on the master of the house, shakes a few coins from the purse onto the table, picks out a half-louis. 'For two weeks,' he says.

Monsieur Monnard accepts the coin, pinches it and tucks it into a pocket of his waistcoat. 'You are welcome here,' he says, his expression that of a man who has just sold a rack of good knives to a priest. 'Be sure to tell Marie all your needs.'

For a second or two the lodger and the servant lock eyes; then she lights the candle stub on the table with the candle she has carried upstairs.

'If you bring your candle down in the morning,' she says, 'you may leave it on the shelf by the street door. There's flint and steel there.'

'You'll hardly need to leave here,' says Monsieur Monnard, nodding to the shutters, 'to do that survey of yours.'

'I may see it from here?'

'You have not had a chance yet to walk in the quarter?'

'No, monsieur.'

'Well, daylight will make it plain enough.'

With a little flurry of nods and smiles, the men take their leave of each other. Monsieur Monnard and Marie quit the room, pull the door shut behind them. Quite suddenly Jean-Baptiste is alone in a strange house in a city where he knows almost no one. He reaches over the bed to the shutters, folds them back on the stiffness of their hinges then, seeing only himself and the candle flame in the glass, he leans again, turns the oval handle and gives the window frame a little shove. There is nothing now between him and the night sky, nothing between him and the church of les Innocents, for surely that black hulk, just discernible against the eastern sky, is les Innocents. And below it, the span of blackness between the church and the street, that, evidently – for what else can it be? – is the burying ground. If he were to climb over the bed and leap from the window, he would be in it, this place that is poisoning Paris! Certainly it is poisoning the rue de la Lingerie. The stink that creeps through the open window he has already smelt something of in the breath of all the Monnards, in the taste of their food. He will have to get used to it, get used to it quickly or get out, take the coach home, wait on the Comte de S—, beg for another bridge . . .

He shuts the window, puts the shutters over. The candle on the table will not last much longer. He undoes the straps on his trunk, rummages, pulls out a copy of the Comte de Buffon's *Histoire Naturelle Volume II*, pulls out a long brass ruler, a little box of writing implements, a small rosewood box containing a pair of brass dividers. Wrapped in a woollen shirt is his engraving of Canaletto's view of the Rialto Bridge. He looks for a nail in the wall, finds one above the empty fireplace, hangs the picture and stands a while to study it.

He lays his watch on the table next to Buffon, puts the purse under the bolster, suspends his wig from the back of the chair and undresses to his shirt and stockings, both of which he will keep on for warmth. There is no water, nothing to wash with. He gets under the covers, thinks briefly, uneasily, of the red-haired musician who slept there before him, then blows out the guttering candle and lies in a darkness so complete his sight, utterly baulked, draws on it odd shapes, odd fancies. He shuts his eyes – darkness either side! – and after a pause begins to speak quietly not a prayer but a catechism of selfhood.

'Who are you? I am Jean-Baptiste Baratte. Where are you from? From Bellême in Normandy. What are you? An engineer, trained at the Ecole des Ponts. What do you believe in? In the power of reason . . .'

It is a habit begun in the weeks following his father's death, and had about it at first something defiant, almost jubilant. *He* was alive, young and alive. *Ecce homo!* But later – perhaps when he started at the mines in Valenciennes – the questions seemed more, truly, to be questions, and ones whose very simplicity gave rise to instants of confusion, momentary vertigos that made the practice – the putting of the questions – more necessary than ever. He should give it up, of course. It was childish. A source of private embarrassment, almost a vice. But for now, for tonight, in this place . . .

'Who are you? I am Jean-Baptiste Baratte. Where are you from? From Bellême in—'

Someone or something is raking the wood of the door. He holds his breath, listens. The cat with the questionable morals? Had his predecessor let the creature sleep on the end of the bed? Well, he has no objection, would in truth be glad of the company, but the moment he sits up, the scratching ceases. Below his door, the soft movement of a light. Then nothing.

6

In the church of les Innocents, the light of a Paris morning falls in thin grey ropes from high windows, but does little to disturb the building's permanent twilight. Pillars, black or nearly so, rise like the remnants of a petrified forest, their tops lost in canopies of shadow. In the side-chapels, where no candle has been lit in five years, the darkness has gathered in drifts. Saints, madonnas, infant saviours, all the large, second-rate paintings of martyr-dom, of doves alighting on coiffured, vaguely Italian heads, the locked treasure boxes with their knucklebones or splinters of holy wood, all these might simply have never existed, so thoroughly are they now hidden.

The organ (three manuals, forty speaking stops), German-built and very old, is found off the north aisle, that side of the church that lies along the rue aux Fers as the rue aux Fers wanders onto the rue Saint-Denis. The door of the loft – about a third the height of a normal house door – is open, and from it, preceded by some coughing and throat-clearing, comes a man's head. He pauses there, exactly as a dog might hesitate before crossing some uncertain open space, then disappears back into the loft to be replaced a moment later by a pair of long, bootless legs, a large, tightly breeched arse, then the trunk and finally the tousled head again.

There is no ladder – someone has used it for firewood – and he slithers down, pours himself from the loft door until his toes touch a makeshift step built from missals, crack-faced Bibles, lives of saints (he has already made many weak jokes to his friends about climbing the ladder of religion to the heaven of music). When he reaches the slabs of the aisle – his feet on the tomb of a Baron somebody, the baron's wife and several extinguished children – he brushes himself down, spits soot into a handkerchief, puts on his coat and settles himself at the keyboards. He cracks his knuckles; some pale bird is startled into flight under the roof. Even in this light the man's hair has a faint coppery glow. He pulls out stops. Trompette, tierce, cromorne, voix humaine. On the music stand, he has Gigault's *Livre de Musique* and, next to it, a book of cantatas by Clérambault, but to read music he would need candles and he cannot be bothered to light them. He has a candle in his head, all the light he needs, and he begins to play a Couperin trio from memory, his spine and neck arched slightly backwards as though the organ was a coach-and-six and he was hurtling through the centre of les Halles, scattering geese and cabbages and old women.

There is no sound, nothing but the dull clacking of the keys, the clumping of the pedals. He has no air, though for Couperin it would take more than air – the old organ really isn't up to it any more. For other pieces, less demanding on warped metal and old leather, he now and then hires a market porter to work the pump, or that big mute boy who hangs around on the rue Saint-Denis. *Then* les Innocents is driven almost mad, the brass eagles, the tattered banners, the million bones in the crypts, all of it forced back for a few minutes towards something like life. That is his job – there is no other reason to play: no congregation comes, no masses are said, no weddings celebrated, and certainly there are no funerals. But while he plays, and while the priest, that haggard old soldier of Christ, is allowed to haunt the place, then the Church retains an interest in les Innocents, one which, like interests anywhere, it may trade for hard advantage.

He is leaping octaves, modulating furiously, his very white fingers dancing across the keyboards in pursuit of Couperin's fawn, when he hears – surely not! – the door in the north wall being opened. The priest, when he leaves the place at all, has other ways of coming and going, but if not Père Colbert, who?

He twists on the bench, squints down the aisle to where, in the open doorway to the rue aux Fers, a man is standing. A man, yes, a young man, but the organist, who knows most of the faces in the quarter, does not recognise him.

'You need some assistance, monsieur?'

The intruder stops mid-stride. He turns his head, seeking the origin of the voice.

'You see the pipes? Walk towards them. You will soon see me . . . A little more . . . A little more . . . There! A being of flesh and blood like yourself. I am Armand de Saint-Méard. Organist at the church of les Saints-Innocents.'

'An organist? Here?'

'Here is the organ. Here is the organist. There is really no cause for astonishment.'

'I did not mean to . . .'

'And you, monsieur? Whom do I have the honour of addressing?'

'Baratte.'

'Baratte?'

'I am the engineer.'

'Ah! You have come to mend the organ.'

'Mend it?'

'It limps, musically speaking. I do what I can, but . . .'

'I regret, monsieur . . . I do not know organs.'

'No? And yet it is the only machine we have. I would suggest that you have come to the wrong place except that I see you have a key in your hand. The bishop has sent you?'

'The bishop? No.'

'Then?'

In a quiet voice, and after a moment of hesitation, Jean-Baptiste speaks the minister's name.

'So they have something in mind for us at last,' says the organist.

'I am here to make a—'

'Shhh!'

High above them, on the narrow gangway of the triforium, a noise of shuffling feet. The organist draws Jean-Baptiste to the shelter of a pillar. They wait. After a minute, the sound fades. 'Père Colbert,' whispers the organist. 'Unlikely to look kindly on an engineer sent by the minister. Unlikely, really, to look kindly on anyone.'

'A priest?'

'Old but strong as an ox. A missionary in China before either of us was born. I have even heard he was tortured there. Did something to his eyes. The light pains him now. Wears tinted spectacles. Sees through a glass darkly. Murderous temper on him . . .'

Jean-Baptiste nods, and glancing at the red of the other's hair, says, 'It was you who lived at the Monnards' house?'

'The Monnards? And how would you, monsieur, know about such a thing?'

'They still speak of you.'

'*You* are there now? The little room above the cemetery?'

'Yes.'

'You are lodging there?'

'Yes.'

'Well, well. Ha! I'd say it was cold up there now.'

'It is.'

'A word of advice. When you lie in bed, look up at the ceiling. You will notice a small— Oh, oh. Careful my friend. You are unwell?'

It occurs to Jean-Baptiste, listening to the drumming of his heart, that since coming inside the church he has been trying not to breathe. He allows the organist to guide him to the organ bench, hears him, as though from the far side of a wall, say how he too, in the beginning, was similarly affected, how he could only enter the church with a cloth soaked in cologne pressed to his face.

'I marvelled anyone could live within a half-day's ride of the place. And yet you see, they do. Numerous as bees. You get used to it. Try to breathe through your mouth. The taste is easier to support than the smell.'

'I am supposed to find Manetti,' says Jean-Baptiste.

'The grave-digger? You really are up to something. But don't worry. Manetti is the easiest man to find in Paris. Let's get you into the air. You can buy us both a glass of something restorative.'

Leaning – there is really no help for it – on the organist's arm, Jean-Baptiste returns to the door in the north wall. Not that he can blame the church entirely. It was a disturbed night, the whole house restless as though a gale was blowing, though none was. He imagined he heard more scratching at the door, even, at some unearthly hour, scratching on the window. And then, in the early morning, Lafosse standing in the Monnards' drawing room with the keys of les Innocents in his hand. No comfort to be found in *that* face . . .

When they are out in the street and the church door is closed and locked and Jean-Baptiste can trust his own feet again, his own strength, they turn left towards the rue de la Lingerie, then right towards the market. Every ten paces or so, the organist is greeted by someone, usually a woman. At each encounter, their eyes flicker over the young man beside him, the new companion.

'Over there,' says the organist, waving an arm, 'you can eat well and cheaply. There on the corner, they'll mend your clothes without stealing them. And that's Gaudet's place. Gives a good shave, knows everyone. And here . . . Here is the rue de la Fromagerie, where you come when you need to breathe in something other than the perfume of graves. Go ahead. Fill your lungs.'

They have entered one end of a curious clogged vein of a street, more alley than street, more gutter than alley. The top stories of the buildings tilt towards each other, just a narrow line of white sky between them. On both sides of the street, every second house is a shop and every shop sells cheese. Sometimes eggs, sometimes milk and butter, but always cheese. Cheese in the windows, cheese laid out on tables and handcarts, cheese piled on straw, cheese hanging on strings or floating in tubs of brine. Cheeses that must be sliced with a knife big enough to slaughter a bull, cheeses scooped with carved wooden spoons. Red, green, grey, pink, purest white. Jean-Baptiste has no idea what most of them are or where they have come from, but one he immediately recognises and his heart lifts as if he had caught sight of some dear old face from home. Pont-l'Evêque! Norman grass! Norman air!

'Want to try some?' asks the girl, but his interest has moved to the stall next door, where a woman in a red cloak is buying a little cake of goat's cheese, the rind rolled in ashes.

'*That*,' says the organist, leaning across Jean-Baptiste's shoulder, 'is the Austrian. So called on account of her likeness to our beloved queen. And not just the blond hair. Hey, Héloïse! Meet my friend here, whose name I have unfortunately forgotten, and who has come from God-knows-where to turn our lives upside down.'

She is counting out little coins for the cheese. She glances over, first at Armand, then at Jean-Baptiste. Does he blush? He thinks perhaps he has frowned at her. Then she looks away, takes her purchase, starts to move through the crowd.

'The women here,' says Armand, 'despise her, in part because their husbands can buy her for an hour, but mostly because she doesn't fit, doesn't belong. If she was over in the Palais Royal, no one would blink an eye. You've seen the Palais, I suppose?'

'I have heard of it. I have never—'

'What a study you are, man! You are like one of Montesquieu's Persians. I shall write about you in the newspaper. A weekly column.' He strides ahead and, as they pass below the buttresses of Saint-Eustache, he launches into a loud, airy, impromptu lecture on the history of the Palais, how it was once the garden of Cardinal Richelieu and how the Duc d'Orléans had given it to his son, who filled it with cafés and theatres and shops, and how it was always crowded and unspeakably elegant and the biggest bordello in Europe . . .

He is still describing it when they come to the thing itself, one of its several entrances, a passage no wider than the rue de la Fromagerie, and through this they are jostled into an arcaded courtyard, in the middle of which a marionette show is coming to an end amid hoots of laughter. To Jean-Baptiste, it appears that the puppets are being made to fornicate. When he looks more closely, he sees that they are.

'The police patrols never come here,' says the organist. 'The duke makes them little presents and they find something else to do. Lewd puppetry is the least of it.'

Who are these people? Do none of them have trades, occupations? Their movement, their costumes, the sheer noise of it, suggests carnival, and yet there is no obvious centre to any of it, no sense of structure. It is, seemingly, all spontaneous, the moment's continual self-invention.

'Come,' says the organist, tugging at the elbow of Jean-Baptiste's coat, urging him towards the door of a café halfway down one of the galleries. 'We'll try our luck in here.'

Inside is as crowded as outside, but the organist, with a well-aimed greeting to one of the waiters, is soon provided with a little table, a pair of battered cane chairs. He orders coffee, a bowl of sweet cream, two glasses of brandy. The clientele is exclusively male, mostly young. Everyone speaks at the top of his voice. Now and then someone reads aloud from a newspaper or raps on the window to draw the attention of a passing acquaintance, perhaps some woman he wishes to grin at. The waiters – small, concentrated men – navigate tightly winding paths between the backs of the chairs. An order is shouted, acknowledged with the barest nod. Two dogs leap at each other's throats, are thrashed by their owners, caged under the tables again. Jean-Baptiste pulls off his coat (hard enough to do in such a space). The café is the warmest place he has been in for weeks. Hot, smoky, slightly damp. When his brandy arrives, he drinks it out of pure thirst.

'Better?' asks the organist. His glass is also empty. He orders two more. 'You may call me Armand,' he says. 'Though I'll leave it up to you.'

Now that they are sitting opposite each other, and now that he does indeed feel better, Jean-Baptiste can start to take him in, this

Armand, especially as the organist has the restless habit of looking past him at all the other faces in the café. He wears no wig, nor is his hair powdered: powder in such hair would serve little purpose. His clothes – expensive-looking, though more so from a distance than close to – belong to no fashion Jean-Baptiste can recognise. Trousers, striped and worn tight as a second skin. A waistcoat half the length of his own, a coat with lapels so large the points extend almost past his shoulders. A cravat of green muslin, metres of it. When he drinks, he has to hold it clear of his mouth, his big, purplish lips.

'You did not expect to find an organist at the church,' says Armand, returning his gaze to Jean-Baptiste. 'In fact I am the director of music.'

'You have been there long?'

'Eighteen months.'

'Then you were appointed when the church was already closed.'

'Can a church be closed like a baker's shop?'

'If the order is given, I suppose.'

'You suppose, eh? Well, no doubt you are right. My predecessor drank himself to death. I dare say he found the situation . . . unsettling.'

'And you do not?'

'Positions, as perhaps you know yourself, are never easy to come by.'

'But there is no one to play for.'

Armand shrugs, picks up his second brandy. 'There's myself, Père Colbert, God. Now you. Quite a good audience really.'

Jean-Baptiste grins. Though it troubles him that he is sitting in a café drinking brandy rather than making a survey of the cemetery, troubles him that he could barely breathe inside the church, he is not sorry to have discovered this flame-haired musician. And after all, he may learn something to the purpose. The work that has been entrusted to him will not be a simple matter of digging up bones and carting them away. He has understood that much. It will be the living as much as the dead he will have to contend with.

'If I can stay in with the bishop,' says Armand, 'then one day I'll get something better. Saint-Eustache, perhaps.'

'Even there,' says Jean-Baptiste, 'you will be able to smell it.'

'The cemetery? It is as I said. You get used to it. Which is to say you never really get used to it, but it becomes bearable. One adjusts. Tell me, what did you notice about the Monnards?'

'That they are . . . respectable people?'

'Oh, yes. Very respectable. And what else?'

'That they like to talk?'

'The only way to silence them would be to put a tax on words. Something our masters may be considering. But come now. Be open. What else?'

'Their breath?'

'Exactly. And you have probably noticed that mine is not much sweeter. No, there's no need for politeness. Anyone who spends time at les Innocents gets to be the same way.'

'Is that what I have to look forward to?'

'You are thinking of staying so long?'

'I do not know how long I shall stay.'

'You do not care to speak of your work.'

'I am sure it would not interest you.'

'No? I suspect it would interest me greatly, though I shall not press you on it now. We will speak of something else. Ziguette Monnard, for example. You had a good look at her?'

'I sat across from her when we ate.'

'You were not impressed? She's one of the prettiest girls in the quarter.'

'I'll admit she's pretty.'

'Oh, you'll admit it? How grand! You have someone at home, perhaps? Wherever home is.'

'Bellême. Normandy.'

'In Bellême, then. No, I can see you do not. Well, watch out, my friend. If you stay, they will certainly try to marry you to her.'

'To Ziguette?'

'Why not? A young engineer. A confidant of the minister.'

'I have never claimed to be his confidant.'

At the next table, a man with a network of silvery scars about his throat glances up from the backgammon board, looks at the young men, looks slowly back to his game.

'And what of you?' asks Jean-Baptiste. 'They tried with you?'

'Musicians are less eligible. People like the Monnards consider a musician little better than an actor.'

'Her father runs a cutler's shop. Can they afford to look down at musicians?'

'It costs very little to look down on people. And yes, they considered me.'

'You liked her?'

'As one likes the company of any attractive woman. But with Ziguette, one must be careful.'

'How so?'

Armand scoops a gob of sweet cream from the bowl, sucks his finger, wipes his lips. 'Ziguette grew up in that house. She has lived there all her life. In that air.'

'That should make me wary of her?'

'To marry Ziguette,' says Armand, 'would be like marrying the cemetery. It is more than simply a matter of breath. Now, little Marie . . .'

'The servant?'

'I'm not talking about marriage, of course.'

'You? And Marie?'

'Poor girls from the faubourg Saint-Antoine are freethinkers. Her mind might be as empty as the Saviour's tomb, but she's more modern than the Monnards will ever be. More than you too, perhaps. Don't be offended. Anyway, I've half a mind to modernise you myself. The project has just occurred to me.'

'And if I do not think I need instruction?'

'From a church organist? It is exactly such an attitude we will need to root out if we are to secure you for the future. The party of the future.'

'Such a party exists?'

'It has no meeting place, no subscriptions, and yet it exists as surely as you or I. The party of the future. The party of the past. There may not be much time left to decide what side you are on. I think we should start by changing your costume. You feel a particular affinity with brown?'

'You find some fault with my suit?'

'Nothing. If you belong to the party of the past. I shall introduce you to Charvet. He will know what to do with you. Charvet is modern.'

'And what is Charvet? A writer?'

'A tailor.'

Vexed, intrigued, tipsy, Jean-Baptiste makes what he hopes is a face expressive of scorn, but the organist has gone back to his study of the other faces in the café. When he has finished, he says, 'I hope you don't object to paying for this. And then we must find somewhere to eat. Nothing is more damaging to incipient friendship than brandy on an empty stomach.'

*   *   *

In the galleries, in the courtyard, the shoving, the shouting, the lifting of hats, the cocking of eyebrows, the tireless pursuing of something, anything, goes on with no sign that it will ever lose its momentum. Is *this* modern? And these people, are they the party of the future or of the past? Does one always know to which party one belongs? Can one be sure? Or is it, thinks the engineer, like his mother's religion – some destined to be saved, others damned, and no sure sign either way?

They are burrowing through the crowd (occasionally having to advance sideways, occasionally having to stop or even retreat a little) when Armand clutches Jean-Baptiste's coat again and steers him through the portal of Salon No. 7. In the lobby, a tightly stayed woman is perched on a stool behind a table on which there is nothing but a small tin and a bell.

'You have to give her four sous,' says Armand. Jean-Baptiste gives her four sous. She rings the bell. A man in a rose-tinted wig appears, holds back a rose-coloured curtain. Clearly, he is already well acquainted with Armand. They bow to each other like courtiers, though it is all mockery.

'Just Zulima today,' says Armand.

'As you wish,' says the man.

'This gentleman,' says Armand, gesturing to Jean-Baptiste with his thumb, 'is from somewhere in Normandy. One day he'll be the greatest engineer in France.'

'Naturally,' purrs the man. He leads them along a softly lit corridor. On either side, heavy drapes conceal what are, presumably, the entrances to rooms, but the last drapes have been imperfectly drawn and Jean-Baptiste, pausing, has a glimpse of a man, part of a man, a naked arm and naked leg lashed to a cartwheel, a face, heavily bearded, one large eye wide in a wild stare. Who was it meant to be? Damiens? Damiens who they spent half a day killing in the place de Grève for grazing the king with a penknife? Racked him, cut him, poured lead into his wounds, flogged horses to rip his limbs from their sockets, though the horses could not do it – poor innocent beasts – until the executioner cut through some of the dying man's muscle. Thousands, it was said, looking on that day from the buildings around the square . . .

At the end of the corridor, the guide is waiting for him. He lifts another curtain. Jean-Baptiste stoops, passes under his arm.

'Zulima,' begins the man, breaking into speech as if he was some manner of automaton, 'was a Persian princess who died, like Cleopatra, from the bite of a viper. She was but seventeen years of age and unhappy in love. Her purity –' another, finer curtain is drawn back – 'and the arts of the Persian priests have preserved her perfectly for more than two hundred years.'

She is lying on a platform that is half catafalque, half daybed. There are two candles by her feet, two more by her head. Her body is wrapped in a shroud, a winding-sheet of some diaphanous stuff – tulle, organza, who knows. She is nubile. She is perfect. The young men stand either side of her and gaze. The older man waits by her feet, head bowed as though in prayer.

'Remind you of anyone?' whispers Armand.

'No one,' says Jean-Baptiste, but he knows who the organist has in mind. There is indeed, in the wax face, the ample figure, a marked resemblance to Ziguette Monnard.

From the Palais they go to an inn near the Bourse to eat. They are seated at a common table and fed the ten-sous dinner of bread soup and boiled beef. A brisk fire burns at the back of the room. They are drinking wine, red wine that is neither good nor bad. They are drinking and talking, their cheeks growing red. Armand, with no sense of shame or awkwardness, confesses to having been abandoned in the baby-wheel outside the Hôpital des Enfants-Trouvés. There, his talent brought him to the notice of the intendants who, in turn, brought him to the notice of the commissioners, those charitable men and women who liked to go fishing among the scabby, shaven-headed children who lived and died in those halls, for one worth saving.

'There are no youthful illusions in such a place. You do not mistake the world's character. By the age of seven we were all as cynical as abbots.'

Together they agree that the losing of illusions is an indispensable preparation for those who hope to rise in the world. On a third bottle, they confide to each other that they are ambitious, madly ambitious, and that through luck and hard work they intend to die famous men.

'And wealthy,' says Armand, picking a shred of beef from between his teeth. 'I do not intend to die famous only for my poverty.'

Jean-Baptiste speaks of his former patron, the Comte de S—, of his two years at the Ecole des Ponts, of Maître Perronet, of the bridges he dreams of building, structures light as thought spanning the Seine, the Orne, the Loire . . .

Wine and unsuspected depths of loneliness have produced in him an effusiveness he would not, sober, trust or like in another. Nearly, very nearly, he tells Armand what he is in Paris to do, for surely Armand would be impressed, would see what he himself (in the ruby light of tavern wine) has come to see – that destroying the cemetery of les Innocents is to sweep away in *fact*, not in rhetoric, the poisonous influence of the past! And would Armand then not have to admit that he, Jean-Baptiste Baratte, engineer, belonged, beyond any quibbling, to the party of the future, indeed, to its vanguard? Or would he be alarmed? Horrified? Furious? What exactly is Armand Saint-Méard's relationship with the bishop? What has His Grace been told of the minister's plans?

Outside, they piss against a wall, button themselves and sail on through what is left of the afternoon. They are still talking, still gabbling about politics, Paris, the irreducible dignity of the peasants (*But I know about the peasants*, Jean-Baptiste wants to say, *I'm related to dozens of them*), but neither is really listening to the other any more, and anyway, he is being urged inside again – immediately feeling more drunk inside than out – and presented to a man, a kind of exquisite monkey, who is, it transpires, Charvet the tailor.

The shop, if such a space could be called by so modest a name, is fitted out with dainty furniture and oil paintings and is not remotely akin to the pungent atelier where Jean-Baptiste's father sewed his gloves. No obvious sign of *work* here at all, other than the table by the window where a pair of young men are dreamily cutting lengths of some material that glitters and shivers like spring water.

Charvet wastes no time. A few words from Armand, a shrug from Jean-Baptiste, are all he needs to begin. He circles the engineer, touching, tugging, stepping back to better assess the length of a leg, the slight roundness of the shoulders, the slender waist. It is not unpleasant to be the focus of such intense professional surveillance. Jean-Baptiste does not even notice when Armand slips away. The whole day has had some strange impetus of its own. He is past trying to wrestle it. He will think about it later.

'I believe, monsieur,' says Charvet, 'I believe that we shall be able to do something very interesting with you. You have, if you will allow me, the figure necessary for the new styles. You are not one of those portly gentlemen I am forced to disguise more than dress. You, monsieur, we may dress. Yes. Something that will flow with the natural movements of the body. Something a little more informal, though, of course, in its way, perfectly correct . . . We must tell a story, monsieur. We must tell it clearly and beautifully. I will dress you not for 1785 but for 1795. Cédric! Bring the gentleman a glass of the Lafitte. Bring the bottle. And now, monsieur, if you will do me the honour of following me . . .'

Two hours later, Jean-Baptiste is examining himself – examining someone – in a large, brilliantly polished oval mirror. He is wearing a suit of pistachio silk, a silk lining of green and saffron stripes. The waistcoat, cut at the top of the thigh, is also pistachio, with modest gold-thread embroidery. The cuffs of the coat are small, the collar high. The cravat – saffron again – is almost as large as Armand's. For a long time, Charvet and Cédric have been pulling pins from between their lips, have been snipping and sewing and handling him with that freedom reserved to their trade, to that of body servants, surgeons and executioners. They are almost done. They stand back, careful to exclude themselves from the mirror's scope. They look at him looking at himself. It is, Jean-Baptiste is perfectly aware, far too late to refuse the suit or even to criticise it. To do so would be to denounce not just Charvet but the future itself. Impossible! He will take it and he will pay whatever Charvet wants. It turns out to be a lot. He blushes. He does not have such an amount on him. The tailor spreads his hands. Of course, of course. Tomorrow will be quite soon enough. But there is something else. Is the young gentleman a young gentleman of an *intellectual* persuasion? Aha! He had thought it all along, but one does not wish to appear impertinent.

He glides to the gleaming walnut of the escritoire, removes

from one of its drawers a little picture in a frame and brings it to Jean-Baptiste. 'Voltaire,' he says, and smiles at the picture as if, alone, he might address fond words to it. 'You see what he is wearing? The robe? It is known as a banyan. Intellectual gentlemen find it something they can barely do without. I have one here in red damask. I would not mention it to most of my customers; it would not be understood. But in your case . . .'

'Yes,' says Jean-Baptiste.

'Yes?'

'I will take it.'

'And, monsieur, you must wear your own hair. In five years the wig will be perfectly extinct. In the meantime, I have an excellent bag wig, all human hair, and rentable by the week . . .'

'That too,' says Jean-Baptiste.

'And shall I keep your old suit as a deposit, monsieur? I have a smaller establishment on the rue du Bac catering to my . . . hmm, more conservative customers. I could perhaps sell it for you there?'

'As you wish.'

'As *you* wish, monsieur.'

'Then yes.' He shrugs. 'Yes.'

Released from Charvet and his shop, the engineer crosses the place des Victoires, turns down the rue de la Feuillade towards the market and the Monnards' house. The wind has got up. It blows the dust into his face and makes him sneeze. The new suit is not as warm as the old. Neither is the new suit a gift from his dead father. He hugs the packaged banyan to his chest. At each step the stink of the cemetery grows stronger, but in spite of this he is several times forced to hesitate, peer forwards, look over his shoulder, take his bearings from a gate, a pillar, a bare tree, a stone trough. Has he seen them before? Then he finds himself standing at the end of the rue de la Fromagerie. The little shops are shuttered, the carts resting on their handles, the cobbles damp with slops. There is a beggar kneeling at the corner, but otherwise the street is deserted. The beggar looks up, slips back a hood to show his sores, but in the coolness of his new pockets Jean-Baptiste has no change for him. They mutter to each other (an apology, a curse).

He has his supper with the Monnards. Can they see he has been drinking, that he has spent the day drinking? Perhaps they are too dazzled by his appearance to notice. Pistachio silk, it seems, can provoke something near astonishment. The women want to touch it but do not quite dare to. Monsieur Monnard looks perplexed. He pulls, ruminatively, at the lobes of his ears as though he were milking a pair of tiny udders.

They sit at the table. Jean-Baptiste has no appetite. He drinks some glasses of Monsieur Monnard's wine, but after the Lafitte at Charvet's, it tastes of what it is, mostly water.

After supper, Madame invites him to stay and hear Ziguette play the pianoforte. 'Getting it in, monsieur, I swear it gave me a nosebleed just watching them! And such a crowd outside. They all cheered when it was swung through the window. I said to my husband, I said, "You'd think they was at a *hanging*!"'

He stays, bathed in his own pale green light, while Ziguette picks her way through a melody he does not recognise. Can the instrument be in tune? Can a sound like that really be intended? She is wearing a low-cut dress of lemon wool and studies the movement of her hands with a pout of concentration, one blond ringlet dangling over her brow and bobbing like a spring each time she raises her head to squint at the music. He thinks of Zulima, dead two hundred years, nipples like peach stones. The music stops. He applauds with the others, is required to sit through a second piece, a third. Madame Monnard beams at him and nods. Before the commencement of a fourth piece, he gets clumsily to his feet, claims he is feeling indisposed, begs to be excused.

'It is nothing serious, I hope?' asks Madame.

He assures her it is not.

In his room, it is as cold as on the previous evening, which is to say, a degree or two colder than the world outside. He still has no wood. He will speak with Marie when she passes on her way to the attic, ask her to make the necessary arrangements, though from what he has seen of her, he thinks it quite likely she will do nothing about it. A symptom of her freethinking? He is not sure – though the thought immediately embarrasses him – how much he cares for modernity when it leaves his fireplace and his wash-basin empty.

He unwraps the parcel, spreads the banyan over the bed, takes off his pistachio coat, carefully folds it and draws on the banyan. There is a lot of it. It swathes him. It might, he thinks, swathe two of him. And there is a cap too – compliments of Monsieur Charvet – a tarboosh, made from the same red material. He takes off his wig, puts on the cap. In the mirror, in candle dark, he looks like a Venetian senator. Also, somehow, like a child who has stolen into his parents' room and put on his father's clothes. Not that his father would ever have possessed a garment like this. He would not have approved of it, would not in the least have been pleased to see his oldest son wearing it, might, indeed, have been moved to ridicule, to anger.

He turns from the image of his face to the print of the Rialto Bridge on the nail above the mantelpiece. If he is going to wear this thing, then he must inhabit it with high thoughts. It will not do simply to *act* the philosopher. He must read, work, think. He hauls up the banyan's skirts, much as he has seen women do on a mired street, and sits at his table, pulls close the candle and opens his copy of Buffon's *Histoire Naturelle Volume II*. A piece of pale straw is his bookmark. He frowns over the page. The taxonomy of fish. Good. Excellent. He manages an entire paragraph before the words swim away from him in black, flickering shoals, leaving behind bare images of the day he has just passed, that shameful, that inexcusable waste of time and money. He sees the interior of Les Innocents, sees Armand as a great imp perched on the organ bench, sees the pair of them hiding from the priest, sees the woman, the Austrian, buying her little piece of cheese and looking at them, looking for a moment *straight at him*, this woman out of her place, who does not belong. Then the Palais, the puppets thrusting their wooden hips at each other, the wax princess. And Charvet, his smile bright with pins . . .

He replaces the straw, shuts the book, turns the brass ruler in his hands. Heaven knows where Marie has got to. He will speak to her in the morning. He cannot wait any longer.

He takes off his shoes, his pistachio breeches. He is interested, slightly disconcerted, to discover that he has an erection. Some strange after-effect of the drinking, the libidinous wine. He grips his cock through the material of his shirt. Is the life of the body the true life? The mind nothing but a freakish light, like the St Elmo's fire sailors see circling the tips of their masts in mid-Atlantic? He is savouring this little pensée (in which he does not believe at all), holding his cock like a pen he might use to note it down with, when he is startled by a noise from the passage, the slow dragging of claws across wood, a sound he is starting to be familiar with. He waits. It comes again. He goes to the door.

When he opens it, Ragoût looks up at him with yellow, unreadable eyes, eyes that seem to possess their own luminescence, as certain flowers do at dusk. He crouches, strokes the creature's head, the mangled ear. 'Very well, my friend. But mind you don't stick those claws in my throat in the middle of the night.'

From the other side of the unlit passage a movement silences him. He squints. It is Ziguette Monnard. She is in her nightclothes. Her hair is unpinned, brushed free.

'The cat,' he says.

'Ragoût,' she says.

'Yes.' He cannot stand up; he is still hard. Even in this light it would be impossible to disguise the fact. 'It must be late,' he says.

'I hope you are happy here,' she says.

'I am sure I shall be.'

'You have begun your work?'

'Some . . . preliminaries.'

She nods. 'Then good night, monsieur.'

'Good night, mademoiselle.'

She turns away, slips into her room. Jean-Baptiste stands, rubs his back, looks down at the absurd puppet now, at last, making its slow bow between his thighs. On the end of the bed, Ragoût is licking his paws. Jean-Baptiste shrugs off the banyan, folds it over the back of the chair, puffs out the candle, feels his way between the slight dampness of the sheets. Then . . .

'Who are you? I am Jean-Baptiste Baratte. Where are you from? From Bellême in Normandy. What are you? An engineer, trained at the Ecole des Ponts . . .'

Some nights more convincing than others.

7

A girl is crossing the burying ground of les Innocents. In one hand, from a length of twine knotted about its feet, she carries a hen; in the other a wicker basket full of vegetables, some fruit, a dark loaf. She was, as usual, one of the first at the market, her slight figure, the thick auburn hair, a familiar sight among the servants who make up the greater part of the early trade. Where she stops, the stall-holder never tries to cheat her. Nor does she need to squeeze and plump the produce, to sniff or haggle like the cook's maids with their chapped fingers, or those bony matriarchs of pared-down households who live a peg or two above destitution. She is served quickly, respectfully. Perhaps she will be asked about her grandfather's health, his stiffening joints, but no one will detain her long. It is not that they dislike her. What is there to dislike about Jeanne? But she comes from the other side of the cemetery wall, a place, in this last quarter of the eighteenth century, many people would prefer not to be reminded of. She is sweet, pretty, well mannered. She is also the little auburn-haired emissary of death.

The morning is cold, beautifully bright. Her shadow and the hen's glide over the stiff grass as she follows the path – a path unmarked by anything other than her own feet – from the door onto the rue aux Fers to the sexton's house by the corner of the church. In places the ground she passes is uneven, the grass lying in shallow hollows where a grave has subsided. A careless visitor, one who did not know his way, might plunge into one of these, plunge in up to waist or shoulders, even vanish entirely. But not Jeanne.

She stops by the preaching cross, that pillar of stone and iron where once wild-eyed men must have leaned to harangue the crowd. By the bottom of its steps is a clump of honesty, the seed-pods bright as money in the sunlight. She bends to pick some, to snap the dry stalks, and puts them in her basket. Not much grows in les Innocents any more. The earth is exhausted from its work, though her grandfather, sexton for fifty years, has told her that when he first came there the cemetery in spring was like a country meadow and that in his predecessor's time the priest and the locals had grazed their animals in it and the grass was cut for hay.

She picks up her hen. Upside down again, it immediately returns to its stupor. She takes a line that keeps her just beyond the heavy shadow of the church. She dawdles, listens to the city beyond the walls, to Paris going about its morning business, hears the geese in their pens at the market, the shrimp-girl singing her wares, the babies crying in the wet-nurse's house on the rue de la Ferronnerie . . .

As a young girl – she was nine when the last interment took place – the cemetery made its own sounds. The tap-tap of the mason, the rhythm of a spade, the tolling of the bell. Now – for how much noise can a girl and an old man make? – the place is silent unless its peace is disturbed by some visitor, the sort who slides uninvited over the walls at night. A winter dawn two years ago, a duel was fought in the corner by the rue de la Lingerie. From the house, she and her grandfather could hear it plainly enough, the brief clash of weapons, the shouting that ended it. Grandfather waited until it was full day before going out. All they had left behind them was trampled grass and a piece of cloth torn from a shirt, bloody.

And then there are the lovers: there is little she has not seen in that way. Just this last August, under a hazy yellow moon, she watched a boy – one of the porters, from the way he was built – with a girl pretty as an elf queen and no older than herself. When he did it to her, she mewed like a cat. And they did not do it once but three or four times, only stopping to look a little at the moon and drink from the bottle they brought with them and which she found the next day leaning against the Peyron tomb they had used as their bed. There was a spit of wine still in it and she had tasted it, felt it run down her throat, then hidden the bottle in a hole under the tomb.

Sometimes – rarely – she sees the old priest in his glasses, a big wingless bat in the dusk. And sometimes the red-haired musician, who comes out to relieve himself and always waves when he sees her. She would like to look at his hands. His hands must be special because only special hands could make the sounds he makes, that music that once or twice a month seeps through the black walls of the church and makes her heart race.

Outside the house, she looks up to let the autumn sun rest its warmth on her face, then, revived, comforted by its touch, she goes inside. Grandfather is in the kitchen. She brings the bird to him, holds it up for him to put his fingers into its feathers. He makes a little grunt of approval, then tilts his chin towards the room off the kitchen, the sexton's office, a whitewashed room with a narrow, arched window where who knows how many volumes of records with their dust, their mouse droppings, their crazy marblings of damp, are lined up on sagging shelves. A man is standing at the desk with one of the volumes open in front of him. He stares at it, turns a page, presses a cloth to his face, shuts his eyes, inhales deeply, then pushes the cloth back into the pocket of his coat. The coat is unbuttoned and beneath it she can see a line of his suit, green like the heart of a lettuce.

The hen clucks; the man turns towards the kitchen. He nods to her, and when she says nothing, he tells her his name. 'I am looking at the records,' he says.

'I can see it,' she says.

He nods again, returns to the book.

'We can offer you wine, monsieur,' she says. 'And we have a little coffee too.'

He has put the cloth to his face again and shakes his head. There is a perfume in the cloth she finds almost offensively strong. Grandfather takes the hen outside.

'Are you a foreigner?' she asks.

'I am from Normandy,' he says. He is running a finger down a meticulously inked column. Seven Flaselles expired, one after the other, in the autumn of 1610. Seven in less than a month.

'I thought so,' she says.

'Why?'

'I have not seen you before.'

'You know everyone in Paris?'

'In the quarter,' she says.

'You know a family called Flaselle?'

'No,' she says. 'There are no Flaselles here.'

'There were once,' he says. He closes the volume and walks

towards her. From outside comes a frenzied clucking, an abrupt silence.

'You are Jeanne?' he asks.

'Yes,' she says, grinning at the lilt of his voice.

'Your grandfather said you would show me the cemetery. That you know where the pits are.'

'The pits?'

'The common graves.'

'They are everywhere,' she says.

'But you can show me?'

She shrugs. 'If you wish.'

The old man comes in, the bird's head in one hand, the softly kicking body in the other. Drops of blood fall like seeds onto the stone of the kitchen floor.

They start with the south charnel, a gallery of blackened stone adjacent to the rue de la Ferronnerie. Of the arches into the gallery, some are barred with man-high gates of rusted iron; others are open. Above the arches – and immediately visible to anyone coming into the cemetery – are garrets where bones, some black as the stones, have been packed behind iron grilles.

After a second of hesitation, Jean-Baptiste steps through one of the arches. On the stone beneath his feet is an inscription. He crouches, touches the lettering with a fingertip. Henri something, struck down, and his son also, beloved something, wife to, late of, devout, fleeting, merciful, the flesh, eternity, 14 something.

He stands and walks a little way along the gallery. Light falls oddly, shows some things clearly, others not at all. He sees the delicate tracery of stone flowers, sees a stone woman holding a stone veil across her face. Narrow steps presumably lead up to the garrets. His shoe kicks a fragment of masonry, the sound of it followed immediately by the sudden scuttling of live things, invisible but close. He turns, hurries back into the open.

He has a notebook with him, a roll of linen tape. When he takes measurements, he asks Jeanne to hold one end of the tape; then, with a steel-tipped pen, a portable inkwell, he writes and sketches in the notebook. He has many questions. She answers them all, and he scratches her replies onto the paper. Sometimes he shuts his eyes and takes out the cloth. He asks if she can read.

'A little,' she says, and points to the inscription on a stone. '"*Hic Jacet*,"' she says. 'And there, "*Hic Requiescit*." And there, "*Hic est Sepultura*."'

He nods, almost smiles.

She says, '*You* can read.'

'I'm an engineer,' he says. 'You know what that is?'

'A kind of priest?'

'We build things. Structures.'

'Like a wall?'

'Like a bridge.'

He asks her the location of the most recent of the common graves. She leads him to it. He looks down, looks around. There is nothing obvious to distinguish it from the patch beside it.

'You are sure?'

'Yes.'

'And it was closed, sealed, five years ago?'

'Yes.'

'You were a child then.'

'Yes.'

'But you remember?'

'Yes.'

They go on. (He needs to keep moving.) Pit after pit.

'And this? It is older than the last?'

'Yes.'

'And this one?'

'Older still.'

He makes a map. She watches how he can make a line thinner or thicker with a little adjustment of the angle of the nib. And the figures and the little words. There's a beauty to it.

'What's that?' she asks, pointing to a squiggle, one of several she has seen him make, a shape like a half-skull.

'A question mark,' he says. 'For when there is some uncertainty.'

Her face falls. 'Then you have not believed me,' she says.

He tells her that he has, but that what is under the ground is hidden. What is hidden cannot accurately be known.

'Not by you,' she says. There is no pertness in her reply. He seems to consider it a moment, then shuts the book, the inkwell, wipes the nib of the pen.

'We are finished for today,' he says. As they walk back to the sexton's house, he asks, 'Wouldn't you like to leave here? Live somewhere else?'

'I don't know anywhere else,' she says. 'And who would look after them?'

'Them?'

She gestures to the ground around them. 'The dead,' she says.

When he has parted from the girl, from the old sexton, he goes into the church. The girl has pointed out a door he can use, not the big door the corpses and the mourners must have come through, but a smaller one to the side of it, its lintel low enough to make him bow his head. For a few strides he is in a vestibule, black as Hell, then a second door lets him into the body of the church. He is at the back of the south aisle. Ahead, he can see part of the rose window above the altar. There is no sound or sign of any presence other than his own. He starts to navigate, right to left, passes behind the backs of pews, passes dreaming pillars, crosses the nave, passes a large, railed tomb on the top of which an armoured man lies beside his metal wife, their slim hands gathered in prayer. He reaches the north wall, walks down to the organ. There is no Armand Saint-Méard today. He is a little disappointed, a little relieved. It might have been reassuring to have heard the organist's admiration of the new suit. It might also, of course, simply have been the prelude to another wasted day of drinking and rambling.

He sits on the organ bench, lets his fingers move above the keyboards. To the right and left are rows of stops, knobs of elegantly turned wood, some seemingly of ivory. He slides one out, leans to try and read what is painted there, but the script is too elaborately Gothic and is, anyway, abbreviated after the manner of chemical compounds. He slides it back in. The instrument is the only thing in the entire church he feels any interest in, any liking for. Could it be saved? Dismantled, wrapped, stored, reassembled?

He gets off the bench, steps down into the aisle and is trying, among the masonry and plaques, the substantial and insubstantial shadows, to see the door to the rue aux Fers when a voice, one that almost crushes him, falls from some impenetrable part of the darkness above.

'*You! Who are you?*'

Horrible to be seen like this, seen but unable to see back. He stares upwards, grimacing, as if in expectation of the thudding of leathery wings.

'*You are not the musician! I know his footfall. Who are you?*'

Echoes, black flocks of them under the vaulting. Impossible to locate the origin.

'Answer me, rogue!'

He sees the door now, gets his key into it on the third attempt, finds it is the key to the Monnards' house, fits another key, turns it, pulls at the door . . .

'Who are you? Who!'

And then he is out; out on the rue aux Fers. The street is not consumed with fire. There are no abominations out of Hieronymous Bosch, no pale women consorting with demons, or stranded whales spewing tormented souls. A half-dozen laundry wives are at work by the Italian fountain. The ground about them glitters. A pair of them glance over, perhaps surprised to see anyone coming out of the church, a man, one they haven't seen before, but soon they look back to their work, cold arms plunged into cold water. Linen will not wash itself.

8

He sits in his room, wrapped in damask, and looking through the unshuttered window to the church. The sun is setting, but the stones of les Innocents give back little of its light. The windows are briefly livid with a fire that seems more the show of some holocaust *inside* the church than anything as distant, as benign, as a red late-October sun. Then the light flares, ebbs, and the whole façade is joined in uniform darkness.

He rises from the chair to see if he can spy the glimmer of the evening's first candle in the sexton's house, but there is nothing, not yet. Perhaps they retire like Norman peasants, like the beasts of those peasants, as soon as it is too dark to work.

Was the girl simple-minded? He does not think so. But can he depend on her description of what, under the rough grass, he will find when he starts to dig? He supposes he must, for he has little else to guide him. The memories of an aged sexton, records that have made a dinner for generations of mice . . .

He turns the chair, sits facing the table. He fusses with his tinderbox, lights his own candle and slides it close to the edge of the book in which, in the morning, he made his notes. He studies his sketches, runs a finger by the figures, tries to see it all as a problem of pure engineering such as, at the school, Maître Perronet might have thrown among them as he passed on his way to his office. So many square metres of ground, so many cart loads of . . . of debris. So many men, so many hours. A calculation. An equation. *Voilà!* He must not forget, of course, to leave a little room for the unexpected. Perronet always insisted on it, some give, some slack in the rope for that quantum of uncertainty that bedevils every project and which the naïve practitioner always ignores until it is too late.

From the back of the notebook he carefully tears out a sheet of plain paper, opens his inkwell, dips his nib and begins to write.

My lord,

I have made an initial examination of both the church and cemetery and see no reason to delay the work that Your Lordship has entrusted to me. It will be necessary to recruit at least thirty able-bodied men for the cemetery and as many more for the church, some of whom should have experience in the art of wrecking. In addition, I shall need horses, wagons, a good supply of timber.

In the matter of the cemetery, beyond the removing of the remains from the crypts, charnels and common graves, I recommend that the entire surface of the cemetery be excavated to a depth of two metres and sent out of the city to some unpopulated place or even taken as far as the coast and cast into the sea.

May I ask if somewhere suitable has been prepared for the reception of the human material? And what in the church other than those objects of a sacred character, relics, etc., is to be preserved? There is, for example, an organ of German origin that might, if Your Lordship wished it, be dismantled in such a way as to preserve it.

I am, my lord, your obedient servant,

J-B Baratte, engineer

He has no sand to sprinkle on the wet ink. He blows on it, cleans the nib of the pen. From below there comes the flat ringing of the supper gong. More dead men's food. He shrugs off the banyan, reaches for the pistachio coat, then, before going down, halts a moment at the window with the candle in his hand. It is just a piece of fancy, of course, an impulse entirely whimsical and one he should not much like to try and explain to anyone, but he moves the candle, side to side, as if signalling. To whom? Who or what could possibly be down in that dark field, watching? Jeanne? Armand? The priest? Some hollow-eyed watchmen of the million dead? Or some future edition of himself, standing in the time to come and seeing in a window high above him the flickering of a light? What baroques even a mind like his is capable of! He must not give play to them. It will end with him believing in that creature the minister spoke of, the dog-wolf in the charnels.

✻

Over Paris, the stars are fragments of a glass ball flung at the sky. The temperature is falling. In an hour or two the first frost flowers will bloom on the grass of parade grounds, parks, royal gardens, cemeteries. The streetlamps are guttering. For their last half-hour they burn a smoky orange and illuminate nothing but themselves.

In the faubourgs of the rich, watchmen call the hour. In the rookeries of the poor, blunt figures try to hide in each other's warmth.

At the Monnards', in the box room under the slates, the servant Marie is kneeling in the dark. She has rolled up the rug and has her eye to the knothole above the lodger's room, the lodger's bed. She watched the musician like this too, but she did not make the hole. She found it with her toe a week after she was taken on.

The air from the lodger's room rises in a warm, slightly smoky column that makes her eye itch. He has had a fire tonight, and it still burns, enough at least for her to see him by, his figure under the covers, his pale mouth, the softness around his shut eyes. On the table by the bed is an open book, a length of brass for measuring. Implements for writing.

What she likes to see is the moment, the precise moment when they fall asleep. She is, in her way, a collector, and while more fortunate, more moneyed girls may collect thimbles or fancy buttons, she must collect what is free. She has to be careful, of course. The little hole must not betray her. They must not look up and see above them the liquorice shimmer of a human eye.

This one, the new one, the grey-eyed foreigner, is lying on his back, his body twisted a little to the right, right arm and hand extended downwards, outwards, above the covers. The hand is palm up, the fingers loosely flexed. Do they tremble, or is that a trick of the embers? She wipes her eye, looks again. It is, she thinks, as if from that open hand he has let himself go, his mind like a ball of black wool rolling over the floor, unwinding, unwinding . . .

Ten quiet streets to the east, a second-floor apartment on the rue des Écouffes, Armand Saint-Méard is sprawled in a large bed with a large woman, his landlady and paramour, Lisa Saget, widowed mother of two living children and two who went into the ground before their fifth year. More asleep than awake, she slips from the bed, squats over a bucket, pisses, dabs herself with the rag, gets back into bed. When she lies down again, the organist's hand strolls drowsily up her thigh, plays a single slow arpeggio on the heat of her skin, then settles, rests.

To the west – west of the cemetery and the silent market, and close enough to the church of Saint-Eustache for normal speech to be unintelligible when the bells are swung – Héloïse Godard, the Austrian, is sitting fully dressed on the edge of her bed reading *The Sorrows of Young Werther* by Johann Wolfgang von Goethe.

The book, like others in her collection, was part-payment from Monsieur Ysbeau, a pleasant, scholarly sort of gentleman who runs two large bookstalls beside the river. On the first Tuesday of the month, she selects a book from the boxes while he sits on the stool behind her, his breeches round his ankles. When she turns to him, she is required to feign scandal, to rebuke him in choice language, after which he apologises, pulls up his breeches and, with a half-dozen neat movements, wraps the book.

She learnt to read courtesy of her parents, innkeepers on the Orléans–Paris road. They intended her for the catering business and had her instructed in her letters by a certain *curé* who, leaning over the primer with her, made himself familiar with the underside of her petticoats. Later, she received the same treatment from several other of the inn's more regular, more free-spending customers, often under the very gaze of her parents, who seemed to consider such handling an acceptable consequence of their trade, and chose to ignore her tears, her glances of mute appeal, until at last she learnt to expect nothing of them, to hide from them and from all the world any show of what she felt.

Candles are her great luxury. She reads only at night, in the hush and privacy of the night. She burns two, even three at a time. She cannot appear in the morning with bloodshot eyes. In the cold seasons, she keeps her cloak on against the room's chill. Poor Werther is in love. ('"I shall see her today!" I exclaim when I wake with gladness of heart.') Will it end badly? Ysbeau would not tell her, only smiled as if he found it surprising a woman like her should have a taste for love stories. Certainly she is no dreaming girl, no innocent. She knows about men, knows a good deal of the world's character. But it is hard, whatever you have endured, to give up on love. Hard to stop thinking of it as a home you might one day find again. More than hard.

She licks a finger, turns the page.

Inside the church of les Innocents, in the vestry, Père Colbert is also awake. He has a bed of sorts, a truckle bed with a mattress of rags, but mostly he sleeps sitting in the wooden armchair, his big head dawdling on his chest. He drools when he sleeps. The black cloth on his chest is damp with it when he wakes. It does not signify. There is no one to see him and he should not care if there was. On the table he keeps a small lamp burning, a wick floating in oil, a small flame (blue through his glasses) that once flickered in the chapel of Saint-Sebastian. At night, in this very city, the Devil and his servants are abroad, and Père Colbert does not wish to meet them in the utter, unrelieved dark that would exist without the lamp. That he will meet them, that he must, this he is reconciled to. It may even be that he surprised one of their scouts creeping about by the organ this morning. Did the whole church not grow uneasy? Did he not hear the sleepers in the crypt let go a soft moan of fear? As for any help, anyone to share the burden of vigilance, he cannot hope for it (they say the bishop has a mistress, has fathered children). He is alone at his post, as alone as when he spent his days in the dust of Hunan Province and where one morning they dragged him to the public square and he saw, perfectly clearly among the faces in the crowd, the eyes of the Adversary, and afterwards could see nothing clearly again . . .

He watches the doors, the one leading out to the street, the other to the apse behind the altar. They are shapes, barely shapes, but he shall know if they are tried, if they are opened.

Jeanne's bed – where she is sleeping soundly – lies along the heavy, carved foot of her grandfather's bed. On her last birthday, her fourteenth, he carried the new bed up the stairs and told her she was too old, too womanly, to decently share a mattress with any man other than a husband. It made her weep when he said it, shake with grief, for she had slept beside him since her infancy when, between one Sunday and the next, both parents and two sisters died of a sweating fever. To be made to lie alone brought back to her a sudden blind memory of that loss, and for many nights she waited for the old man to relent, but he did not, and she has grown used to it, the new arrangement, her new status as a woman.

She is dreaming now of the cemetery carpeted with flowers, white and pink and yellow and crimson. It was a lovely dream, rich with promise, and she is smiling at it, while above her, above cracked, smoke-black beams as old as the church, the cat Ragoût sits beside the warmth of a chimneypot wiping a licked forepaw, meditatively, across his damaged ear. In the cemetery, in an archway of the south charnel, something catches his attention. He stares, grows perfectly still, then flattens himself to the tiles.

9

'The minister,' says Monsieur Lafosse, 'accepts your proposals. You may obtain the men you need. Likewise the horses, the timber. This purse – you will sign for it, here and here – contains five hundred livres. And these are bills of exchange. You may draw on them at the house of Kellerman the goldsmith on the rue Saint-Honoré. We expect every sou to be accounted for. I assure you the minister will not be amused if, for example, he were to discover you have spent fifty livres on a new coat.'

Jean-Baptiste reddens. He has a mind to defend himself but cannot immediately think what the defence is. That he was drunk and wished to be modern? To be thought modern?

'As for your enquiry about what is to be saved in the church, the answer is the same as you were given before. Nothing.'

'And the old priest?'

'We are not suggesting you demolish a priest.'

'I mean, will he not protest?'

'Why? It is not his church.'

'But he will not take kindly . . .'

'You cannot manage an old priest?'

'I can . . . of course.'

'Then there is no difficulty.'

'And there is a musician. The church organist.'

'What of him?'

'When the church is gone, he must lose his position.'

'One imagines so.'

'I am told he is very skilled. Perhaps the minister . . .'

'You are asking for the minister to concern himself with the fate of a church organist? You will be pleading next for the sexton.'

'I had thought—'

'You seem confused, Baratte, as to what you are here to do. You will begin your work as expeditiously as possible. You will allow no petty obstacle to impede you. If you have not commenced your work by the New Year, you will be replaced with someone more effective. Is that clear?'

'Perfectly, monsieur. May I speak of what I am to do? My presence here gives rise to suspicions, rumours.'

'Rumours will not be stopped by explanations.'

'And the disposal of the remains?'

'The bones? You will hear on the matter shortly.'

There is a moment of inhospitable quiet between them. Lafosse's small eyes take in the room and briefly settle on the pianoforte. The contemplation of it seems to afford him some private amusement.

'You find your new lodgings to your taste?' he asks.

10

How hard to find thirty men? Not hard, in such times. But thirty good men, men who will be able to bear the work?

He has already decided where he will look for them: the mines at Valenciennes. There, in receipt of their pittances, are men inured to the type of labour that would kill others inside of a month.

He writes to Lecoeur. Lecoeur is – or was – one of the managers at the north seam. When Jean-Baptiste worked at the mines, the two of them, isolated from all society, half hidden in that damp, remote pocket of northern France, their nerves wound tight by the smoke, the noise of the gear, the occasional savagery of the place, made a sort of compact, an intimacy, though one that entirely ceased upon Jean-Baptiste's departure.

It was their habit, particularly during that first interminable winter, to invent utopias where all that offended them, their ears, eyes, their young hearts, was made good in the imagination. Their favourite creation, the most detailed and satisfactory, was Valenciana. In Valenciana, economics and morality, virtue and industry were threaded together to the benefit and improvement of all. There were squares of small, neat houses for the families, dormitory blocks for the single men, parks where the air was clean and the children could play as others do, play and perhaps grow up less misshapen than their fathers. In Valenciana, no child under twelve would be sent down a shaft. None younger than ten would be employed on the surface as carriage-pushers, gug-winders or the like. There would be schools run by benign and educated men – men like Jean-Baptiste and Lecoeur. There would be no churches in Valenciana (an evening of especially passionate debate), though in the open spaces there would be statues of the relevant classical deities, an Athene, an Apollo, a Prometheus, though no Dionysus, no Aphrodite. Nor, at Lecoeur's insistence, would there be anywhere men could gather to consume strong liquor. It was more than a game. They even discussed the possibility of presenting Valenciana in the form of a book and, for one night at least, shared a vivid dream of themselves making their way, shy yet assured, through the salons of the capital.

Was Lecoeur still at the mines? Would he be interested in les Innocents? The letter goes off by the midday coach to Lille, 7 November 1785.

When he enquires after horses, he is, by small degrees, directed to a young officer, who meets him in an inn by the Sèvres porcelain works on the road to Versailles. The young officer will, apparently, provide everything. It does not have to stop at horses.

In his blue coat and cream leggings (and what long, long legs he has!), the young man, who goes by the name Louis Horatio Boyer-Duboisson, seems very at home in the world. There is passing mention of a father, an estate in Burgundy. He seems to know more about Jean-Baptiste's work than Jean-Baptiste can remember telling him. Is he connected to the minister? To Lafosse? Some neat, circular arrangement by which state funds are channelled back to the state, or at least, to its representatives? They agree to meet again in a week's time for Jean-Baptiste to view a sample of the animals. They bow to each other, and though the engineer does not like or trust the soldier, who reminds him of a young Comte de S—, he cannot keep himself from wishing a little that he *was* the soldier, that he wore life like a good shirt and might, if the weather picks up, ride down to the woods and rivers of his father's estate in Burgundy.

The weather does not pick up. Clouds tangle in the Paris chimneys. The wind is from the east. By the middle of most afternoons, it is too dark inside to read comfortably.

Every day Jean-Baptiste forces himself to go into the cemetery, to walk inside the walls, sometimes alone, sometimes in the company of the girl, who speaks of the dead beneath their feet as if of some vast extended family. She even pretends to be able to identify many of the bones that litter the ground – that jawbone belonging to a Madame Charcot, that femur from a Monsieur Mericourt, a farrier who died of a cold.

For his part, Jean-Baptiste prefers not to think of bones as having owners, names. If he has to start treating them as former people, farriers, mothers, former engineers perhaps, how will he ever dare sink a spade into the earth and part for all eternity a foot from a leg, a head from its rightful neck?

On the rue de la Lingerie, his evenings with the Monnards turn out not to be quite as devoid of pleasure as he at first had anticipated. With Monsieur Monnard, he talks a vague, guarded politics. Taxes, shortages, the national finances. Monsieur is, unsurprisingly, no liberal. He speaks slightingly of Voltaire, of Rousseau, of head-in-the-cloud ideas, the salons, the agitating. He is, it seems, in favour of order, firmly imposed if necessary. Of trade too, the busyness and respectability of shopkeepers. In reply, Jean-Baptiste confines himself to general remarks about the desirability of reform, the sort of comments nobody but the most reactionary aristocrat could be troubled by. Things somehow getting better and fairer, though how, practically, it can be done, other than by some form of intellectual radiation, he does not know. Does anyone? He nearly mentions, one evening, his old utopia, Valenciana, but bites it back. A man like Monnard who reads only the newspaper could not be expected to understand, and anyway, the recollection of those nights beside the never-quite-adequate coal fire in Lecoeur's parlour is not without a certain awkwardness. That younger, more garrulous version of himself, their two heads hung close in the room's shadows, the strange urgency of it all . . .

With Madame, he discusses the intricacies of the weather. Did the wind blow somewhat harder today? Was it colder in the morning or in the afternoon? What is Monsieur Baratte's opinion of the likelihood of snow? Does he *care* for snow? All kinds of snow?

And then there is Ziguette. Conversations with Ziguette – sometimes at the table, sometimes on the settle by the fire or sitting by the window overlooking the cemetery – require greater effort. He tries music, but she knows even less of it than he does, has not heard of Clérambault or any of the Couperin family. Theatre is equally hopeless – neither of them knows much – and as for books, it is evident she makes no more use of them than her parents. He asks about her own history; the subject seems to bore her. She asks about his work and he is forced to obfuscate. He wonders if she is in love, not with him, of course, but with someone. He wonders if he desires her. He is not quite sure. His interest in her seems no more marked than his interest in the little hairy-armed servant who brings in the supper plates. As for *marriage* . . . could he? The daughter – the very pretty daughter – of a well-set-up Paris shop owner, most people would think it a fair match, one that offered advantage to both parties. He conducts little thought-experiments, sometimes while speaking to her, in which the two of them are together in a room, a cabriolet, a canopied bed, her breath made sweet by his eradication of the cemetery, a parcel of her father's money in a locked box underneath the bed . . . Such thoughts are not disagreeable and yet the images are thin as tissue. None of it persuades.

As for the Monnards' food, it goes on as mysteriously unpalatable as ever. Even an apple tart manages to put him in mind of those little silvery mushrooms that grow in the dampest corners of a cellar, and yet he always clears his plate. It is, in part, a practice instilled in him in earliest childhood by the back of his father's hand, and later confirmed by the sticks and sanctions of the brothers of the Oratorian Order in Nogent, but in part, after nearly five weeks in the house, he is simply getting used to it, used to it all. And when supper is over, he retires to his room, the banyan, a page or two of Buffon. Then into bed, candle out, the catechism. He does not ask himself if he is happy or unhappy. The question is postponed. On the roof of his mouth, he has a pair of ulcers, which, lying in the dark, he probes with the tip of his tongue. Has *his* breath turned? Would he know if it had? He cannot, for the life of him, think who he might count upon to tell him.

*   *   *

On the 15th, he meets again with Louis Horatio Boyer-Duboisson. It's almost dusk and they are in a field behind the inn where they met before. The horses, five of them, stand in light rain, their halters held by two soldiers, neither of whom, in their ill-fitting uniforms, look more than children.

Jean-Baptiste walks round the horses, then asks that they be walked round him. His father had a good eye for horses. Perhaps the knack has been passed on in the blood, but standing there in the drizzle, he feels he is doing nothing more than imitating his father's posture, those little movements of the eye and mouth that tokened judgement.

'I will not pay for any that are lame or sick.'

'Naturally,' says the officer. 'Who would?'

'And you will stable them until I need them?'

'They will be waiting for you.'

The young soldiers are left in the rain while Jean-Baptiste and Boyer-Duboisson retire to the inn to finish their business. They ask for a private room and are shown one. Jean-Baptiste makes a down payment of a hundred livres. He asks for a note of receipt. The officer cocks an eyebrow, then smiles as though remembering who he is dealing with, what rank of man. They drink a glass of indifferent wine, then walk out to where, in the field, the horses and the boy soldiers stand together like a single complicated creature dressed in a coat of dull rain.

Two letters arrive. They are handed to Jean-Baptiste on the stairs by Marie. She has a small but effective range of facial expressions, all of them faintly unsettling.

He thanks her, takes the letters to his room. On the corner of the first, there is a soot-black thumbprint. He breaks the seal. It is from Lecoeur. The handwriting, scattered with ink blots and looking as though it had been set down at great speed while riding on a horse, is, in parts, illegible, but its drift is plain enough. How delighted he was to hear from his old friend! Life at the mines is quite as disagreeable as it ever was, though now without the solace of intelligent company. The new managers – no one seems to last much longer than a year – are feebly educated, narrowly commercial, while the miners and their terrifying wives continue to live like half-tamed dogs. As for hiring them, there is the usual surplus of labour and much hardship attending upon it. Thirty men, or sixty, should present no difficulty. What is this project so tantalisingly dangled? In Paris too! Might there be need of someone who knows the men, who can direct them about their tasks efficiently? Someone conscientious, discreet? A fellow philosopher no less?

The other letter, on good paper and written in an irreproachable script, comes from someone called de Verteuil at the Academy of Sciences. The matter concerns certain preparations being made at a quarry near the Porte d'Enfer, south of the river, for the reception of the remains removed from the church and cemetery of les Saints-Innocents. A house has been acquired, its cellar steps extended to reach the old workings, and in the garden there is a well with a circumference above three metres that empties into the same workings, which are tolerably dry and quite suitable for the purpose. When everything is made ready, the bishop will consecrate the relevant passages and chambers. Once this is done, Monsieur l'Ingénieur will be free to commence the first transports. Would Monsieur l'Ingénieur like to give his estimate to the number of bones that may be expected?

Jean-Baptiste folds the letter, places it inside his notebook. The number of bones? He has not the faintest idea.

11

Before he leaves for Valenciennes, he finds Armand and tells him everything. He is not used to carrying secrets, and the undisclosed truth sits in his gut like one of the Monnards' savoury jellies. It is, he knows, the inescapable influence of his mother's religion, that deadly emphasis on conscience, on tireless moral book-keeping. It is also the desire to offer something to the one person in Paris he has any reason to think of as a friend, for they have met together three or four times since that first day, have confirmed their interests in each other, their pleasure in the other's difference. And anyway, all of it must come out soon enough. Better now than when thirty wild-eyed miners troop through the church with picks and hammers.

He finds Armand (the middle of a cold morning) on the rue Saint-Denis, the organist bantering with a shrimp-girl, and now and then – without taking his eyes from the girl's – reaching up to help himself to one of the little pink bodies on the tray on her head. He greets Jean-Baptiste, takes his arm, walks him up and down the street, listens to his clumsy preface, then interrupts him to point out a pair of mournful dogs copulating in the gutter outside a hatter's shop and, before Jean-Baptiste can continue his confession, invites him to come and eat that night at his lodgings.

'Lisa's brats will be there, but the food is always decent. Certainly it does not taste of cemeteries. And there will be some company later.'

They arrange to meet by the Italian fountain at seven sharp. Jean-Baptiste is there ten minutes before the hour but has to wait another forty before Armand appears. There is no apology, no excuse. They set off together, striding from one little bay of light to the next, while the organist, waving his long, white fingers, delivers a panegyric in rags of Greek and ecclesiastical Latin on the beauty, the sheer *scale*, of his landlady's breasts.

The rue des Ecouffes is a twenty-minute march in the direction of the place Royale and the Bastille. On the ground floor of the house is a shop specialising in the manufacture and repair of mirrors, and the two men pause a moment in front of one of these in the window, though it is too dark to see more than the briefly arrested suggestion of themselves. They grope their way up three flights of steep wooden steps to the door of the apartment. Lisa Saget and the children are in the kitchen. Here there is light, a fire, the smell of food. Armand greets his landlady with a loud kiss on her brow, ruffles the children's hair. There is a chicken roasting on a spit; the girl has the work of turning it. She glances at Jean-Baptiste, smiles at Armand. Other than for the flatness of her chest, she is the perfect miniature of her powerful-looking mother.

'Monsieur Baratte,' says Armand, speaking into the cupboard in which he is searching for glasses, a bottle, 'who has my old billet at the Monnards'.'

It is evident the woman has heard of him. She is sitting at the end of the kitchen table doing something with the consumable part of the chicken's innards. She looks up and looks him over, this grey-eyed man lost in a green coat. 'Is he eating with us?' she asks.

'Of course,' says Armand. 'He hasn't had a decent meal since coming to Paris.'

Jean-Baptiste takes a stool at the table. He is facing the fire, the little girl. Her brother, scratching his backside, watches her from behind Armand's shoulder, her envious work by the food.

'So what of the Monnards?' asks the woman, busy with her knife.

'I believe they are quite well,' says Jean-Baptiste, aware that is not really what he has been asked.

'We shall need to find him somewhere else,' says Armand, 'if he's planning to stick around.'

'And is he?' asks the woman.

'Who knows,' says Armand. 'He doesn't say much.'

Jean-Baptiste studies his pistachio cuffs, wonders if the table is quite clean, if it would be wise to take off his coat.

'I shall stay for a time,' he says. 'I cannot tell yet how long.'

'I could not live on a cemetery like that,' says the woman. 'I cannot think what kind of people do it, year after year. Bad enough having Armand coming back with the smell of the place on him.'

'She washes me with lemons,' says Armand. 'With a soap made of sage leaves and ashes. Smokes me with rosemary . . .'

'Would it not be good,' says Jean-Baptiste, 'if the place was removed?'

'Removed?' The woman snorts. 'And how do you remove a cemetery like les Innocents? You might as easily remove the river.'

'It could be done,' says Jean-Baptiste quietly. 'Either could be done.'

Armand, who has been examining the boy's scalp, parting the brown curls in search of vermin, pauses and looks across.

'Is that what you are up to? The cemetery?'

'It will not be easy, of course,' says Jean-Baptiste. 'It will take many months.'

'He's like the rest of your friends,' says Lisa. 'Tell you the moon's a bowl of soup if they think anyone could be made to believe it.'

'Yet to me,' says Armand slowly, 'he looks perfectly serious.'

'It can be done,' says Jean-Baptiste. 'It will be done.'

'The whole cemetery?' asks Armand.

'The cemetery. The church.'

'The church?'

'It will not be touched for a while yet. Perhaps for as long as a year.'

'So,' says Armand softly, 'the moment has come.'

'I would have preferred to tell you sooner. I was instructed to keep the matter to myself.'

The woman has stopped her work now. 'And his position?' she asks. 'Is *that* to be removed?'

'I have . . . spoken of it,' says Jean-Baptiste.

'To the minister?' asks Armand.

'To one who represents him.'

'And may I hope for something?'

'I will speak of it again.'

There is a silence between them, broken at last by a sharp word from Lisa to her daughter, who, caught up in this interesting business between the adults, has stopped rotating the chicken.

'I think,' says Armand, 'I think that I should thank you.'

'Thank him?' asks the woman. 'For what?'

'The church, my gentle one, has been shut for five years. I cannot continue indefinitely playing Bach to bats.'

'It's all wind anyway,' says the woman, snatching up her knife again. 'You must have stopped at Djeco's place on the way here.'

'If it was not me,' says Jean-Baptiste, 'they would have sent another. Though I cannot blame you for . . . resenting it.'

'Who said anything about resenting?' asks Armand, stretching for the bottle. 'One does not resent the future. Nor its agents.' He fills their glasses. 'Come now, we will drink to that shadowy country we are all travelling towards, some on their feet, some on their backsides, squealing.'

The little girl laughs. A moment later, the boy joins her. Lisa ignores them.

They eat. The food is indeed the best Jean-Baptiste has tasted since coming to the city, though his enjoyment of it would be greater still if he could find some way of winning over the woman, who served him his chicken as if she would rather have chased him through the door with the spit. The subject of the cemetery does not come up again. Armand is thoughtful, somewhat distant, somewhat distracted, but good-humoured.

When they have finished eating, Armand teaches the children a song, which they sing back to him, sweetly. He asked Jean-Baptiste to teach them something, a little arithmetic perhaps, and for half an hour he endeavours to do so. They listen; they understand nothing. He draws geometries for them on a slate, triangles within circles, circles within squares. These are immediately admired. The children stand either side of him, watching to see what new cleverness will appear from under his fingers. The girl rests her hand comfortably on his shoulder.

The spell is broken by the tap of some small thing thrown up at the window. Lisa – whose manner towards the guest has been slowly thawing – gets up with a tut of irritation. She takes one of the candles and goes with the children into a back room. Armand exits through the other door and returns a minute later with three men. They look like students, though all are much too old to be students. One has a tattered silk rose pinned to his lapel, the next has his thin neck wrapped in a collar of ginger fur, while the last wears a pair of wire-rimmed spectacles on a nose intended for comedy.

'Messieurs Fleur, Renard and de Bergerac,' says Armand. The men bow, mockingly. 'I am now Monsieur Orgue and you . . . well, let's see. You are . . . hmm. Monsieur Triangle? Monsieur Normand? Or Bêche? Yes. Bêche is better. You shall be named after one of the spades you will use to dig up the dead.'

'I see you sent him to Charvet,' says Monsieur Fleur.

'Naturally,' says Armand, returning the other's grin.

Their conversation is not easy to follow. It appears to consist of gossip about men and women who also possess names like characters in a farce. When the wine is gone, something stronger is found. No one seems quite sure of what it is. It tastes faintly of almonds and burns agreeably in the chest. There is some giggling. De Bergerac dabs at his nose; Renard fingers a hole in the bottom of his shoe, tenderly, as though fingering a hole in his foot.

Has Lisa Saget gone to bed with the children? Jean-Baptiste has been waiting for her in the hope he might then be able to excuse himself and find his way back to his lodgings. It is pleasant enough to sit by the fire sipping liquor, the taste of chicken grease on his lips, but he has done what he set out to do and tomorrow he must begin his journey to Valenciennes. He does not want to travel with a thick head.

Catching him peering round at the door, Armand settles a hand on his arm. 'Do not think you can escape us, Monsieur Bêche. We have not finished yet.'

They drain the last drops of the liquor and fall silent, staring into the embers of the fire. The room is growing colder. Nothing happens. Is it midnight? Later? Then, with no warning, Armand gets to his feet. He goes out but comes back almost immediately with two large glass pots wrapped in plaited straw.

'I assume, gentlemen,' he whispers, 'you are all armed?'

From the depths of their coats, Renard, Fleur and de Bergerac, produce paintbrushes. They show them, then quickly stow them again.

They descend to the street. It's raw now. Raw and damp, a true winter's night, no romance to it. Jean-Baptiste has his horsecoat buttoned to the chin but wishes, once again, he had his old suit below it.

Following Armand, they pass into the small streets behind the rue Saint-Antoine. The city is theirs – they see no one, hear no one. It is that brief hour, the turning of the city's tide, when the last of the wine shops have thrown out their rabble but before the market carts appear, the big six-wheelers with their lanterns swinging from their sides, or the strings of packhorses, miserable beasts that have walked all night from farms and country gardens, their panniers creaking.

On through the rue Neuve, the rue de l'Echarpe, into the colonnades of the place Royale . . . Whatever it is they are doing, drunkenly doing, hurrying across the square with their pots of paint, it will not be easy to explain should they meet a patrol. And if he – the newly appointed engineer – had to explain himself to Lafosse? To the minister? (*I felt constrained, my lord. I did not, under the circumstances, think I could refuse what appeared merely an excursion. Had I known what these men, whose acquaintance I had so recently made, intended . . .*)

They drop onto the rue Saint-Antoine, cross to the far side, pass the church of Sainte-Marie, where a dozen indigents are curled on the steps waiting for first mass at five o'clock, the hope of a coin from the hand of some pious widow.

Ahead of them now – a distance of some hundred and fifty metres – is the fortress of the Bastille, its walls and turrets black shapes cut clumsily out of the night. It looms over everything, yet somehow gives the impression of being cornered, trapped, the last of the basilisks, rearing, fearful, full of useless strength. And behind those walls? What? Scores of wretched men chained in underground cells, buried alive? Or just more stone, stone and volumes of dank air, with a few locked rooms occupied by bored though not greatly discommoded inmates, gentlemen scribblers who, having penned some satire on a royal favourite, found themselves removed from their studies by a *lettre de cachet*.

They pause in the doorway of a workshop. The street ahead is scoured, hats are pulled lower, then a quick word from Armand and they flit, a hunched running, across the front of the fortress to the three-arched gate beside it, the Porte Saint-Antoine. It is here, on the stone of the gate, that the government posts its notices and decrees. A rise in the salt tax, a new penalty for illegal fishing in the Seine, for emptying pots of human ordure into the street between six in the morning and six at night. The date of a sermon to be preached by the royal chaplain at Sainte-Chapelle. The date, the hour, of a branding, a hanging.

Defacing such notices is part of the trade between government and people. Occasionally, a persistent offender is pounced on by the watch, but for the most part the scrawling of an obscenity about the queen – *La pute Autrienne!* – or some notoriously gouging tax-farmer, attracts little official attention.

Tonight, on freshly posted notices, it is the turn of Renard, Fleur, de Bergerac, Orgue and Bêche. It is all done in less than a minute. Jean-Baptiste holds one of the pots for the furiously swishing Renard and feels his cheeks being spattered with paint. He cannot even see what they are writing, or only the single word – 'PEOPLE!' Then, with their brushes and pots, they are scurrying away like mice from a larder.

Breathless, back on the rue des Ecouffes, Armand invites them upstairs to celebrate the night's action. He thinks there may be another bottle of that almond liquor somewhere, perhaps under the bed. Jean-Baptiste makes his excuses. The lateness of the hour, his journey in the morning . . . He nods to them, politely, friendly even, but they are already turning away from him, offended perhaps by his lack of solidarity, of party spirit.

Holding his coat at his throat, he crosses the street. A mist is rising off the cobbles, has already swallowed the thigh-high street-posts and the ground-floor windows, and is soon sucking at the shop signs, those wood and iron exemplars – a giant glove, a pistol like a small cannon, a quill big as a sword – that dangle over the street from gibbets. He is not perturbed. He knows his way well enough, has learnt to navigate the quarter, though it may be he has forgotten that a city at night is not quite the same place as a city by day. And he is distracted by his efforts to decide what he thinks about running through the streets with a paint pot. Was it exciting? Now that it is over, he can admit that it was, a little. Exciting, but also tiresome and absurd and childish, for what will ever be changed by men flying about the town painting slogans on the walls? And such odd men too! Something freakish about them, something he does not think he should associate himself with, some quality of desperation. Surprising that Armand should trouble himself with such people, though for Armand, it is perhaps nothing but an excuse to spend the night drinking. The woman was interesting, likeable in spite of her brusqueness. And the children too. He enjoyed their company, the sweet attentiveness with which they watched him draw calm shapes on the slate.

He stops and frowns into the mist. He should by now have come out onto the rue Saint-Denis, a little above the rue aux Fers. Instead he is . . . where? A street he does not recognise at all. Has he come too far north? He looks for a left-hand turning, walks what seems a good half-kilometre before he finds one that appears serviceable, sets off along its length, becomes with each step a little less confident of where he is, has the fantasy that he is walking not through the heart of Paris but through the rutted alleys of Bellême, then sees, rearing in the air above him, the buttresses of a church, a big one. Saint-Eustache? The mist is thick as wood smoke now. He goes on slowly, cautiously. If the church is indeed Saint-Eustache, then – in theory – he knows exactly where he is, but he is afraid of being fooled again, of spending what is left of the night trailing through unreadable streets, past buildings like moored shipping.

Ahead of him, the sudden sound of footsteps. Someone else is out here, someone who, from the quick, light clip of his feet, is very sure of his way. There is nothing sinister in it, nothing obviously so, yet the fear grows in him quickly. What manner of man is about at such an hour on such a night? Could he have been followed? Followed all the way from the Porte Saint-Antoine? He digs in his pockets for something he might defend himself with but finds nothing more dangerous than one of the cemetery keys. Too late anyway. The weave of the mist is unravelling. A shape, a shadow, a cloaked shadow . . . A woman! A woman deep in reverie, for she is a bare metre from him when she comes to a halt. For three, four seconds they are fixed in some primitive watchfulness; then the stance of each softens a little. He knows her. There can be no mistake. The cloak, the height, that steady gaze lit by the mist's own odd lucency, a faint blue-like light radiating from everywhere and nowhere. Does she remember *him*? He cannot think why she should.

'I was walking home,' he says quietly, almost a whisper. She nods, waits. She does remember him! He believes she does. 'I became lost.'

'What is your street?' she asks, her voice as soft as his.

'The rue de la Lingerie.'

'By the cemetery.'

'Yes.'

'It is not far,' she says. 'You can walk through the market.' She looks past his shoulder towards the turning he must take.

'I have seen you before,' he says.

'Yes,' she says.

'You remember?'

'You were with the musician.'

'You are Héloïse,' he says.

'I was not told your name.'

'Bêche.'

'*Bêche?*'

'Jean-Baptiste.'

He takes a step towards her. Then, after a heartbeat, takes another step. They stand there, quite private in the mist. He lifts a hand and touches her cheek. She does not flinch.

'You are not frightened of me?' he asks.

'No,' she says. 'Should I be?'

'No. There is no reason.'

His fingers rest on her skin. He could not say what he is doing, what he is guided by, he whose experience with women is so little. Is it her being a whore that lets him do it? But in this unlooked-for hour, words like whore, like engineer, like Héloïse or Jean-Baptiste, are empty as blown eggs.

'So I turn there?' he asks, suddenly waking to himself, his hand falling to his side.

'At the corner there,' she says.

He mutters his thanks, walks away from her. He finds the market easily enough. It is already a city within a city, bantering, spotted with lanterns and rush-lights, though it will be another two hours before any customers arrive. On the other side of it, the corner of the rue aux Fers, the black wall of the cemetery, the fog-damp cobbles of the rue de la Lingerie . . .

When he opens the door of the Monnards' house, something darts in ahead of him. He fumbles with the matches on the hall table, eventually gets a candle to light. Ragoût is by the door to the cellar, his blunt face pressed to the crevice at the bottom of the door. He looks up at Jean-Baptiste as if in hope of some assistance. Jean-Baptiste reaches down, feels the air flowing through the crevice, cold air, cold like the breath of a man in the last stages of a fever. He sets his candle on the board next to the door. Immediately the flame sickens and, before he can raise it again, goes out.

12

In what is left of the night he lies awake, the inside of his head shiny with the clarity of sleeplessness and unlabelled liquor. Again and again he recalls his meeting with the woman, with Héloïse, until the whole scene becomes impenetrable and he enters some other state, vaguely hypnogogic, in which he is watching the cellar door swing slowly open and himself move, as if compelled, to the top of the cellar steps, steps he has never even seen . . .

He dresses in the first of the dawn. Twice he wipes the mirror with his hand before realising the black spots are on his face, not on the glass, his reward for holding Monsieur Renard's paint pot. He has no washing water. He curses and creeps out of the house.

He is the last to board the coach on the rue aux Ours. He climbs up and sits opposite a silver-haired priest. Beside the priest (who, under his black cape, is gently palpating some discomfort in his belly) is a foreign couple, English it turns out, the woman neat, solidly dressed, comfortable as a hen; the man red-faced, big as an old prizefighter. The remaining passenger is a woman, one of those elegant, mysteriously sad women of a certain age, who travel unaccompanied on the public stages and who immediately become the focus of all manner of speculation for the other passengers. She gazes from the window as if in lingering hope of some figure, someone like Louis Horatio Boyer-Duboisson, riding out of the rags of last night's mist to beg her to stay. No one comes.

In the doorway of the coaching office, the coachman is taking his morning dram. The English couple share a boiled egg. The priest reads a little book, the pages almost touching the end of his nose. The elegant woman sighs. Jean-Baptiste – who has eaten nothing since last night's chicken – shuts his eyes and falls so profoundly asleep he is dead to everything until, abruptly waking three hours later, he sees, through mud-spattered windows, the winter countryside passing by, Paris already leagues behind them. The Englishwoman smiles at him, bobs her head. Her husband and the priest are side by side, snoring, each to his own rhythm.

They come to a hill. The horses struggle. The coachman, peering down through his hatch in the carriage roof, asks if the gentlemen would object to walking to the top. The gentlemen oblige, pick their way through the mud while making observations on the character of the mud-coloured country either side of them. They join the coach again at the crest, spread their mud over the floor, then cling to the straps as the horses make their long, slithering descent into the next village where, to everyone's relief, they stop for lunch.

In the afternoon, all of them having drunk a good deal of white wine with the food, there is an hour of harmless conversation followed by an hour of napping, the coach rocking like a boat, the world outside the windows passing by, unconsidered and nameless.

They get to Amiens two hours after dark, riding in through one of the old city gates and craning their necks to get a glimpse of the shadow of the cathedral. There is a party of pilgrims staying at the inn. The newcomers must make the best of what space remains. Jean-Baptiste shares a bed in the attic with the priest and is invited, before the candle is put out, to join him in a prayer. He does not wish to pray, would prefer to announce that he is a philosopher, a rationalist, a freethinker, but he politely adds his amens to the priest's and feels the old comfort of it. They shake hands and snuff the light. The priest's guts rumble. He apologises. Jean-Baptiste assures him he is not troubled by it.

In the morning, he wakes with his head rolled against the priest's shoulder. They sit up in the bed, shake hands again. This is life; this is travelling.

A new coach, a new coachman, fresh horses. They reach Douai by early afternoon. Here, the company divides. The old priest is met by young priests from the seminary, the English couple cross the yard to the waiting Calais coach, the sad and elegant woman makes hushed enquiries about the next conveyance to Brussels. Jean-Baptiste, clutching a small valise, is hurried into a crowded box aimed at Valenciennes. Two hours later, he climbs down, stiff with cold, onto the rue de Paris. There is always traffic between the town and the mines. For ten sous, he buys a ride on a cart delivering barrels of high-smelling butter, and they come to the edge of the miners' colony just as the daylight gutters behind them.

Even in the gloom, it is evident that Lecoeur was right and that nothing important has changed since Jean-Baptiste was last here. The same thick rind of shacks and hovels, like the encampment of a besieging army, one that clings on grimly without the slightest faith in victory. Scores of small fires burn, each attended by its gang of silhouetted men and women. On the verges of the road, children play laboriously, some pausing to look up, wan and incurious, at the passing wagon. The roads were built by the company. The first were given names such as avenue de Charbon, avenue de l'Avenir, even avenue de Richesse. Later roads were simply given numbers: rue 1, rue 2. In the centre of it all, discernible as a darker, denser zone of smoke and muffled din, are the works themselves.

The managers have a compound of their own a little to the east of the works. The prevailing wind brings a steady drift of soot and rock dust. The style of the compound is that of a provincial barracks, each block divided into six, each sixth the home of a manager, most of them single men. It is not a place to bring a wife; it is certainly not a place you might hope to find one. The senior managers live in Valenciennes. The owners and shareholders are in Paris, where the mines might feature in their thoughts as marvellous holes in the ground from which one can simply scoop money.

Snow has been threatening for hours. Now, just as the engineer enters the compound, it begins to fall. He remembers Lecoeur's place; his own was next to it for nigh on a year, the second and third divisions respectively of the second block. Outside his front window, Lecoeur used to have a small garden, a patch of worked ground in which, in summer, he grew onions and lettuces, some marigolds. There is no trace of it now.

He raps at the door, waits, knocks again. Snow is settling on his shoulders, the brim of his hat. He is about to knock for a third time when the door is dragged open and there is Lecoeur, candle in hand, the flame streaming, flickering.

'Comrade!' he cries. 'Oh, dear comrade! I am almost deranged with waiting!'

The candle blows out. They go down the little passage in the dark. They come to the parlour. The candle, after some searching for the necessary materials, is lit again. Lecoeur stands in the middle of the room, triumphant, fumy, a little unsteady.

'You remember it?' he asks. 'Mmm? Can you not see your old self in that very armchair?'

'I can,' says Jean-Baptiste. He takes in the room – the chair with its blooms of human grease, the mean little fire, the silhouette portraits of mother and sister . . . A constancy, a changelessness that, like that of the miners' colony, is not of a good type.

On the table, a meal has been set out. Some slices of a soused calf's head, potatoes undressed, bread spread thinly with a previous consignment of the high-smelling butter. At the centre of the table is a bottle containing some clear liquid that Lecoeur now pours into two glasses, draining his own immediately, then passing the other to Jean-Baptiste. They sit opposite each other. Jean-Baptiste saws at the slice of head on his plate (it tastes, poor thing, as though pickled in its own tears). He sips at the stuff from the bottle, sees black flakes of snow collide soundlessly with the window glass.

Three years since they last met – a hurried embrace in the drizzle by the coach-stop in Valenciennes. What rigours have those years imposed that this man should be so hollowed out? He is no more than thirty-five, possibly younger, yet looks fifty and ill. Most of his teeth have gone. His nose is swollen, pitted, strung with swollen vessels. He is pitifully thin and nervous. Once he has started talking, he cannot stop, and what began breezily enough becomes, by degrees, a lament, then a bitter complaint, that has at its heart the mine, that leviathan, that grinder of men's bones.

Is this how he passes his nights? Alone with a bottle, indicting the air? He has on a waistcoat of clotted brown wool, a garment knitted perhaps by a circle of unmarried female relatives for whom the young Lecoeur, the Lecoeur with teeth, once represented the family's last great hope. By the time he falls silent and reaches, with a lover's sigh, for the bottle again, Jean-Baptiste has already decided he must take him to Paris if he can. Here he will not last another winter. And can he *really* have lost all his former ability? All that good activity of mind he once possessed? With the minister's money, the minister's authority, it should not be impossible to extricate him. There is a risk, of course. How far gone is he? But in good conscience, he cannot be left in Valenciennes.

He is thinking it through, trying to construct in his imagination a credible picture of the first day of excavations at les Innocents – himself on some kind of dais or scaffolding, the men below in neat rows with their tools – when Lecoeur suddenly asks, 'Have you married?'

'No,' says Jean-Baptiste, into whose mind – absurdly! – comes the shadow of Héloïse, the whore Héloïse.

'I thought not,' says Lecoeur. 'A married man does not wear a suit such as that.'

'And you?' asks Jean-Baptiste. 'There is some . . . involvement?'

Lecoeur smiles, shakes his head, glances into the fire. 'I have had nothing to do with women for a long time now.'

In the morning, the tocsin rings at three thirty. First shift, first descent, is at four. Jean-Baptiste wakes in the upstairs room. He is looking towards the window, but there is no hint of any light. He swings his legs from the bed. The room is laughably cold. He remembers it all, perfectly.

In the parlour, he finds Lecoeur fully dressed, his face a mask of concentration as he uses both hands to pour himself a glass from the now almost empty bottle. He sets the bottle down, then leans his mouth to the rim of the glass and sucks in the first mouthful while the glass is still on the table.

'Shall I pour one for you?' he asks.

'Later, perhaps,' says Jean-Baptiste.

They have, the previous evening, talked a little about the scheme for les Innocents, about the men who will be needed. Lecoeur was reassuringly businesslike. He had prepared a list of names and, going down the list (Everbout, Slabbart, Block, Rape, Cent, Wyntère . . .), gave Jean-Baptiste a quick assessment of each of them, the approximate age, length of service, moral character so far as it was known, could be known. Nothing was said about adding his own name to the list, but now, in the snow-cold parlour, Jean-Baptiste asks if he might consider it.

'*Consider it!*'

In his rush to clutch his friend's hands, Lecoeur strikes the corner of the table with his thigh, almost upsetting the precious bottle.

'They will name squares after us!' he cries. 'The men who purified Paris!'

He breaks into a jig; he cannot help himself. Jean-Baptiste laughs, claps time. He has saved a life today and has not even had his breakfast.

For almost an hour, having rediscovered their old intensity of speaking, the thrust and parry of the Valenciana days, the two of them discuss the preparations they must make. The transportation of the men, their lodging in Paris. Hygiene, discipline, pay. All imaginable difficulties, from inclement weather to a terror of ghosts.

'And this place,' asks Lecoeur, 'where the remains will be taken . . . ?'

'An old quarry.'

'The arrangements are complete?'

'They will be soon enough.'

'And it is dry? We have been using a new pump here after the English model. Much faster than anything we have used before.'

'My responsibility is the cemetery. Once the carts have left les Innocents . . .'

'How deep must we go?'

'They say some of the common graves are thirty metres.'

'So deep?'

'Most, hopefully, are less so, but for the men, it will not be very pretty work.'

'It cannot,' says Lecoeur, 'be any worse than slithering into the earth with a pick and not knowing when you might crawl into choke-damp or when the tunnel behind you will fall. We lost three this last week. Buried alive. They will not shore up the tunnels properly, for they know they will not be paid for it. Only for coal.'

Beyond the window, the day does not seem to be getting any lighter. Thin gusts of snow are striking the glass again. Jean-Baptiste bestirs himself. He does not intend to be trapped here.

'I will leave you money. Use what you need. And you may use the minister's name where it is necessary. But everything must be done without delay. If we drag our feet, I am assured that none of us will be needed. They have been most particular on that point.'

'*Amicus certus in re incerta cernitur,*' says Lecoeur, grinning and rubbing his palms together. 'Now, will you take a mouthful of food? A few slices of the head perhaps?' He reaches it down from the meat safe on the wall, holds it like a darling. The poor, hacked-about head.

13

There is snow in Paris too. Snow churned with ash, soot, mud, dung. On the better streets, outside the better houses, it has been swept into grey pyramids. Elsewhere, cartwheels, hooves, sabots have cleared their own paths. In the cemetery, the snow lies along the arms of the preaching cross, sits discreetly on the stone heads of the *lanternes des morts*, lines the tops of the walls, the sloping roofs of the charnels.

With a spade borrowed from the sexton's house, Jean-Baptiste prods at the ground, feels its resistance, hears it, the dull ringing, as if he had struck iron. At least the stink of the place is much reduced. He feels no nausea. No active disgust.

Armand appears from the church, ducking under the low door, then crossing the cemetery, his hair like the one thing of vivid colour left in the world.

'I see,' he says, nodding to the spade, 'you are staying true to your name, Monsieur Bêche.'

'On ground like this,' says Jean-Baptiste, 'I would do better with an axe.'

'You know it could stay frozen for months,' says Armand, cheerfully.

'It will not.'

'Because the minister won't permit it? Very well. But I do not think you will be digging up any bones this side of Christmas. You should go home. Remind yourself of who you are.'

Jean-Baptiste nods, taps around his toes with the edge of the spade. Home. He would like nothing better. He aches for it.

'And you?' he asks.

'Christmas? I shall stay drunk for three days. Lisa will berate me for the dog I am. Then I will grow sober, make love to her for hours, go with her and the children to Saint-Eustache for mass. Have ungodly thoughts about the young wife in the pew ahead of me. Perhaps find a way to press against her at the communion rail.'

'And your friends? Renard? Fleur, de Bergerac?'

'Ah, you did not like them much, did you? In fact, there is not much to like about them. By the way, that paint on your cheek will wash off eventually. In the meantime, you can pretend they are beauty spots. Now, talking of beauty . . .'

The girl Jeanne, a heavy shawl over her shoulders, is walking towards them from the sexton's house. She raises a pink hand in greeting.

'You are back,' she says.

'Yes,' says Jean-Baptiste.

'I wondered where you had gone.'

'I had some business,' he says, 'in another place. I travelled.'

'That's nice,' she says. 'Was it nice?'

'It served its purpose,' says Jean-Baptiste.

'And does she know,' asks Armand, 'what its purpose was? Does she know what you have in mind for us?'

Jeanne looks at Armand, then at Jean-Baptiste. 'You have something in mind for us?' she asks.

'Others do,' says Jean-Baptiste. 'Important people.'

'Oh,' she says.

'Oh, indeed,' says Armand.

'You must have wondered, Jeanne, what I was doing here. When you were helping me, you must have wondered.'

'I enjoyed helping you,' she says. 'I will help you today if you wish.'

'I will not need it today,' he says.

'The cemetery,' says Armand, 'for I shall tell her if you won't. The cemetery is to be got rid of, Jeanne. The cemetery and the church.'

'The matter was settled long ago,' says Jean-Baptiste. 'The place is to be made new. Pure. It is what the king himself wishes.'

'The king?'

'You have nothing to fear. The remains, the bones, will all be taken to a place, a consecrated place, where they may be kept safely.'

'All of them?' she asks.

'Yes.'

'And you can do this?' She looks at the spade.

'I will have others to help me,' he says.

She nods several times. 'If it is what you want,' she says quietly.

'You and your grandfather, you will be provided for. You have my word on it.'

'You want to be careful what you promise,' says Armand.

'The cemetery,' says Jean-Baptiste, ignoring him, 'cannot just be forgotten about, can it?'

'Oh, no,' she says, 'it cannot.'

'And you know how the people complain of it.'

She frowns. 'Grandfather says they used to be proud to live by such a famous place. They boasted of it.'

'People's noses,' says Armand, 'have grown more delicate.'

She nods again, more emphatically, as if the matter was entirely proved.

'And the house?' she asks.

'You will have a new one. Perhaps even here when the land has been cleared.'

'Here?'

'Yes.'

'Grandfather will be well if I am with him,' she says.

'Of course. You must be with him.'

For a quarter-minute they stand without speaking. They look about themselves. They can see nothing to suggest that anything will ever be other than the way it is now.

An hour later, warming themselves with brandy and hot water in a mirrored booth at the Café de Foy, Armand says, 'She agrees only because it is you. You have used some Norman enchantment on her. But have you not misled her? Once your miners get to work, they will fling the bones around like firewood. And this house you have promised her. Did you not invent it on the spot? You have no more power to give her a house than you have to give me the organ at Saint-Eustache.'

'I will do what I can,' says Jean-Baptiste.

'You will do what you are told,' says Armand. 'Isn't that more like it?'

'The minister . . .'

'Your great friend the minister.'

'I do not believe he is . . . unfeeling.'

'And you think he will feel something for Jeanne? Or is it you who feels something for her? I can see that it might be nice to curl up with a girl like that on a cold night.'

'She is barely more than a child.'

'Barely will do. Our beloved queen was wed at fourteen. And she'd go with you. You could smuggle her up to your room at the Monnards'. Though no doubt it would put Ziguette's nose out of joint.'

'It is you, I think, who is interested in Ziguette.'

'If you mean would I *do* it with her if the opportunity presented itself, the answer is yes. So, I assume, would you. Which makes me think we should go and ogle our Persian princess. What do you say?'

'Not today.'

'No? You are being very dull, Monsieur Bêche. You want to beware of dullness. It is not modern. But it shall be as you wish. When you've paid for the brandy, I will do you the honour of escorting you to your lodgings.'

At the edge of the market, as they are crossing the top of the rue des Prêcheurs, they encounter the Austrian. She is carrying a small parcel of books, wrapped and neatly tied with black twine. She gives the impression of being only a very little disturbed by the cold, the slush on the cobbles, the eddying wind others scowl into. Armand salutes her, then catches something of the glance, the second's worth of to-and-fro between the whore and the engineer.

'Oh, no. Not her as well?' he asks. And starts to laugh.

SECOND

One day I shall mourn for those who are dear to me, or I shall be mourned by them . . . At the thought of death, the oppressed soul longs to open itself completely and envelop the objects of its affection.

J. Girard, *Des Tombeaux, ou de l'Influence des Institutions Funèbres sur les Moeurs*

1

The poverty of the villages is almost picturesque from the windows of a coach that is not stopping. How much has changed in two hundred years? Did the people not live much like this in the days of Henri IV? They may have lived better, with fewer of them and the land less tired and the lords, with their just glimpsable chateaux, less numerous.

He is going home! Home for the first time in eleven weeks, though in his heart it might as easily be eleven years, himself a grizzled Ulysses straining his eyes for the blue shadow of Ithaca.

The roads, thank God, are passable. Last week's snow has thawed and the new weather – a low, icy sun, the air cracking at night – has turned the mud to stone.

He has changed coach twice. The driver of this one is worryingly drunk, but the horses know their way. He looks out at the wall of a forest, frets when they are held up by a flock of geese being herded on the road ahead by some dreaming girl with a stick. Then a final hill, a church tower purple in the afternoon light and the coachman's voice bellowing, 'Bellême! Bellême!'

He climbs down in the market square. His bag is unlashed, dropped into his arms. As ever, a small group of townsfolk are stood nearby, arms folded, watching. In Bellême, curiosity will never go out of fashion. One of these watchers, a widow who deals in cures for the toothache, for palsy, wet ulcers, recognises him and he speaks to her and hears of the deaths of two or three whose names he knows, of the wedding of a local girl to a cloth-shearer in Mamers, of a man caught poaching on the cardinal's estate and sent for trial at Nogent. Nobody, it seems, is making any money. The soil grows only stones. And yet somehow every-one is managing and the church clock is being repaired and God will grant them a better year next year, for they are not bad people and their sins are only small ones.

'And what of you?' she asks, finally drawing breath. 'You have been somewhere?'

He has some distance still to go. He shoulders his bag, marches down the hill, crosses the stream on the stepping stones, walks warily through the corner of a field where once he was pursued by a white bull. From the woods at the side of him, he smells the smoke of the charcoal-burners' fires, those mysterious people who belong only to themselves; then he passes the holly tree – thick this year with berries – crosses Farfield, hears the dogs begin their clamour, and there is the house, the yard, the patched outbuildings, all the stone and mud of home exactly where it should be, must be, and yet, at the same time, all of it somehow surprising. He quickens his pace; a figure appears in the doorway. He raises an arm; she raises hers. For the last minutes of the walk he is watched by her. It is as if her gaze was the path he was walking up, as if at the end of it he might walk clean into her grey eyes.

When they have greeted, he sits by the fire, holds his hands to the heat. There is a moment, a little span of seconds, in which he is simply and passionately happy and nothing in the world is any more complicated than a picture in a child's book. He is home! Home at last! And then the moment passes.

His mother is making things for him, bringing things to him, asking him questions, thanking him for the money he has sent. She looks, he thinks, a little pinched about the eyes and mouth. And is there not more grey to be seen under the linen scallops of her cap? He would like to ask if she has been quite well, but she would only smile and say she has been well enough. Suffering is a gift from God. It is not a matter to complain of.

His sister comes in, Henriette, cold hands tucked under her arms. She has been in the dairy and smells like a wet-nurse. She wants, she says, to know everything. Her interest flatters him and he listens to himself with some astonishment, his fluent refashioning of the recent past. To hear him, anyone might imagine he and the minister spent their mornings together strolling between the fountains in the gardens of Versailles. The Monnards become a simple bourgeois family, amiable, irreproachable, while Armand is exactly the sort of companion his mother – who has always fretted that he will be lonely – would wish for him, and one who could never be suspected of living conjugally with his landlady or having a taste for preserved princesses. About his work at les Innocents he repeats only what he has already said in his letters, that he is charged with improving the health of a populous quarter, and with some structural alterations to an ancient church there. There is no good reason not to tell them everything, nothing forbids it, the work is not *indecent*, yet when it comes to it, he is afraid he will see something in their faces, will glimpse some imperfectly concealed reflex of disgust.

His sister wants to know if he has seen the queen. 'Yes,' he says, the bluntest of his lies so far. Naturally, he is required to describe her, in detail.

'She was at some distance from me,' he says, 'and surrounded by her ladies.'

'But you must have seen something?'

He describes Héloïse. Mother and sister are delighted, his sister especially.

'She cannot have been so far away,' she says, 'for you have made a perfect portrait of her.'

An hour later, amid the banging of doors, the reckless jollity of dogs, his brother, Jean-Jacques, bursts in on them, as alike in his looks to their dead father as Jean-Baptiste is to their living mother. He leans his gun – father's old Charleville musket – against a side of the dresser and greets his brother with an undisguised and manly affection that has the immediate effect of strengthening in Jean-Baptiste that sense of strangerhood that has been growing in him almost from the moment he sat down.

'I hit a rabbit,' says Jean-Jacques. 'Just a small one, up by the hollow. Blew the poor thing to pieces. Let the dogs have it.'

'To have hit anything . . .' says Jean-Baptiste, nodding to the musket.

'The secret is to aim half a metre to the left. You could calculate it for me, brother. A bit of your Euclid.'

'It'd be easier to buy a new gun. Something with rifling.'

'But I'd miss the old one,' says Jean-Jacques, settling himself on the opposite side of the fire, stretching his legs out in front of him. 'So what's the news in Paris, eh?'

'This and that.'

'You've got skinny.'

'And you've grown a belly. That waistcoat will need letting out.'

'A belly suits him,' says Henriette. 'Don't you think?'

It does. It suits him perfectly. How well he fits into this Norman world! Big shoulders from working the farm. A good high colour in his cheeks, his dark hair tied with a length of old blue ribbon. A country beau. A man adapted, a man in his rightful place. No wonder he has never shown much envy of his older brother's success, his education, his being taken up by powerful men. His ambitions were always of a different order – less fancy, more easily grasped. And which of them now is the freer? Which has more pleasure in life? Which, to some clear-eyed judge of such things, would seem like the man arrived, the one whose wheel has risen?

That night the brothers share their old room, are carried into sleep by the calling of owls and wake together in the light of a late-setting moon. In the kitchen – that scrubbed and orderly world where even the light seems to lie like lengths of rinsed muslin – their mother is rousing the fire, dropping small wood onto small flames. She scalds cider. They drink it hot enough to make their teeth ache, put bread and apples in their pockets and set off with the mare to saw a fallen tree, an old elm uprooted in the autumn storms.

It is lovely work, sane work, though not easy for Jean-Baptiste to keep up with his brother. They sweat, laugh at nothing, compete with the saw, hint in their stories at sex, come home, the mare loaded with aromatic timber, their throats parched.

A week of this and he starts to forget about the Monnards, Lecoeur, les Innocents. He discovers in himself a great appetite for forgetting. He lets his accent thicken, rediscovers his country trudge, that considered slowness of movement and gesture that was the mark of the men he grew up among.

On Christmas Eve, they go to mass at Bellême. They put on their best things, compliment each other, though Jean-Baptiste is not wearing his pistachio suit, having, at the last moment in Paris, not quite had the nerve to face his family in Monsieur Charvet's vision of the future. He had considered, briefly, going back to the place des Victoires and seeing if his old suit was still there (his mother has already asked after it), but let himself be unnerved by the anticipation of Charvet's scorn, the unvoiced judgement that the young engineer was one of those timorous creatures who leap forward one day only to scurry back the next. Instead, he has on a suit borrowed from Monsieur Monnard, something pigeon-coloured and respectable, the sort of costume that might be worn to the annual Guild of Cutlers dinner. It fits him well; better perhaps than he would have wished it to.

In church, they sit in their usual pew, opposite the chapel of Sainte-Anne. Everyone, except the dying and those who have already drunk themselves into oblivion, is present. The priest, Père Bricard, is popular in the town for the shortness of his masses, his fathomless indifference as to how the members of his flock choose to damn themselves. When it's done and neighbours have lingered in the cold by the church door and the children can find no more ice to crack with the heels of their boots and the town's dogs have grown hoarse from barking, the Barattes go home across stream and fields. At the farm, the brothers look to the animals, peer into stable and byre with light held high, make out the shifting of cattle, the stillness of the horses, then come inside and sit and drink and join in the gossiping. (Who was that gentleman with the Vadier family? Did he not show a most particular attention to Camille Vadier? And what a curious little hat Lucile Robin was wearing! Surely she never meant it to look like that?)

At last the fire is smoored, the table cleared, and the house retires. In their room, the brothers lie speaking into the darkness above them, exchanging stories of their father. It is a ritual between them, a thing they must always do, the dead man's life and character in a dozen worn anecdotes picked from a shared hoard, like that time in the middle of the market he told old Tissot what he thought of him, and the night he dragged the pedlar half drowned from the river and carried him home over his shoulder, and how, at his workbench, with his needles and grommets and waxed thread, he looked like a bull making a daisy chain . . .

Such tales comfort the brothers. Such stories make it possible not to tell other stories, like those in which their father is making free with his fists or his belt, his ashplant, his boots, with strips of hide or a pair of newly stitched gauntlets, thrashing the brothers or Henriette or his wife until he fell back, spent and shuddering. Nor do they speak of the last year of his life, though it is *this* Jean-Baptiste thinks of when they have fallen quiet and Jean-Jacques begins to snore. How their father became lost inside his own head, forgot the names of his tools, then forgot how to use them. How he took to addressing his wife as though speaking to his mother, called Henriette by the name of a long-dead sister. When the crisis was close, Jean-Baptiste was summoned home from the Ecole des Ponts and sat for hours on the stool by the sickbed talking of Maître Perronet, of roads and the grey wings of bridges, while his father lay with his head motionless on the bolster, eyes open, mouth slightly agape. The white lilac was in bloom. Bees and butterflies drifted through the narrow window and, having circled the room's shade, found their way out again. Twice a week the doctor came from Eperrais, fussed uselessly over his patient. In the family they took turns attending to the glover's needs, spooning soup into his mouth, propping him on the side of the bed to piss into the pot, wetting his lips, calming his fidgeting. All summer it went on – a whole summer viewed through the green diamonds of the sickroom window – until one afternoon, the air thickening for the last big storm of the season, the stricken man suddenly sat up in bed, grappled Jean-Baptiste's hands into his own, stared into his face and with a voice hauled from the ice within him said, 'I do love you.'

Love? Nothing of the kind had ever been said between them before. None of the children would have expected to hear such words from their father. So who, in that little resurrection, did he imagine he was speaking to? Did he know it was his eldest son? Did he think it was Jean-Jacques? Or perhaps his own brother, Simon, with whose absence he had several times held long, muttered conversations? There was no sequel, nothing that might have made anything clearer. Two days later the glover was gathered into an immense and private silence. Two weeks after that, he was dead, a man who, to all appearances, no longer knew his own name.

On Christmas morning – and early even for the country – Jean-Baptiste goes with his mother to the house-on-the-hill, the Protestant house, where she and a clutch of others will pray in the way they prefer. The few who see them on the road pretend not to know where they are headed. Madame Baratte is a decent woman, and there are plenty in Normandy for whom the gospel of Jesus Christ means nothing at all. Let her have her little heresies.

They pass through a well-swept yard, are admitted to the house the moment their faces are seen. To the left of the door is a broad flight of stairs, the stones so well trodden they are like the cast of an ancient riverbed. At the stair's turning is a pillar, a plain cross scored into the stone, and here there is space enough for six or eight to gather together. A small window gives a view of the road – a view that must once have been more necessary. The pastor is a Dutchman. He speaks French with an accent Jean-Baptiste has always found faintly comical. He is smooth-shaven, has eyes like a child's. He opens his Bible. The pages are worn to a grey nothing, but he does not need to read from them. He recites.

'"Beware the Lord will empty the earth and turn it upside down and scatter its inhabitants . . ."'

No infants? No stables? No shepherds or journeying kings?

'"The earth dries up and withers, the whole world withers and grows sick, the earth's high places sicken, and the earth itself is desecrated by the feet of those who live in it . . ."'

Ezekiel? Isaiah? The others will know.

'"Desolation alone is left in the city and the gate is broken into pieces . . . If a man runs from the rattle of the snare, he will fall into the pit; if he climbs out of the pit, he will be caught in the trap . . ."'

He does not spare them. He would not consider it kind to spare them. At length – great length – he shuts the book and the little congregation is left to pick through their consciences in silence, while Jean-Baptiste, hat in hand but head unbowed, looks out at the sky and is lost for a time in the beauty and mystery of what is most ordinary. When it is over, the company embrace one another, stiffly, solemnly, then quit the house in pairs, melt into the brightening day.

At the farm, the kitchen is already strewn with relatives. Children – a boy and girl Jean-Baptiste only vaguely recognises – clamber onto his back the moment he sits down. Cousin André is there, of course, looking prosperous, masonic, entertaining the women with tales of small-town scandal. And there too the poorest of the relatives, old Dudo and his wife – pure Baratte peasantry – their eyes untellable from those of the beasts they husband on their scrap of Norman mud. They speak only old Norman, understand no French, and sit at the end of the table smuggling slices of white sausage under their smocks. A plate of it is always left near them for this purpose. Even the children know better than to notice what they do.

In the midst of this, this amiable hubbub, Jean-Baptiste works at his cider. The visit, like all visits home for a long time now, has been an obscure failure. When is it we cease to be able to go back, truly go back? What secret door is it that closes? Having longed to escape Paris, he is anxious now to return. Whatever his life will be, whatever fate it is he is pressed against, it will be lived out somewhere else, not here among the still-loved fields and woods of his boyhood. He drains his mug, chews at something in the bottom of it, and stretches for the jug. His sister settles on the bench beside him. When they were younger they used to fight, and she had seemed to him spiteful, proud, yet now – plain and twenty-three – she is all kindness, and with a wisdom she has pulled down from who knows where, an enviable wisdom. She asks him more questions about Paris, about the fashions, about those Monnards he lives with. He knows she knows he has not told her the half of it. She asks more particularly if he has been in good health. A little fatigued, he says, shrugging. He has not been sleeping as he used to. And then it occurs to him what she might be referring to.

'You mean I do not smell as sweet as I did?'

'We wondered if it was the air in Paris, Jean. That it is not as good as here.'

'It is not,' he says. 'Not at all.'

'Then when you return here, you will recover,' she says. 'Already I think it is somewhat improved.'

He thanks her, drolly.

'When do you go back?' she asks.

2

Armand and his mistress must have been busy, Jeanne too perhaps. When Jean-Baptiste returns to Paris he is pointed out in the street, or simply stared at as if he might reveal a fringe of angel wing above the collar of his coat, or a nub of horn on his brow. In the marketplace, the morning before the Feast of Epiphany, an old man, one of the ragged, grimacing sort who haunt any public space, waves a withered arm at him and warns him to leave alone 'the field of our fathers lest the wrath of the Almighty . . .' Two days later, a stall-holder on the rue de la Fromagerie makes him a gift of honeycomb, wishes him luck. He starts to hear a new word at his back. 'Engineer.' He wonders how many of them have any clear notion of what an engineer is.

But of all the reactions he encounters in the first cold days of the New Year, none is more perplexing than that of the Monnards. Coming back to the house, he had felt almost pleased to see them, had been most particular in his thanks to Monsieur Monnard for the loan of his suit, assiduous in his enquiries as to how Madame and Mademoiselle Monnard had enjoyed the festivities, but by dinner on the second evening, it was clear that all was not well with them. It was Madame Monnard (having first ejected a piece of gristle from her mouth to the top of her fist) who raised the matter that was evidently the source of their disquiet.

'Monsieur,' she began, 'is it the case what we hear about the cemetery?'

'Madame?'

'That it is . . . to go?'

He set down his knife and fork. 'In a manner of speaking, madame, yes. It is to be removed, the land made clean. The church too, in time, will be removed.'

'It comes as a shock to us,' said Monsieur Monnard. 'We had not suspected it.'

'I am sorry for it, monsieur. But the church and cemetery have been closed these last five years. They could not be left to . . .'

'It is hard for us to think of it,' said Madame, a strange shrill voice.

'I hope it is for the public good, madame,' said Jean-Baptiste. 'And this house will no longer overlook a place of public interment. Will no longer have to suffer the consequences of that.'

'What consequences?' asked Monsieur Monnard.

Jean-Baptiste glanced down at his plate, where, in the coolness of the room, his food was already starting to congeal. 'Can it be entirely healthy, monsieur?'

'Do we seem unhealthy to you?'

'No. Of course. I did not mean to suggest . . .'

'Well then?'

And Ziguette began to cry. A thin whining followed by a gulp, then a sob rising out of her bosom, all of it accompanied by a vigorous working of her face so that she looked to Jean-Baptiste like someone he had never seen before. She fled the room. Madame and Monsieur exchanged glances.

'If I have . . .' began Jean-Baptiste, half rising from his chair.

'Poor Ziggi so dislikes any commotion,' said Madame, and then made certain remarks, incomprehensible at first, but which Jean-Baptiste finally understood to mean that Ziguette had started her monthly bleeding and was, as a result, unusually sensitive.

The sequel to this uneasy scene took place later the same night. Jean-Baptiste was in his room, wrapped in the red damask of his banyan. He was reading a few lines out of Buffon, something about the manner in which certain non-poisonous creatures mimic the markings of their poisonous cousins, when he heard the familiar scratching at the door and, opening it, expected to greet the muscular Ragoût but found instead Ziguette, white as death, and dressed in her nightclothes. That she was uncorseted was apparent each time she sighed.

She wanted to explain, or to apologise or both or neither. After some whispering at the door, he invited her inside, and as there was only one chair, he offered it to her and sat on the bed. She did not seem startled by the banyan, did not comment on it. He put another stick on the fire. He tried to reassure her.

'When it is done, think how nice it will be. In place of what you have now, a pleasant square. Gardens perhaps.'

She nodded. She seemed to be attempting to follow his reasoning, but her eyes had filled with tears again. 'It is,' she said, after a pause, 'as though you wished to dig up my childhood.'

'Childhood?'

'Innocent, girlish days.'

'I shall be digging only the cemetery. Earth and old bones. Many old bones.'

'You did not grow up here,' she said softly. 'If so, you would feel differently.'

Sitting a little lower than her, his gaze had somehow settled on her lap. He imagined a slow effusion of blood, a blood-rose blooming in the pale stuff of her nightgown, spreading across her thighs then, perhaps, starting audibly to drip onto the floorboards . . .

'When it is done,' he said, raising his eyes to hers, 'when it is over, it will be you who feels differently. The initial discomfort will quickly pass. You will be pleased.'

She did not argue against him. She began, discreetly, to look around his room, the bed, the trunk, the table with its books, the brass ruler. Then she stifled a yawn, apologised for disturbing him, and with a sweet, watery smile, the kind one bestows on a person who, through no fault of his own, is unable to understand what ought to be plain as day, she excused herself.

As she pulled the door shut behind her, he glanced at the ceiling, at the little hole over the bed, for once or twice during their interview he had heard the boards above them creaking.

He got onto the bed, stood on it. From such a perch, the ceiling was comfortably within his reach. He peered into the hole – nothing, no light, nothing at all. Then slowly, tentatively, he inserted the first finger of his left hand, much as the Comte de Buffon might have investigated the nest of some dubious insect, one that may or may not be merely mimicking its venomous nature . . . He could not swear to what he felt then, yet it seemed to him someone had softly blown on his finger, and for a while, balanced on the bed, he examined it.

3

He meets with Lafosse. January is burning low; nothing has started; not a bone has been shifted. He explains himself, endeavours to show himself a victim of circumstances which, in truth, he believes himself to be. He cannot begin without the miners and the miners have not arrived. They are coming, coming very soon, but they have not yet arrived. Halfway through his explanation, his somewhat hot-faced justification of himself, he realises that Lafosse does not really care about a few weeks here or there, will not remove him from his post or even threaten it. Who else, at short notice, would take on work like this? He presents his accounts. He is not unhappy to see that Lafosse is suffering with a cold.

What he can do alone, he does. From Louis Horatio Boyer-Duboisson he obtains canvas, wooden poles, rope, ship's chain. He arranges with a toothless man called Dejour the supply of firewood, and works beside him and his sons when the first consignment is delivered. He cannot set foot in the market without tradesmen approaching him with offers and promises, sometimes with whispered warnings about a fellow tradesman who is nothing but a thief. Straw for bedding comes from the stables behind the coaching office on the rue aux Ours. It is dry and tolerably clean. Thirty spades, thirty picks arrive, also from Louis Horatio Boyer-Duboisson. At Valenciennes, the miners are not permitted to own their own tools. A man with his own spade may start to think of himself as independent.

On the fifth day of February, he receives a message from Lecoeur informing him that all is at last ready, that he is on the point of proceeding to Paris with the men and that he hopes to be there within a week. As the letter has taken two days to reach him, Jean-Baptiste starts his vigil two days later, standing hour after hour by the junction of the rue Saint-Denis and the rue aux Fers, though not so close to the Italian fountain as to make himself a target for the ribaldry of the laundry women.

The weather is cold but bright, thick frosts in the morning but then in the middle of the day almost warm. He sees the same faces again and again, sees how the streets have their currents, their little tides. He has a glimpse of Héloïse walking away from him towards the faubourg Saint-Denis. He sees Père Colbert – it can be no one else – the blue glasses, the greeny-black of his soutane stretched across the big, hunched back. He sees Armand, who tells him to hire a boy, but Jean-Baptiste does not wish to rely on a boy, a boy's powers of concentration, nor does he want to sit idly in the Monnards' house, waiting for something he sometimes thinks will never happen.

And then, at about two in the afternoon, precisely a week from the day the letter from Valenciennes was dated, Lecoeur is suddenly, improbably there, riding a wagon from the direction of the river and lifting his hat in elegant salute as he catches sight of Jean-Baptiste.

There are three vehicles in all, uncovered, and with large, mud-encrusted wheels. When the wagons stop, knots of locals, including the laundry women, gather to look up at the strangers, who look back, some of them with the wide and frightened eyes of driven cattle, others simply wonderstruck, their faces, perhaps, like those of Hernán Cortés's men entering the golden city of Tenochtitlan. All traffic on the rue Saint-Denis comes to a halt. The horses droop their heads. One voids itself, noisily and greenly, onto the cobbles. Lecoeur clambers down from his bench at the front of the first wagon and strides over to Jean-Baptiste. In a flood of mutual relief, they clasp each other's hands, firmly.

'We have had several adventures on our way,' says Lecoeur. 'Not quite Circe or the Cyclops but enough to contend with. Yet here we are, ready to do your bidding.'

For a man who has been on the road in the company of thirty miners through all the inclemencies of deep winter, Lecoeur appears marvellously neat and fresh. A little brown wig on his head, his face decently shaved, a handsome red cloth round his throat, and on his breath just a whiff of the strong drink any man travelling in the cold might take, prophylactically.

'You have them all?' asks Jean-Baptiste, nodding to the wagons.

'Thirty men and hand-picked. I believe you will find no fault with them.'

'I am grateful to you,' says Jean-Baptiste, 'most grateful, but we must move the wagons into the street here.' He points into the rue aux Fers. 'We shall be shouted at otherwise. People here are not slow to make their feelings known.'

It is done in four minutes, the wagons and horses lined up along the north wall of the church. The men get down, stand in clumps, looking from Lecoeur to Jean-Baptiste as if silently weighing the authority of each, silently reaching their conclusions.

Jean-Baptiste unlocks the door into the cemetery. Here, then, is the first test. The men must be got into the cemetery, a place disturbing even to a mind as well-lit as his own. Will they baulk? And what then? Force them in? How? With the point of a sword? He does not have a sword.

'If you would lead them,' he says quietly to Lecoeur. 'They are used to you.'

'Very well,' says Lecoeur. He goes through the door without hesitation. The miners shuffle in behind him. When the last is inside, Jean-Baptiste follows them, pulls the doors shut, joins Lecoeur.

'It is as you promised,' says Lecoeur, 'a somewhat powerful impression.'

'You become used to it,' says Jean-Baptiste. 'At least a little.'

'It will inspire us to do our work more swiftly,' says Lecoeur, attempting a smile.

Wood for a large fire has for days been piled in readiness between the church and the preaching cross. Now, with embers from the sexton's kitchen, they light it. Smoke spirals into the still air; there is a sound of snapping in the fire's heart; the smoke thickens; a dozen flames leap out from between the timbers. The miners make a circle round it, holding their hands to its warmth.

Jeanne comes out. Jean-Baptiste introduces her to Lecoeur. Are the men hungry? she asks. Oh, undoubtedly, yes. Very hungry. Then she will go to the market and fetch soup and bread for them. There is a stall that sells wholesome soup by the pail. It will not take her long.

Her offer – the good, practical sense of it – is quickly accepted. Lecoeur picks out three men from the circle to assist her. Jean-Baptiste counts money into her hand.

'They are quite tame,' says Lecoeur, indicating her helpers. 'Tell them what you want of them and they will do it.'

They watch her go, the men plodding behind her.

'She will be a great asset,' says Lecoeur. 'I foresee she will become their little virgin mother.'

'When the men have eaten,' says Jean-Baptiste, 'they must put up their tents. Here, I think, in two rows of five. You, if you have no objection, will have your billet in the sexton's house. It is only the old man and Jeanne there. I think you will be quite comfortable.'

'I am here as a tool,' says Lecoeur. 'It matters very little where I am laid down at night.'

Jean-Baptiste nods. He is listening to the low voices of the men and remembering what, unaccountably, he had forgotten. At least half of the miners at Valenciennes speak only Flemish. When he worked at the mines, he learnt two dozen words of it but has long since lost them all.

'You have their tongue?' he asks Lecoeur.

'I do not think I could court a lady with it,' says Lecoeur, 'but for our needs I believe I have what is necessary.'

After half an hour, Jeanne returns with the miners. Two of them carry steaming pails of soup. Jeanne and the third miner have their arms loaded with bread. Behind this party comes Armand, who strides towards Jean-Baptiste and Lecoeur and, while still some way off, calls, 'I saw your smoke. I had begun to believe that you were merely an amiable dreamer. I shall always take you at your word now.'

'Allow me to present,' says Jean-Baptiste, 'Monsieur Saint-Méard.'

'Are you of our number, monsieur?' asks Lecoeur.

'I think I may be called so,' says Armand, looking at Jean-Baptiste.

'Monsieur Saint-Méard is the organist at the church,' says Jean-Baptiste.

'Former organist,' says Armand, 'once these gentlemen have started their work. But I intend to participate in my own destruction. Is that not the right of us all?'

'The ancients believed that, monsieur,' says Lecoeur.

'And we are the new ancients, are we not?'

'We are the men,' says Lecoeur, 'who will purify Paris. I said as much to my friend here when last we met. It will be a type of example.'

'We will dispose of the past,' says Armand, a voice pitched between earnestness and comedy. 'History has been choking us long enough.'

'I much approve of these sentiments,' says Lecoeur, lowering his voice.

'Then let's approve of them over a bottle,' says Armand.

'It will be dark in two hours,' says Jean-Baptiste. 'The bottle must wait.'

'Already he has turned tyrant on us,' says Armand.

Lecoeur looks uncomfortable. 'But he is right, monsieur. Quite right. There is much to attend to here. We will need our wits about us. Later, perhaps?'

The soup and bread are consumed without ceremony. The miners lick their spoons, wipe clean their beards with the side of a hand, spit, scratch, yawn.

Seeing them done, Jean-Baptiste climbs the winding steps to the narrow, railed pulpit on the pediment of the preaching cross. He is followed by Lecoeur, then, entirely at his own invitation, by Armand. With three of them in the pulpit, they have to stand with their shoulders pressed hard against each other. With his free arm Jean-Baptiste gestures to the miners. They stand and slowly approach the cross. Something else he had forgotten about these men: years of stooping in the tunnels means that many are permanently hunched. They gather below him and tilt their heads awkwardly to look up. To Lecoeur he says, 'I shall speak to them a little. Then you, if you will be so kind, can repeat the gist of it in Flemish.'

He clears his throat. He does not have a strong speaking voice, wants to be heard but does not wish to shout at them. 'You are welcome here,' he begins. 'It may be that I knew some of you in Valenciennes. Our work here will be very different. All this ancient cemetery and the church behind you is to be destroyed. The whole surface of the cemetery will be dug out. All the bones, all those you can see in the charnels, all those underground and in the crypts, will be removed and taken to another place. You must handle the bones as you would those of your own ancestors. We will start tomorrow on the first of the big pits. We will, at all times, have fires burning to purify and circulate the air. The doctors are agreed that fire is the best defence against any vapours our digging may release. Your pay will be twenty-five sous for a day's work. There will be one hot meal a day plus a litre of wine. You must not leave the cemetery without permission from myself or Monsieur Lecoeur. Your first task is to put up your shelters and dig the latrines. You must not foul the ground. We will work every day. You will each be responsible for the care and maintenance of your tools.' Then, an afterthought, 'I am Baratte. The engineer.'

'Excellent,' whispers Lecoeur.

'Functional,' says Armand.

Lecoeur begins his translation. He is evidently much more fluent than he has admitted. As he speaks, Jean-Baptiste scans the broken ranks of the miners. There is one who stands out; taller than most of the others, bare-headed, his gaze seems to move coolly across the faces of the triumvirate on the preaching cross. One might almost guess that he was amused, as if he had seen such sights, witnessed such moments too often not to find in them some hint of the absurd. For a few seconds he settles a hand on the shoulder of a much older miner in front of him, and though it is hard to see clearly across twenty metres of air, the hand is evidently not quite as it should be, is, in some way, deformed.

When Lecoeur has finished, the three of them, at some risk of tumbling over each other, descend the winding steps. Boyer-Duboisson's poles and canvas are carried to the level ground in the middle of the cemetery. Once the first tent is erected, its construction understood, the others go up swiftly enough.

The wood merchant arrives with fresh timber. He peers in at the miners, sucks his gums, nods approvingly. Supplying les Innocents will be the best work of his life: once the fires are lit, they'll stay that way for months. The new wood is stacked close beside the tents. It is both valuable and stealable. Already a size-able quantity has found its way over the walls at night.

Jean-Baptiste inspects the work on the latrines, approves it. Inspects each tent, tugs at their ropes. Several times he is called away to the cemetery doors to deal with a tradesman, work he eventually gives to Armand, who seems to want it.

Even in digging the latrines and the fire pits they have unearthed some hundred or more large bones and countless frag-ments, some of them chalk-white, others grey or black, or yellow as a chanterelle. Jeanne collects one of the smaller skulls, dislodges with her thumb a gob of earth from its brow and settles it in the grass again as though returning a fledgling to its nest. There is in these actions of hers something faintly repellent, yet it is obvious to Jean-Baptiste that her example will impress the men far more than any words of his own.

As he passes them in the deepening gloom of early evening, he tries to fix their faces in memory. Not many will look him in the eyes. Those who do he stops and asks their names. Jacques Everbout, Joos Slabbart, Jan Biloo, Pieter Molendino, Jan Block. He does not find the man he noticed from the preaching cross, the one who looked up so coolly. Whoever he is, he seems to have the knack of making himself invisible when he chooses to.

When Jean-Baptiste built the bridge on the estate of the Comte de S—, he had some twelve men under him – servants from the house and gardens, together with a pair of journeymen masons and a master mason from Troyes. The master in particular made no effort to hide his impatience with the 'boy' who commanded the project. The journeymen were not much kinder, and even the house-servants would come and go as they pleased and missed no opportunity to humiliate him, in that way servants in great houses become adept at. It is not good to be humiliated. It is not good to be the master in word only. Here, at les Innocents, he must somehow impose his will, must do it even if in the privacy of his own heart he is as uncertain of himself as he was then. And yet he would like them to like him. Or at least, not to despise him.

Once it has become too dark for any useful activity, the men sit by the openings of their tents. They have been fed a second time, have been given drink. Jean-Baptiste – who has eaten only because Jeanne insisted on it, standing beside him with bread and bowl – makes a last round with Lecoeur, the pair of them bidding the men a good night and receiving in reply a few guttural responses. Impossible to know what they are thinking, whether half of them intend to run away in the night. Can they be trusted? There were, on occasions, incidents at the mines, violent incidents. Imagine the minister's face when he is told that the men have absconded and are ravaging Paris!

Away from the tents, Lecoeur reassures him.

'You are paying them considerably more than they received at Valenciennes. And they are decent sorts in their way. One might raise a very creditable company from them.'

'With you as their captain,' says Jean-Baptiste.

'You, dear Baratte, are our captain. I think you should look quite dashing atop a white horse.'

'I would need to improve my Flemish.'

'Advance, attack. Ten sous for every enemy head. That would be enough, I think.'

They are crossing the corner of the cemetery towards the sexton's house. Lecoeur has a burning torch, though they hardly need it. There is lamplight from the windows of the house and a broad, red light from the big fire.

'My first view of this place,' says Jean-Baptiste, 'was from the window of my room, up there. I looked down at night and it was a region of the most impenetrable dark. Now it is almost festive.'

'Festive? Forgive me, but I do not think such a place could ever be festive.'

'How do you find the stink now?'

'Tolerable, just. I have no large sense of stinks. Some effect of the mines. My skull is packed with coal dust.'

'There is said to be an animal,' says Jean-Baptiste, 'part dog, part wolf, that has its lair in the charnels on this side.' He gestures ahead of them to the south wall, the archways leading into the galleries.

'I would not allow such a story to get among the men.'

'No, you are right,' says Jean-Baptiste.

'But should it prove more than an old story, I have come

prepared.' Lecoeur stops and pulls a shape from the pocket of his coat. 'You see?'

'Is it loaded?' asks Jean-Baptiste.

'I have powder and balls among my things. And I have practised with it. I can hit a coal scuttle at thirty paces.'

'Lecoeur's wolf-destroyer,' says Jean-Baptiste. They laugh, softly. Lecoeur extinguishes the torch with the side of his boot and they enter the sexton's house.

The old man is asleep by the grate, the silver curls of his beard crushed against his chest. Armand is at the table with Jeanne. Jeanne stands as soon as the others enter. 'We have been waiting for you,' she says.

'We have been making our rounds of the camp,' says Lecoeur. He is looking at the brandy bottle on the table by Armand's elbow.

'How is your grandfather?' asks Jean-Baptiste.

'Weary,' says Jeanne, smiling at the top of the old man's head. 'Yet glad, I think, that it has begun. And he sees that I am content.' To Lecoeur she says, 'Your men are very nice.'

Lecoeur makes a little bow. 'You have become a favourite of theirs already, mademoiselle.'

'Now,' says Armand, yawning, 'perhaps we will be permitted to have that drink. Jeanne, we will need two more glasses.'

The glasses are fetched, filled, raised. Even Jeanne takes a little; the heat of it makes her cheeks burn. Armand tops them up. Jean-Baptiste puts his glass aside.

'We start to dig tomorrow,' he says. 'It would be best we do not sit up with the bottle. I shall be here very early, Jeanne. And I believe Madame Saget will be coming?'

'Lisa will be here,' says Armand. 'It seems she is quite reconciled to you.'

'I will go to the market for bread as soon as it is light,' says Jeanne. 'Grandfather will come, and perhaps Madame Saget.'

'And I have arranged for fifteen nice old hens to join us for dinner,' says Armand. 'A sack of potatoes, a sack of carrots, a man's weight in green lentils. Onions. And I took the liberty of ordering a hundred and twenty litres of Burgundy wine. Chateau Nothing-in-Particular. I suggest we keep the wine locked in one of the church offices. I doubt Père Colbert will drink it.'

'Good,' says Jean-Baptiste. 'Thank you.'

'We are a machine!' exults Lecoeur, whose glass, emptied twice, is somehow full again. 'We have been wound and now we are running!'

'Tick, tock, tick, tock,' says Armand. Jeanne giggles.

'Are you coming?' Jean-Baptiste asks Armand.

'I think perhaps I shall stay a while,' says Armand.

A pause.

'Very well. Then I wish you all a good night.'

He goes out, irritably tugging at the collar of his coat. Is Armand trying to make a fool of him? Is he up to something with Jeanne? He can only hope that Lisa Saget keeps him on a tight rein.

At the door to the rue aux Fers, he turns back to look at the strange, flickering stage he has created. From one of the tents comes the sound of singing, something muted and repetitive, a ballad, perhaps a lament. He listens a few moments, then goes out onto the empty street, shuts and locks the door. If Armand intends to leave at all, let him fumble his way out through the church.

At the house on the rue de la Lingerie, he avoids the Monnards, goes with his candle as quietly as he can past the drawing-room door. They, like everyone else, will have seen the fires – they could hardly have a better view of them – and given their inexplicable opposition to his work, the sight is unlikely to have occasioned any celebration. If he sits with them, they will rebuke him with silences, batter him with sighs. He has no idea any longer what to tell them.

In his room, he tugs off his boots. The brandy sits in a little stinging pool in his chest. He belches, then leans over the bed to look out of the window. A light rain has started to fall. There is nothing to see but the points of fire, the darkness close around them.

He closes the shutters and sits at the table, draws his note-book towards himself. He has had, this last week, some thoughts of starting a journal, a record of the destruction of the cemetery, something technical but also philosophical, witty even, that he could one day present to Maître Perronet at a small ceremony at the school. He toys with the pen, turning it round in his fingers. He should have stayed with the others, drunk more brandy, laughed a little. It would have done him good, would have been better than sitting up here on his own, oscillating.

He takes the cork from the ink bottle, dips his nib, writes at the top of a new page the date, writes below it, 'They came today, thirty poor men led by one whose presence I may have cause to regret. Already the work disgusts me and we have not even begun it. I wish to God I had never heard of Les Innocents.'

He closes the book, pushes it away, sits there blankly like a man under sentence. Then he draws the book to him again, opens it, reads through what he has written, dips his nib and, working methodically across the page, scratches a glistening X over each letter until the lines are hidden, unreadable, buried.

✳

One of them speaks; the others listen. It is raining still but not heavily enough to douse the fires. A dull red light finds its way through the open flap of the tent. It illuminates their lower bodies but leaves their faces in shadow. The one who speaks is dressed all in pale clothing, sits upon a throne of logs; the rest squat or kneel in the straw. A sermon? A story? Anyone unfamiliar with that language, which even spoken softly is like the rubbing and tapping of shale on shale, might guess at some manner of law-giving, the soft issuing of orders. Now and then the listeners offer a response, a hummed assenting. The speaker moves his hands, joins them, parts them. The third finger of his left hand is absent above the middle joint, ends in a blunt nub of bone and wrapped skin.

He pauses, then stretches for something by his boots, lifts it like a living thing, something that might wake and fly. It is a length of cut wood, or the hollow stem of a plant perhaps – fennel, hogweed. He tilts back his head and blows gently at the base of it. At its tip, a glow becomes a spark becomes a flame, a tongue of flame, its light settling over the man's upturned features, his narrowed eyes. The others sit, watch. Something is absorbed. Then words again, three or four weighty words, which his listeners repeat in voices no louder than the rain. And then it is done; it is over. They rise from the straw, file out of the tent, some of them glancing at the old church, some at the charnels. Quiet as ghosts they go into their own tents. Night, in the blue hulls of rain clouds, passes softly above them. The cemetery settles.

4

In the morning when he opens his eyes, there is already light around the shutters. He fumbles for his watch, flicks up its lid (the all-seeing eye) and holds it beside one of the fragile lines of daylight. A quarter past eight! He wrestles open the shutters and looks down. The tents are still there, the big fire burning briskly, figures moving between the latrines and the tents. That patch of colour crossing the wet grass is Jeanne, and the big-shouldered woman beside her surely Lisa Saget. There is Lecoeur, talking to one of the men. And there is Armand! Armand making himself useful while he, the engineer, the captain, is still in his bed!

There is not much dressing to be done; there was not much undressing the night before. He buttons his waistcoat, pulls on his boots, his hat, and clumps down the stairs three at a time, passes the cellar door, a door that always seems to find itself behind a fine curtain of shadow . . .

At the cemetery, he is grinned at; grinned at particularly by Armand, but no one is so unkind as to make a remark. Everyone is busy, calmly busy. He is pleased, relieved, more grateful to them than he dares to express. Jeanne puts a bowl of coffee into his hands, and before he can thank her, she has gone out of the house to help her grandfather and Lisa Saget with the construction of a little kitchen annexe – a firebox, a grate, some irons for hanging the pots, a canvas awning to keep off the rain. He should himself have foreseen the need of it: you cannot cook for thirty-five souls in a kitchen sized like the sexton's. What else has he failed to anticipate? He drinks the coffee, lets the heat of it almost scald his tongue and throat.

The office next to the kitchen has become Lecoeur's quarters. Jean-Baptiste leans in, sees that the bed is already neatly made, either by Lecoeur or Jeanne. There is a bag at the end of the bed, not large, some books visible inside. The air of the room, along with the damp-plaster smell of the cemetery records, has an unmistakable whiff of brandy sweat.

He looks for Lecoeur and finds him by one of the old tombs, one of those blocks of weathered masonry eccentrically sunk into the earth like the petrified wreck of a little boat.

'An entire noble family may be found beneath here,' says Lecoeur, patting the damp stone, 'but the lettering is so worn I can hardly make out the name. Can you read it?'

Jean-Baptiste looks. Rohan. Rohring. Roche. 'No,' he says. Then, 'We should begin now.'

'To dig?'

'Yes.'

'Our Alexander has spoken,' says Lecoeur, who is possibly still not quite sober.

'If you will bring the men to where the ground is marked,' says Jean-Baptiste, 'I shall meet you there.'

It is, as far as Jean-Baptiste knows – as far as Jeanne and her grandfather have been able to inform him – the oldest of the extant pits, a square some seven metres by seven that he has marked out with rope and pegs in the northwest corner near to where, beyond the wall, the rue aux Fers meets the rue de la Lingerie. The surface, pale grass, tussocky, gives nothing away. If this *is* the place, then there was no lasting memorial for those who went into it.

He stands by the rope, watching the men approach. He greets them, hopes they have passed a peaceful night; then, with Lecoeur's assistance, he separates them into three groups. Those who will dig, those who will collect the bones, those who will stack them. When it is done, those marked for digging are sent across the rope.

'Earth,' says the engineer, 'will be piled upon this side, here. When the pit is empty, the earth will be mixed with quicklime and returned to the pit. As for the bones, they will, in time, be carted across the city to their new resting place.' He pauses. A few of the men move their heads. The others just look at him.

The day is very still, a wintry stillness. Jeanne and her grandfather stand together quietly a little distance from the rope. Jean-Baptiste looks over to them. He smiles at them or tries to, but his face is cold, and anyway, what would such a smile mean? He turns to the miner nearest him. Joos Slabbart or Jan Biloo. Jan Block, perhaps. He nods. The man nods back, lifts the handle of his spade. The ground is opened.

They dig for three hours before Jean-Baptiste asks Lecoeur to call the first break. There has not, in these first hours, been much to see. The dead appear to have been reduced to shards, fragments, as if the pit had churned them like dry bread in an old man's mouth. Are they digging in the right place? Was the sexton mistaken? He and Jeanne have gone back to the house, but after the break, the pit starts to give up its treasures and every second thrust of the spade levers out some recognisable structure. A jaw with a row of teeth that look as if they might still have a bite to them. All the delicate apparatus of a foot, ribs like the staves of an old barrel. The bone mound becomes a low bone wall. There is no wood, not a splinter, nothing to suggest the men and women who went into the pit had anything more than the shelter of their own winding sheets.

The midday meal is announced by Lisa Saget beating a ladle against the base of a saucepan. Whatever discomfort the men may have felt in their work it does not appear to have affected their appetites. Jean-Baptiste and Lecoeur linger by the edge of the pit. Lecoeur does not look well. He has pulled his neckcloth over his mouth and nose.

'We will light a fire after lunch,' says Jean-Baptiste. 'It may help a little.'

Lecoeur nods.

'Will you eat anything?' asks Jean-Baptiste.

'I should take something to settle my stomach first,' says Lecoeur, the voice muffled, odd and muffled.

'Yes,' says Jean-Baptiste. 'I shall ask Armand to fetch more brandy. We can all take a mouthful before we begin again.'

For the afternoon shift, three of the diggers are transferred to the bone-collectors. Almost all those inside the rope find themselves at some point standing on bones. Besides bones, other things start to be found and passed up. A deformed metal cross, greenish. A brooch, mostly destroyed, in the form of a rose. Part of a child's toy horse cut from tin. Buttons. An antique-looking buckle. Nothing yet of any value. And if something valuable should be found? Who is the legal owner? The man who uncovered it? The sexton? The engineer? Perhaps it is the minister.

At moments, the men – all of them – seem swept by waves of disgust. Their eyes shut, they tremble, they hesitate, then one spits in his fist and a boot or clog drives more resolutely at the edge of a spade, and the rhythm is restored.

By the time the city bells sound four, the light is going and the men, whose bent heads are now below the level of the ground, look, from above, to be excavating shadows. Torches are driven into the walls of the pit. Now, truly, it is a spectacle: a gang of men in a red hole, prising bones from under their feet. The bone wall runs all the length of one side of the pit and is as high as a man's shoulders. The last hour feels like a day in itself. Jean-Baptiste keeps the brandy bottle in the grass beside him. At intervals – intervals that grow shorter – he passes it down, watches it go between them, takes it back, the lighter bottle. At a quarter to six, he stops it. Later, he knows he will have to insist on them working at night, but not now. He could not do it himself; he cannot ask it of them.

He finds Lecoeur and they walk in silence to the sexton's house. They stand by the kitchen fire.

After a minute or two, Lecoeur, speaking to the fire, says softly, 'Sweet Christ.'

'Tomorrow will be easier,' says Jean-Baptiste.

Lecoeur turns, suddenly grins at him. 'Tomorrow will break our hearts,' he says.

5

The second day: they have been hard at it for an hour when the engineer's concentration is broken by a shrill whistle and he turns to see Armand waving him towards the church. He goes. Armand informs him that there are three men to see him.

'In the church?'

'In the church.'

'You know them?' asks Jean-Baptiste.

'Not one,' says Armand, falling into step beside him.

The men are standing in the nave beside a pillar from which the remnants of a broad-brimmed cardinal's hat hang suspended like a glorified soup plate. One of the men is Lafosse. The other two are strangers.

'Monsieur,' says Jean-Baptiste to Lafosse. The other men simply stand there, faintly smiling. Jean-Baptiste introduces Armand.

'An organist?' says one of the strangers. 'You play Couperin, of course?'

'I play them all,' says Armand.

'I should like to hear some,' says the stranger, 'before the organ is broken up. *The Parnassus*, perhaps.'

'Only music is immortal,' says Armand.

'These men,' says Lafosse, fixing his gaze on Jean-Baptiste 'are doctors. They will be conducting certain investigations. You are to afford them every assistance.'

'Disinterment on such a scale,' says the admirer of Couperin, a prosperous-looking, well-padded gentleman of about fifty, 'is quite unique. Every stage of decomposition will be apparent, even to the final handful of dust.'

'Man's journey,' begins his colleague, a more angular, more slightly built man, 'has, historically, been measured from the moment of his birth to the moment of his death. From first breath to last. Yet thanks to the sharp blades of our anatomists, we now know much of those months when we lie invisibly inside our mothers. Your work here, monsieur, will offer us a most complete view of our fate after that event we call death.'

'Our physical fate,' says his colleague in an amused tone, gesturing to where, in the half-dark, the altar crouches.

'Indeed, indeed,' says the other. 'The rest we must leave to the wisdom of Mother Church.'

'Set up a place for them,' says Lafosse. 'Somewhere they may work undisturbed.'

From high over their heads, there comes certain small but distinctly carried sounds that might be nothing but the shifting of those birds that roost there, but Jean-Baptiste catches Armand's eye and quickly offers whatever assistance the doctors may require. He does not care to have Père Colbert's voice fall on him again, to have it made plain how little he holds sway here.

'Then our business is concluded,' says Lafosse. He turns, uncertainly, as if in search of the way out.

'I am Dr Thouret,' says the slighter of the two strangers, realising at last that he will receive no introduction from the minister's emissary. 'My colleague here –' the colleague smiles graciously – 'is Dr Guillotin.'

After the midday meal, the men, under Jean-Baptiste's instruction, build a pulley from three stout poles lashed together, a wheel, a length of chain. They make a canvas cradle to attach to the end of the chain. They make two ladders with broad and strongly fixed rungs. They stoke the fire. They set to work again.

With his plumb line, Jean-Baptiste measures the depth of the floor of the pit at a little over thirteen metres. The bone wall will soon be too high for the men to reach to the top of it. Such a profusion would be less troubling if he had not, the previous evening received a communication from the Porte d'Enfer informing him that they had suffered flooding from an uncharted spring and that it would be some time before they were ready to accept any material from les Innocents. There was no indication as to whether they meant days, weeks or months. Even a few weeks, at this rate, and the cemetery would become a labyrinth. They would lose each other in corridors of bone.

The gangs – diggers, collectors, stackers – are rotated at hourly intervals. It is evident that no one must be left more than two hours at the bottom of the pit. Near the end of the afternoon – it has been one of those days when the light struggles to impose itself, to convince – one of the men, coming up the ladder at the end of his shift, pauses, lets go of the rung and tumbles backwards. Fortunately, he does not break his fall on the heads of his fellows. He is raised to the surface in the canvas cradle.

'It is Block,' says Lecoeur, kneeling by the man's side. 'Jan Block.'

In the surface air, Block stirs, looks about himself and, ashen still, gets to his feet.

'Let him go to his tent if he wishes,' says Jean-Baptiste. He has already heard someone mutter the words 'choke-damp'. All of them know it, and at Valenciennes, all will have seen or heard of a man drowning in some undetectable element. Absurd, of course, to imagine that it could exist in the pit, but he calls a break and lets them pass the bottle. They look at him. He sees in their gazes nothing he can put a name to. After fifteen minutes, he sends a new party down the ladders.

Among the items found in the pit today: a green coin from the reign of Charles IX; a rusted but recognisable gorget; a ring with a cross on it – not valuable; more buttons; the blade of a knife – why? For use in the next world? A curious small piece of coloured glass, heart-shaped, quite pretty.

This last the engineer rinses when he washes his hands in the evening, and on some whim, or simply not knowing what else to do with it, he presents it to Jeanne, who accepts it, a strange solemn smile on her face.

6

A man runs away, runs away with his pack in the middle of the night. No one saw him go; no one heard him. Even the men in his own tent look surprised, uneasy, as if he might have been spirited away, perhaps by something they have disturbed in the pit. Lecoeur offers to lead a party in pursuit of him. He cannot have got far and will surely find it hard to conceal himself in a city he knows nothing of.

'They are not prisoners,' says Jean-Baptiste. 'They are not bonded labour.'

'The men expect a firm hand,' says Lecoeur, who has this morning cut his neck shaving. 'After all, have we not rescued them from the mines?'

'I do not know,' says Jean-Baptiste, more to himself than Lecoeur, 'who we have rescued.'

Of the others, all are accounted for, though the man who fell from the ladder, Jan Block, is not fit to work and Jean-Baptiste visits him in his tent, where he lies on his bed of straw like

Holbein's Christ. His eyes follow the engineer's dark form as it crosses the entrance of the tent and stands above him in the tent's light.

'You have pain? You are suffering?'

Block wets his lips with the tip of a pale tongue, says something, says it twice more before Jean-Baptiste understands.

'You are cold?'

'Yes.'

'We will bring you more blankets. We will bring something hot for you to drink.'

Block blinks. The engineer leaves. When he finds Jeanne, he asks her if she could visit the sick man, take him some coffee or broth. And is there a blanket somewhere? He complains of the cold.

In the pit, under Lecoeur's direction, the men are already at work. Fire, pulley, ladders. The hollow sound of bones laid on bones. A simple call from the men below warns those above that the canvas cradle is filled and ready for hoisting. They are deep enough now to need lights even in the morning, four torches protruding from the walls and burning fitfully. Jean-Baptiste crouches, tries to see the condition of the walls. Does the earth fray? Is there risk of collapse? Could the men be got out quickly if a side of the pit did collapse?

He decides that he must go down and see for himself (it is time he went down), and with no announcement he swings himself onto the nearest ladder and begins to descend. He is aware that both below and above him all work has ceased, that they are watching him. His feet feel for the rungs. The sky recedes. The air thickens.

Stepping off the bottom of the ladder, he suffers a momentary loss of balance and has to grip the elbow of the man nearest him.

Now that he is down here, he should tell them to continue with their work, but there is so little room. He looks at them, their long faces lit from above by fire and the feeble light of morning. He looks at the black walls, looks at what he is standing on, looks up to where Lecoeur's head and shoulders are bent over the pit's edge. He takes a spade from the hands of the man he stumbled against, presses its blade into the earth wall, twists the blade and watches a piece of the wall come away in a damp slab. He tests the opposite wall in the same manner and with the same result. He returns the tool, gets a boot on the bottom rung of the ladder, is swept by a wave of nausea that, thank God, he is able to control, to let pass. He climbs, reaches the top, steadies himself on the grass.

To Lecoeur, who has come up close beside him, he says huskily, 'We will build frames. Box-cribs to secure the walls. Bring the men out.'

There is no shortage of suitable lumber: Monsieur Dejour must have hoarded half the saleable wood in Paris. They shape posts and struts, improvise puncheons and cleats. It is nice to work with the wood, and when the men go down after the midday meal, they go, it seems, in slightly better heart. By mid-afternoon the plumb line measures a depth of nearly seventeen metres. The cradle carries more earth than bone now. By dark they will have done it! Emptied one of the pits of les Innocents!

The last shift of diggers surfaces at half past six. A winter moon shines in their faces, shines on the bone wall that looks now less what it is, the macabre and pitiful residue of countless lives, and more like a good harvest, hard won. Jean-Baptiste takes off his hat, rubs at his hair, his own hair, which he's grown to an almost respectable length, just as Charvet suggested. The miners file away from him, some with their spades over their shoulders like muskets. A good day. A little victory for stubborn hard work, for keeping one's nerve. Quietly, by the side of the pit, he and Lecoeur congratulate each other. They reach out and touch hands.

He is less pleased with the world the next morning. He has slept badly again, waking in some useless quarter of the night, heart racing, and then lying for hours mentally digging pit after pit until he sickened of it and climbed from his bed and dressed in the dark.

At the cemetery, examined by lamplight, Jan Block is obviously worse. There is a sheen on his skin like that on rotten cheese. His breathing is laboured, unprofitable. He may be dying, may conceivably, all too conceivably, be dying of some infection the others could contract, the whole place shut down within the week, the last man living rolling the last man dead into the emptied pit . . .

An hour later, he finds one of the doctors, Dr Guillotin, inspecting the bone wall. He sees him prise out some fragment from the wall and slip it into his coat pocket.

'You don't object, I hope?' asks the doctor, seeing the engineer approach. 'An intriguingly deformed vertebra. Thought I should have it before Thouret beat me to it.'

Jean-Baptiste speaks to him of the sick man, describes the accident and asks if the doctor would be kind enough to examine him. 'If there is an infection . . . something that might . . .'

The doctor is agreeable. The man is nearby? He is. They walk together to the tent, duck inside it. There is someone else in there. The miner with the damaged hand. For a moment the newcomers are kept at bay by the miner's calm regard of them. Then he leaves, silent and unhurried.

'A curious-looking character,' says the doctor. 'Violet eyes. Did you notice? Most unusual.' He turns to the man on the straw. 'What is his name?' he asks.

'This is Block,' says Jean-Baptiste.

'Block? Good morning to you, Block. You have had a fall? You are unwell?'

Jan Block looks startled.

The doctor smiles. 'You need not be afraid of me.' To Jean-Baptiste he says, 'If you would turn him? It is easier to examine a man's back when he is not lying on it.'

Jean-Baptiste takes hold of the miner's shoulders, starts to shift him. The sick man makes no protest, though his flesh trembles. It is not easy to turn him. When it is done, the doctor says, 'Lift up his shirt.'

The skin of Jan Block's upper back has been pierced either side of his spine, and though the puncture marks are small, they are surrounded by angry haloes of inflammation.

Guillotin steps closer. He looks, but like most of his profession is reluctant to touch. He nods. 'You may pull down his shirt. Thank you, Monsieur Block. We will find something to help you, yes?'

When they have walked a few steps from the tent, the doctor says, 'He is poisoned by whatever matter entered him in the fall. The wounds must be cleaned immediately with a solution of brimstone. As for the fever, he should take a dust of Peruvian bark, dispersed in a little brandy. I am not, however, in favour of suppressing fever entirely. Fever is not the enemy. It is the fire in which disease is combusted.' He stops, then looks closely at Jean-Baptiste. 'Even in perfect health,' he says, 'we are remade continuously in a heat of our own generation. You are familiar with the theory of phlogiston?'

'I know something of it.'

'Phlogiston, from the Greek, to set on fire. The combustible element within all things. The latent fire. The potential fire. Passive until roused.'

'Roused by a spark?'

'Or by some shock or friction. Or simply the gradual accretion of heat.'

'Is it possible,' asks Jean-Baptiste, 'that Block's infection is caused by a disease that has continued in the bones? That the bones carry still a residue of the sicknesses that once afflicted them? I mean, afflicted those to whom they once belonged?'

'How quaintly you put it,' says Guillotin. 'You speak as if our bones were mere possessions, like a horse or a watch. But to answer your question, I think it unlikely any disease could so long outlive its victim. I do not suggest, however, that you or your men allow the bones to touch any open sore or wound. I recommend vinegar as a general disinfectant. And purified alcohol. Ethanol. Very effective. Though be careful where you store it. A powerful intoxicant. Also highly inflammable. Even the vapour. Particularly the vapour.'

'And where would I find it? Ethanol?'

'Shall I procure you some?'

'I would be indebted to you. And for the brimstone? The bark?'

'I will write you a note for the apothecary,' says Guillotin, patting the younger man's shoulder. 'Now, let us go into the house together and see if that nice girl will make us some coffee, eh?'

At the kitchen table, Jeanne, Lisa Saget and both of Lisa's children are busy paring vegetables. A chair is brought for the doctor but he prefers to stand by the fire. He is vigorous and good-humoured. He says pleasant, admiring things to the women and children. Jean-Baptiste explains that they have been to see the sick miner. That he is certainly worse today but that the doctor has prescribed some remedies.

'Natalie,' says Lisa, tilting her head towards the girl, 'will fetch them. Wipe your hands, Natalie, and put on your coat.'

'We can make room for him in the house,' says Jeanne. 'I can make a bed on the landing upstairs. He will be better here.'

'You have the cooking,' says Jean-Baptiste, 'and many other duties.'

'Good nursing,' says Guillotin, 'is often the difference between a patient living or dying.'

'Then we must do it,' says Jeanne, turning wide-eyed to Jean-Baptiste.

'Could he not go to a hospital?' asks Jean-Baptiste.

The doctor flares his nostrils. 'Hospitals are very dangerous places. Particularly to one already weakened by illness.'

Natalie, her coat buttoned, is ready for her errand. There are writing materials in the office where Lecoeur sleeps. The doctor writes a little list, squints at it, signs it, folds it, gives it to the child.

'I have added something for you,' he says to Jean-Baptiste. '*Lachryma papaveris*. Tears of the poppy. It will help you with your rest. Have I judged the matter rightly?'

'You go to Monsieur Boustanquoi,' says Lisa to the girl. 'Straight there and straight back.'

The girl nods, grins coquettishly at the doctor, takes her leave.

'Children,' purrs the doctor. He taps a finger on the lid of the coffee pot. 'May we impose, mademoiselle?'

The emptied pit is filled, the black earth leavened with sacks of quicklime. The wind has got up, skirling and gusting between the cemetery walls. The men's clothes, hands and faces are all finely dusted with the lime. Eyes sting, noses run, but filling a pit is better work than emptying one. Quicker work too. By early afternoon, pit one can have a neat line run through it in Jean-Baptiste's notebook. The fire burns down. The pulley and cradle, the timber for the frames, the tools, the men themselves are all moved fifteen strides to the south. Lecoeur and Jean-Baptiste measure out the mouth of a new pit with the pegs and rope. Jeanne and the sexton are brought out to confirm the position. The sexton, after walking about somewhat in the manner of a dog looking for somewhere to sleep, eventually decides the rope square should begin another five strides in the direction of the south wall. The pegs are pulled and driven in again. The sexton nods. A new fire is built, lit. The gang who are to dig step across the rope; those who are to stack stand ready. It starts again, that dull music of blade on earth, then the noise of the bones, the way, when knocked together, they ring like clay pots.

A day's difficulty can be measured by the amount of strong liquor necessary to endure it. Today is a three-bottle day. A bottle per metre dug. A tenth of a bottle per man per metre dug. Is that the equation? It is not one the engineer was taught at the Ecole des Ponts. When they have finished and the miners have dispersed to their tents or to the warmth of the big fire by the preaching cross, Jean-Baptiste and Lecoeur wash their hands in the bucket outside the door of the sexton's house.

'What is it they will do in there?' asks Lecoeur, shaking the water from his fingers and nodding towards the doctors' new workshop, a little, windowless structure of draped canvas propped against the wall of the church.

'God knows,' says Jean-Baptiste, who earlier in the day witnessed a pair of trestle tables being carried inside, along with a heavy leather pouch that jangled as it was carried.

In the kitchen, there is only the old sexton, asleep in his chair, but after a few moments, Jeanne appears at the bottom of the stairs, her face softly radiant as though she had just bathed it in fresh cold water. 'He is resting,' she says, 'and has taken all his medicines.'

'Block?' asks Jean-Baptiste.

She nods. 'The doctor says he will look at him again tomorrow, if he is able to.'

'Good. Thank you, Jeanne. I am grateful to you.'

'And your medicine is on the mantelpiece,' she says. 'There.'

'Yours?' asks Lecoeur.

'Dr Guillotin seemed to think I might need some help with my sleep.'

'Ah, sleep,' says Lecoeur. 'Yes. Morpheus has proved no friend to me recently. I am restless at night as a jackrabbit.'

'Then you shall have half of this,' says Jean-Baptiste, examining the thick, brown glass, corked, unlabelled. 'There must be enough for both of us in here.'

He leaves Lecoeur with Jeanne and her grandfather, returns to the rue de la Lingerie, the half-decanted flask in his coat pocket. He should try to do some accounts before bed, and tomorrow he must draw some more money at the goldsmith's on the rue Saint-Honoré. There are tradesmen to pay, and the men of course, and something handsome for Lecoeur, for Jeanne and her grandfather, for Armand and Lisa Saget. He owes a month's rent to Monsieur Monnard. He does not like to be behind with it, to give Monsieur Monnard any further cause to find fault with him. On the stairs to the drawing room, he meets Marie coming down with a tray of plates. The plates are littered with small bones. She makes a face at him, a little grimace that might have some specific meaning in the faubourg Saint-Antoine. He asks, keeping his voice low, how Ziguette is today.

'Oh, poor Ziggi!' says Marie, in a very passable imitation of

Madame Monnard. Then she brushes past him, shoulder and thigh against his own.

He goes up to his room, sits in candlelight, puts on the table his bottle of medicine, folds his arms, looks at it. How many drops is he supposed to take? Did Guillotin say? He remembers his father towards the end having such a remedy. What was it they spooned into his mouth? Ten drops? Twenty? He decides, simply, that he will take *some*. He will not trouble himself with counting; he is tired of counting. He will take *some* and see how he does, then make his adjustments accordingly.

✳

It is late, late or early. Jeanne, woken by something she has heard in her sleep, leaves the room she shares with her grandfather and looks down at Jan Block, his face lit by the moonlight that slides through the narrow arched window at the end of the landing. It takes a few moments – she has been sleeping deeply – to realise that his eyes are open. She smiles at him, then kneels beside him so that he can see her more certainly. He lifts a hand to her and she catches it before it falls, holds it a moment, then lays it on the shallow panting of his chest. Slowly he shuts his eyes, and there is something so resigned, so final in that shutting she cannot believe he will ever open them again. His breathing suspends a moment, a long moment, a moment that will perhaps extend into eternity. Then, with a little spasm in his chest, a kind of hiccup, it starts again, somewhat easier.

On the stairs, the wood creaks. A head appears, rising out of the darkness of the stairwell into the silver light of the corridor. A shaved nude head, eyes that glitter.

'Don't be afraid,' says the head, very softly. 'It is only Lecoeur.'

'He woke,' she says, 'but he is sleeping now.'

'You are a good girl,' says Lecoeur. 'I believe I was dreaming of you.'

'Is it morning?' she asks.

'No,' he says, uncertainly. 'I do not think so.'

7

Héloïse Godard, reader, woman for sale, daughter of innkeepers on the Orléans–Paris road, a young person recently entered into her twenty-fifth year though not yet quite finished with her long project of debasement, rises with the six o'clock bell from Saint-Eustache, dresses by touch (from white stockings to the green ribbon round her throat), lights her candle for a final brief inspection of herself, blows it out and descends the winding wooden staircase into the public world of the rue du Jour.

Always that small shock of being outside again, that small hardening of whatever, as she lay alone in her bed through the hours of night, had softened, opened . . . She pulls her cloak about herself, pulls up her hood, breathes the cold air.

She has an appointment with Boubon the basket-maker in his workshop on the far side of the market. Boubon is a widower, and a man who, like Ysbeau the bookseller and Thibault the tailor – like herself – does not fit easily among his neighbours. This will be her eighth visit to him. Those whom she sees – there are not many – she sees regularly, on their appointed days, their appointed hours. She does no casual trade. All that talk about her going with anyone who waves a coin under her nose, all that is lies. In most cases she has to approach the gentlemen herself, and even then nothing explicit is discussed. She has learnt to be very businesslike while never speaking to the point. This, she thinks, is a good part of what they like about her: her willingness never to confront them with what they are doing, what they are paying for, what they need. And what they need is not quite what the quarter's vulgar imagination excites itself with. With Boubon, for example, she will sit on his knee among the sheaves and rods of willow. He will tell her about trade, complain of the aches in his back, his thighs. She will listen, all sweet attentiveness, then offer a little wifely advice, a little wifely encouragement. Later, he will observe the tops of her stockings and run a blunt and calloused finger along the garment's woollen hems while she asks again for the difference between slyping and slewing and how exactly slewing is distinguished from randing or waling. None of it is particularly unpleasant. Certainly it is bearable, usually bearable. Then, when her dress and petticoats and shift are down and patted into good order, they will drink coffee brewed on the workshop fire and she will pick up the money left for her in a screw of paper in the niche by the door (she is not one of those Palais Royal hussies who will do or say nothing without money given first), and she will depart, quickly and quietly, both of them relieved to have it over again for another week.

But before Boubon, she needs to eat. You cannot walk through the market in the morning and not pause to break your fast. The air alone – the air despite everything – compels it. So she stops at Madame Forges's stall (that Madame Forges who dyes her hair the colour of a butcher's rag), buys a small, blood-warm loaf and picks off the crust as she goes. At this hour in the morning, she is barely noticed, rarely insulted. Even Merda the drunk, smudge-eyed on a step eating an onion, does no more than glance up at her, mildly. To save herself a few minutes of walking, she cuts through one of the fish sheds and sees the old priest in his blue glasses haggling with a fish-girl over the price of a cod's head. The girl's mother might have offered the head for free to a poor priest, her grandmother certainly, but times have altered. One does not need to be awed by priests any more. Heaven and Hell, angels and devils, there are plenty of people ready to scoff at such things now. And not just the savants at the Café de Foy or the Procope. Plenty of ordinary people who say as much. People like the fish-girl perhaps. People like herself.

She follows the priest out of the shed, loses him in the day's first crowd, makes her way to the rue de la Fromagerie, crosses the market's southern fringe and arrives at the corner of the rue aux Fers. Above the walls of the cemetery – as ever these days, days and nights – the twisting plumes of smoke from the fires. But this morning there is something else to see, something new. Black letters on the cemetery wall. Tall, ragged, unignorable letters extending from the cemetery door almost as far as the rue de la Lingerie: 'FAT KING SLUT QUEEN BEWARE! BECHE IS DIGGING A HOLE BIG ENOUGH TO BURY ALL VERSAILLES!'

In the middle of the street, a half-dozen men and women are looking, discussing, trying to agree on what is written there. They have 'king' and 'queen', 'slut' and 'Versailles'. The rest is less sure. She could tell them, of course, but they would not want it from her, a woman, *that* woman.

They leave (still arguing), and she is about to go herself (she does not wish to make Boubon anxious; Boubon will be anxious enough) when she sees, turning out of the rue de la Lingerie, the young engineer, the one who in the mist called himself by that name now scrawled on the wall. The one who touched her face. He sees her and then, a second later, sees the black letters, reads, visibly stiffens and, with his face flushed, steps up to her and says, 'I know nothing of this.'

She nods, then breaks off a piece of her bread and holds it out to him. He takes it, almost snatching it from her, pushes it quickly into one of the pockets of his coat and hurries away.

8

When he has Armand on his own, the two of them squared off just inside one of the arched entrances to the south charnel, a roof of bones over their heads, the organist splays his fingers to show how they are without the slightest stain.

'Fleur or Renard,' he says. 'De Bergerac at a push. Excess of zeal. I will speak to them. But I think you should be flattered.'

'*Flattered?*'

'You must have made a considerable impression on them. I can assure you they have never written a word about me and I have known them since the hospital.'

'They were foundlings?'

'Were and are.'

'I did not know.'

'No. You preferred simply to dislike them. To feel contemptuous of them.'

'But I must work here! Does that mean nothing to them?'

'Who would make the connection? I assume you have not mentioned your *nom de guerre* to anyone?'

'No. Of course. No.'

'No?'

'No!'

'Then?'

'I will not . . . I do not . . .' The engineer falters, then casts around himself as if, among the memorial slabs, the stone flummery, he might discover what it is he will not or does not. Evidently he should have taken much more of Guillotin's syrup. Another night of sleeplessness has rendered him stupid, his thoughts separated from each other by patches of mental wasteland. Reason, coherence, these seem suddenly finite assets he might, this morning, tonight, next week, abruptly come to the end of. And then that odd, that startling encounter with the Austrian! Was she waiting for him? Waiting there to give him a piece of her bread? Why should she do that?

'Yours,' says Armand, who may have been speaking for some time, 'are the politics of undrawn conclusions. It is pitifully common.'

'What?'

'You see how things are. You have read, you have considered, yet you refuse to reach the obvious conclusions.'

'And they are?'

'They are what men of much meaner capacities have understood perfectly. Men like Fleur and Renard and de Bergerac.'

'Then perhaps my difficulty is that I know the names of my parents.'

'All that has offended you is that the paint on the wall may reflect upon your *professional* character. You are entirely self-regarding. You think yourself a man of elevated thoughts, of liberal sentiment, but your only true ideal is your own ambition.'

'You have given up on yours? The organ at Saint-Eustache?'

'I can see past my ambitions. I am not contained by them. That is the difference.'

Peevishly, they turn away from each other. Jean-Baptiste, his arms crossed tightly over his chest, peers past the blackened stones of the archway to where Lecoeur is crossing the grass towards them. An agitated, stiff-legged gait, body bent forwards, face shadowed by his hat . . .

'A mutiny,' he says, hopping through the archway, not troubling himself with any pleasantries. 'The men have mutinied!' He looks at them, appears hugely satisfied to see their startled faces, then says, 'It may not be correct to say they have mutinied, not yet. But they are unhappy. Most unhappy. They will not work.'

'And the reason?'

'They wish for pipes.'

'Pipes?'

'Tobacco pipes. They will not work without them. They have convinced themselves that tobacco is a specific against infection.'

'Infection from what?'

'The pits, of course.'

'They wish to smoke?'

'They insist on it. All of them. And you need not trouble yourself seeking the origin of such an idea. They wake up with them in their heads one morning. Such notions may even be autogenous.'

Armand chuckles. 'This is more good than bad. It is a demand very cheaply satisfied. And they will think well of you for doing so. They will be comforted.'

While speaking, the three of them have stepped out of the charnel. The miners are bunched by the big fire, watching.

'There is a shop on the rue aux Ours,' continues Armand, 'opposite the coaching office. Several hundred pipes in stock. Enough tobacco to supply the navy. I recommend it.'

'Then,' says Jean-Baptiste, 'then perhaps you would fetch what is necessary?'

'Should I open an account?' asks Armand, reverting with no obvious effort to his role as Scaramouche, Harlequin, Puck. 'Preferential rates? Monthly billing?'

'And if Monsieur Saint-Méard has no objection,' says Lecoeur quickly, 'I could accompany him.'

Armand makes a bow of invitation. Lecoeur replies with a bow of his own.

'How is the sick man this morning?' asks Jean-Baptiste.

'Block? Ah, a ministering angel attends him,' says Lecoeur.

'He is dead?' asks Jean-Baptiste, his concentration still on the men, the wildness of their thinking.

'I mean Jeanne,' says Lecoeur. 'She looks after him. We should not worry about Block. Block will outlive us all.'

It is, by the bells of Saint-Eustache and the restless hands of Jean-Baptiste's own watch, almost two hours before Armand and Lecoeur return to the cemetery. He has already cursed himself for his folly in allowing them to go together, though whether he could have stopped them, whether he has the authority, the right, the necessary force of character, he does not quite know.

That they are both drunk is obvious at a distance of many metres, but they seem to be able to walk without staggering and the parcel in Lecoeur's arms suggests they did not forget the original purpose of their errand.

'You have seen the wall?' hisses Lecoeur, his mouth swaying so close to the engineer's cheek it is almost a kiss. 'Saint-Méard says he knows him. This Bêche. Apparently a man you would never suspect of radicalism. Quite unassuming to meet, yet beneath it, beneath it, cold as ice. Kill without a blink. Saint-Méard calls him the people's avenger. Does that not have a type of beauty to it?'

'Those are the pipes?' asks Jean-Baptiste.

'I bought every pipe in the shop. Quite cleaned him out. There are several spare. Perhaps you would like one for yourself? Shall I choose one for you?' He laughs, starts to rummage in the parcel and looks happy, simply happy, for the first time in days.

When at last the men are gathered and they start back in the pit, there is not a single miner without a clay stem between his teeth. It does not seem to inhibit their ability to dig, collect, stack. Lecoeur stands dangerously near the edge of the pit. He seems to be drifting in and out of sleep. The doctors arrive. Guillotin stations himself beside Jean-Baptiste and, after watching the work for a while, says, 'You have seen what is written on the wall?'

Jean-Baptiste nods.

'There are forces at work,' says Guillotin, 'that our masters ignore at their peril.'

Jean-Baptiste glances round at him, the mild, brown eyes in that large, florid face. Was Guillotin of the party of the future? Did he, along with Renard and Fleur, de Bergerac and Armand, know the conclusions to be drawn? They hold each other's gaze a moment until the noise of a spade striking wood, splitting it, draws both men's attention back into the pit.

The engineer crouches. 'A coffin?' he calls. The miner looks up and, by way of answer, of assent, takes the pipe from his mouth.

They dig it out, lay it in the cradle, hoist it, lay it on the ground.

'I suppose we must open it,' says Jean-Baptiste quietly, as if to himself. He looks at the man nearest him. Guido Brun, or if not Brun, then the one who looks much like Brun. Someone Agast. Englebert Agast? The man drives the edge of his spade under the lid of the coffin, levers it, then levers it more forcefully until the wood, with a small detonation, gives itself up, and much of the coffin, on the instant, disintegrates. Inside is a skeleton, the residue of a man, his bones connected by patches of leathery sinew. Strands of coarse, black hair, like black grass, sprout from the sides of his skull. Several large, brown teeth are on show.

Lecoeur, awake now, very sober, crosses himself, as do several of the men.

'To get the bones,' says Dr Thouret, 'to separate them and have them as you wish, you will need to boil them.'

'Boil the corpse?' asks Jean-Baptiste.

'It is a perfectly normal procedure,' says Guillotin, soothingly. 'There is nothing indecent. You should speak with the sexton. Those gentlemen have their arts.'

The next coffin raised to the surface has inside only a clean litter of bones, so that picked up and shaken it would rattle like a child's toy. The next, but for a little dust, is empty.

'At least,' says Guillotin, looking round at the company, 'one has escaped. There is hope for us all.'

The remark is presumably intended to lighten the atmosphere, but the men look at him stonily, and only Lecoeur, with a kind of courage of good manners, manages a smile in return.

A new system emerges, a new routine. Coffin wood is burnt on the fire, where it provokes brief displays of weirdly coloured flames. Those corpses still stubbornly strung together with ligament and tendon are left inside the charnel, where, from the middle of the afternoon onwards, Manetti, assisted by one of the miners, collects them on a handcart and wheels them away to where he has established his boiling vessel, a copper tub used for a hundred years to finish off what the earth of les Innocents had started, and that now has been dragged from its long retirement in a corner of the cemetery.

For the men in the pit, and the men above charged with the task of opening the coffins, there is at first a palpable tension, all of them seemingly braced for some horror, something abruptly unhidden that might, from its box, *regard* them. Along with the brandy bottle, the tobacco jar is circulated. It is, mercifully, enough to keep them at it. And by the end of the day, as the last coffin is lifted by firelight, it all seems queerly bearable, as if work, whatever its particulars, was in the end just work. Something you bent to for probable reward. Something you did because human restlessness must be harnessed to some purpose if it is not to feed on itself.

He has supper with the Monnards. He cannot avoid them for ever. He sits with them – with Madame and Monsieur – chewing mouthfuls of meat and brown beans. The little fire is livelier than usual: Jean-Baptiste has arranged a delivery from the cemetery of his plentiful wood. The flames ripple in the polished hip of the pianoforte. Ziguette's absence is not commented upon, though now and then her mother glances at the unoccupied seat, the laid but unused utensils on the table.

They have, in fitful conversation, exhausted the weather, the merits of the meat, the rising price of beans, and have, each of them, fallen back upon their private thoughts, their relentless chewing, when Madame Monnard, clearing her throat, asks, 'Is it true, monsieur, what Marie tells us about the scandalous thing written on the cemetery wall?'

'Marie, madame? I did not know she could read.'

'She could not read her own name, monsieur,' says Monsieur Monnard, 'but she has ears. She can hear better than an owl.'

Instantly – unbidden and perfect – an image of Marie with tufted ears, perched on a bough in moonlight, enters the engineer's imagination.

'It was said to her, monsieur,' explains Madame. 'She learnt it.'

'And it is not the only such,' says Monsieur Monnard. 'I had Monsieur Gobel in the shop this afternoon, who informed me he had seen something of a very similar character on a wall opposite the Bourse.'

'There may be hundreds of them,' says Madame. 'Could there be hundreds?'

'That other,' asks Jean-Baptiste, fork in the air, 'the one by the Bourse. It made use of the same name?'

'Bêche,' says Monsieur Monnard, stabbing at a last square of beef on his plate. 'And all manner of threats to the king and his ministers. My wife has been very affected, monsieur.'

'I fear,' says Madame, who does, suddenly, look very affected, 'we shall be murdered in our beds. We shall have our throats slit.'

'I am sure it is all idle,' says Jean-Baptiste. 'Nothing but . . . a type of game.'

'A *game*? You may say so, monsieur. Yes, you wish to comfort me. You are a very considerate young man. But I shall dream tonight of this Bêche climbing in at our bedroom window. Would you come, monsieur, if we called you? Do you have a sword, monsieur?'

'I do not, madame.'

'I thought you would have a sword.'

'I am an engineer, madame. I have a brass ruler.'

'I dare say it might serve,' says Madame, thoughtfully. 'If it is a large one.'

Marie comes in to clear the plates. All conversation stops. The plates are gathered, piled. She has strong red hands like a man, a working man. And that black hair of hers! That slick female moustache that is, surely, no defect. To Jean-Baptiste she seems to possess a vigour no one else in the room can match, as if her roots were sunk into some richer, blacker soil they cannot reach.

When she goes, pulling the door shut with her trailing foot, Madame and Monsieur exchange glances, then turn their gaze on their lodger, as if some explanation – an explanation for every ill and unsettling thing that has occurred since his arrival on the rue de la Lingerie – was now required of him.

'I wished to ask you,' begins Jean-Baptiste, 'to enquire that is, how your daughter does, madame.'

'Ziggi? Oh, it is very trying to have children, monsieur. She seems quite to have melted. You should call on her, monsieur. My husband and myself are at our wits' ends. Ever since – and I pray you excuse us – ever since your work began she will not be comforted. It is as if she felt the shovels on her own skin.'

'I am sorry for it,' says Jean-Baptiste. 'Truly. But the work cannot be avoided. I am trying, madame . . . *we* are trying, to do what is good, what is . . .'

The fire snaps; a spark flies out. Jean-Baptiste, rising swiftly, extinguishes it with the toe of his boot.

'The wood is green,' growls Monsieur Monnard, and he frowns at the fire as though green wood was the green heart of all that vexed him.

*   *   *

Upstairs, shielding his candle from the dozen draughts that live in the air at the top of the house like so many secret, invisible streams, the engineer stops outside Ziguette's room and looks down at the line of light at the bottom of her door. It is late, but he is curious to see her, this melting girl. And he would, if he is able, like to give her some reassurance. As a guest, a type of guest in this place, it surely behoves him to offer her his sympathy, and he is about to tap softly on the door when it is opened and Marie is there, the hint of a smile on her face. For a few seconds they stand, blatantly regarding each other; then she steps back to admit him.

Two candles (in addition to his own) illuminate the room: one on the dressing table, the other in a little holder of painted porcelain on the cabinet beside the bed. The room is spacious, at least three times the size of his own, and with a large shuttered window over the quiet street. Put into good order, it would be a pleasant room, the nicest in the house perhaps, but nothing here is in good order. The place appears to have been subject to a private storm, one that has whirled every dress and petticoat, every linen pocket, embroidered apron and set of stays, every mob cap and straw hat, every frill, stocking and furbelow that a cutler's paternal love can bestow upon an only daughter, whirled it all into the air and then, suddenly ceasing, left everything to rain down in confusion. In the centre of it all, partly covered by it, is Ziguette herself, her body loosely sculpted by a linen sheet, her face flushed with a heat whose source is surely internal. (The room has only a modest fire.) She stares up at the engineer with swollen eyes, her hair – unpinned, uncovered, uncombed – spread over the bolster in a heavy blond tangle. Her mouth has a punched look, and in the stretched white of her neck he can clearly see the pulsing of her blood.

'It is not too late, I hope, to pay a call?'

She does not answer him. He looks round at Marie, who is standing directly behind him, hands clasped at the front of her thighs, her expression now perfectly blank.

'Your mother,' he says, turning back to Ziguette, 'thought you would not object. I have just come from having supper with her. Your father too, of course.' He gestures outwards and downwards towards the sitting room. 'I am sorry to find you unwell. Sorry if I, in any way, unwittingly . . .'

She makes a frantic gesture. Marie drags a large pot from under the bed. Ziguette retches. She does not produce much – presumably her belly is near empty – but the noise, amplified by the pot, is impressive. Marie holds the girl's head, red fingers sunk into the yellow hair, tugging it.

The engineer gets out onto the landing, eases the door shut and crosses quickly to his own room. He sits on the end of the bed, listening for more noises from the sickroom, receives a few faint reports; then the house is quiet, free for a moment even of its habitual small crackings and creakings.

Light a fire? Why bother.

He drags the banyan across his lap like a blanket, looks at the bottle of tincture on the cover of Buffon's *Histoire Naturelle Volume II*, wonders if he should offer some of it, a generous brown spoonful, to Ziguette, then suddenly stands and goes to his coat, the riding coat he was wearing this morning, delves into a pocket, delves into the other pocket and pulls out the piece of bread Héloïse gave to him beside the cemetery wall. It has dried out, has almost the consistency of a biscuit, but he bites it, carefully, lets it soften on his tongue, and is smiling at the memory of that gesture of hers, so graceful, so spontaneous, so simple, when he hears from outside, from below, from – unmistakably – the cemetery, the thrill of a woman's laughter. He unlatches his window, pushes it open, thrusts out his head. There is nothing to see, nothing obvious. Perhaps the fire by the preaching cross is burning more brilliantly than it should at such an hour, but otherwise . . . He leans out further, almost to his waist, focuses his stare. Across the fire's red light shadows flit. Then it comes again, that wild laughter, rising above the walls, ringing clear as a pedlar's bell in the cold, stinking silence of the night.

9

Seven in the morning. Frost on the charnel tiles, a white sun wedged between two houses on the rue Saint-Denis. 'I heard women,' he says to Lecoeur. 'At least, I heard one.'

'Mmm,' says Lecoeur, who today has on the heavy, knitted waistcoat. 'Yes. We must not forget our master has a clear view of us and can spy on us at his leisure.'

'I was not spying,' says Jean-Baptiste. 'I am not in the habit of spying.'

'No? What would you prefer that we call it when you peer down at us from your eyrie?'

'What I would prefer is not to find you drunk in the morning.'

'Drunk? Oh good. Yes. Now you choose to defame me. And what if I was . . . if I was as you say? Would I not have justification? You escape here each night while I must remain surrounded by pits, bones. It is intolerable!'

'You would prefer Valenciennes?'

'I have burnt my ships there, monsieur. And all for your

benefit. All so you can feed the swans at Versailles and keep the company of grandees!'

'I feed no swans! Nor do I ever go to Versailles. I go to that house, there. There and no further. I keep the company of people I can make no sense of.'

Their voices have risen to something close to shouting. Each is dimly aware of being looked at, listened to.

'But I am sorry,' says Jean-Baptiste, alarmed to find himself suddenly on the brink of childish tears. 'Sorry that you find it . . . intolerable. You have always been free to come and go. You know there are keys in the sexton's house to all the doors. If it pleased you, you could go this morning. Walk about the city. I can manage well enough here. And . . . and you should come and have supper at the house. I had meant to invite you before. I am certain my landlord would be happy to make your acquaintance. You could come tonight if you wished it.'

'Tonight?' Lecoeur steps forward, muttering something about forgiveness, about the sweet balm of friendship. He tries to pull Jean-Baptiste into an embrace, but Jean-Baptiste, who has no wish to be folded in Lecoeur's arms, steps back, and for a few moments, as the one advances and the other seeks to avoid him, they appear to be dancing.

'You have not yet told me about the women,' says Jean-Baptiste, bringing them both to a halt by the edge of the second pit.

'The women? Half a dozen of the hardier local moppets. They climbed onto the wall with a ladder. Our men provided the means of their descent. I did not interfere. As a result you will find their morale much improved this morning. Cemeteries, of course, were once notorious for such women.'

'You saw them?'

'Their forms. At a distance.'

'And none . . . none seemed remarkable in any way?'

'I would say they were all of a type. Assiduous. Immemorial.'

'Jeanne saw them?'

'We saw them together. The spectacle seemed quite to animate her.'

'Perhaps she knew them.'

'By reputation you mean?'

'Yes.'

'I have no idea.'

'It cannot be a nightly occurrence,' says Jean-Baptiste. 'There must be some . . . regulation. They could come on a particular night. Saturday, for example. We would admit them by the door. They would have no need of ladders.'

'But how are we to communicate this arrangement? By town crier?'

'Monsieur Saint-Méard. He will know at least one of them. One will be enough.'

'This will be a new part for us,' says Lecoeur.

'Part?'

'There is a name for it, is there not? For those who arrange such matters?'

With a quick handshake they separate – Lecoeur towards the latrines, Jean-Baptiste to the sexton's house, where Jeanne, Lisa Saget and the girl Natalie are about their business at the kitchen table. They will, from the window, have seen his awkward encounter with Lecoeur, but they say nothing. He is longing to ask Jeanne about the women, the moppets, their height, their hair, though he has already tested in his imagination a picture of Héloïse climbing a ladder propped against the cemetery wall, and dismissed it as being no more probable than her spreading her cloak and flying over the wall.

By the kitchen fire, there are now two chairs. The sexton's is unoccupied; in the other is Jan Block, his shoulders hunched under a blanket, his eyes sunk and shadowed, yet he is clearly a man at the beginning of his convalescence. Jean-Baptiste congratulates him. Block nods, glances towards Jeanne, then back to the bobbling flames.

'Good,' says the engineer, talking to himself, to the air, to whoever cares to listen. 'So now we go on.'

That evening – though in his heart it is the last thing he wishes – Jean-Baptiste returns to the rue de la Lingerie with Lecoeur and introduces him to the Monnards. Another place is set at the table. Lecoeur sits opposite Madame. Jean-Baptiste has warned him on their walk over not to speak of the work at the cemetery, that the Monnards were people peculiarly sensitive to change, commotion. Lecoeur promised he would not and remains true to his word, though he talks of everything else, fluently, restlessly, as if words had been massing inside him for weeks and needed only some genteel surroundings, the presence of a pianoforte, to start flying out of his throat.

Monsieur Monnard, however, seems genuinely interested in the mines at Valenciennes, the technicalities of pumps and gear, while Madame seems touched by Lecoeur's description of his mother's demise, extinct from the dropsy some years past and nursed in her last agony by Lecoeur and his sister, Violette.

'Then you and Monsieur Baratte understand each other perfectly,' says Madame. 'For Monsieur Baratte was so unfortunate as to lose his father at an age when he might have hoped still to have one. And who is to say which loss is the greater, a father or a mother? And you are both very feeling young men, are you not?'

'I believe we are, madame,' says Lecoeur. 'Ours is a friendship based on the twin pillars of sensibility and philosophy. We know each other's thoughts, madame.'

'I would say I am so with my daughter, monsieur. Just as you express it.'

'You have a *daughter*, madame? I had assumed *you* were the daughter of the house.' He makes a little flourish with his hand. The doubled cuff of his coat flicks the lip of his glass. Marie is called for. She kneels, collects the broken glass in her apron.

After supper, the friends climb to Jean-Baptiste's room. Jean-Baptiste lights the fire. He offers Lecoeur the chair, sits on the bed. He is glad Lecoeur can see the simplicity of his circumstances, that his room, in size and furnishings, is not unlike the one Lecoeur sleeps in at the sexton's house. He alludes to the fact. The allusion is missed.

'I have not come empty-handed,' says Lecoeur, reaching under his shirt and tugging out a crumpled package. He lays it on the table between them, smooths it. The package is tied with a red ribbon. He teases it apart, lifts away the plain top sheet of paper. Below is a picture of some sort, a complicated diagram drawn in faded ink and much annotated. He smiles at it and passes it across to Jean-Baptiste, who takes it, looks at it and nods. 'Valenciana,' he says.

'Valenciana indeed,' says Lecoeur.

'Our old plans. You have kept them all.'

'Did you imagine I would throw them on the fire? Now that we are older, better versed in the ways of the world, we should review them. *Distil* them.'

'We should?'

'Behold!' says Lecoeur, taking the brass ruler off the desk, holding it horizontally and raising it over his head in the manner of a priest celebrating the Eucharist. 'Valenciana rises from the ashes!'

For an hour and a half – until the candle, burning low, threatens to leave them sitting together in the dark – they pass between them sheets and scraps of paper on which the very handwriting, sometimes Jean-Baptiste's, sometimes Lecoeur's, evokes the excitement of those winter evenings at the mines six years before. There are headings such as 'On the Education of Women', 'Plans for a Modern Sewerage System', 'Sparta and Valenciana', 'On Combustion', 'The Ideal Wife', 'An Investigation into Rational Religion', 'Some Costumes for Women', 'The Purity of Forms', 'A Conveyance for Women', 'Plans for a Bridge'.

'And look,' says Lecoeur, 'we even had a little paper on the disposal of bodies.'

'I had forgotten it,' says Jean-Baptiste. 'I had forgotten much of it.'

'The very reason I brought it with me,' says Lecoeur. 'First ambitions are best. We are less brave later. Don't you think?'

'Or we simply change?'

'Grow older, you mean?'

'Older. Other.'

'But tonight, everything is as it was. Mind speaking to mind, heart speaking to heart. The fountain of youth in our breasts . . . bubbling! You know what it is distinguishes one man from the next? His willingness to remain unspotted while the other, out of a kind of idleness, lets his mouth fill up with soil. Grave-dirt.'

Jean-Baptiste nods to the candle. 'I will walk you down,' he says.

'Or I could stay here?' says Lecoeur.

'I think,' says Jean-Baptiste, getting to his feet, 'we would not be comfortable.'

They part at the front door. There is a clasping of hands. Lecoeur, standing in the street like the shade of himself, a spirit required by the hour to return to the Underworld, lingers and sighs and at last turns away with a reluctance painful to see.

Jean-Baptiste shuts the door, locks it, then stands in the hall awhile, in the dark between the street door and the kitchen door. He has done his duty, has he not? He has offered the hand of companionship, has revisited a past, an enthusiasm that seemed even more remote than he might have anticipated. What more could be expected of him? And yet, as he feels his way to the bottom of the stairs, what sits in his chest is unmistakably a sense of betrayal. He does not investigate it. He gives himself up to the darkness around him, cautiously ascends.

By lunchtime the following day the second pit, emptied and filled, can be crossed from the list, and though it is no easy matter to measure morale in a place like les Innocents, it does seem to Jean-Baptiste that the men have recovered something, have, in the company of the laughing women, been transfused with new vigour. The third pit is marked out to the west of the second, and at one in the afternoon, in steady drizzle that soon turns to steady rain, the men (some of whom have the knack of smoking their pipes with the bowls turned downwards) break open the ground.

The doctors are present again. They raise stout umbrellas against the rain. They are quite comfortable, like a pair of gentlemen anglers at a pond hoping to lift a pike for their dinner, though in truth there has been little at the cemetery to excite their professional interest. They have picked among the bones, have spent the occasional hour with the sexton and his boiling vessel, have sketched and measured and peered cautiously into the charnels, but they might have done as much in any ancient cemetery – Saint-Séverin or Saint-Gervais for example. Then, shortly after three o'clock, two coffins are raised and laid side by side on the wet grass. To look at, there is nothing obvious to set them apart from the forty others they have raised since lunch. The wood, perhaps, is a little less rotten, but there is really no time to waste on close inspection. Two of the miners apply their spades to the lids. Nearly all the men are proficient at this now, prying coffins open like oysters. Then they stagger back. One drops his spade, which falls, soundlessly, onto the damp ground. Inside the coffins are young women. Skin, hair, lips, fingernails, *eyelashes*. All of it, even the woollen shrouds they are wrapped in, looking only in need of some washing, some buffing, a little thread to restore them.

For several seconds no one moves. Rain falls on the dead girls' faces. Then the doctors kneel and with their umbrellas shelter them, anglers who have suddenly become suitors. They make their preliminary examinations. Thouret touches the hay-coloured hair of one; Guillotin gently shifts the lips of the other with the tip of a metal spike he has, a silver toothpick perhaps. They confer. Guillotin orders the coffins closed up and carried immediately to the workshop.

'A form of mummification,' he says to Jean-Baptiste. 'A remark-able instance. Remarkable! Like a pair of dried flowers . . .'

Manetti's handcart is employed. The doctors, walking either side of the cart, escort the coffins on their journey towards the church, the workshop. All labouring has ceased. The men are priming their pipes. The afternoon is still and rain-hushed. Now that death has looked so like life, should there not be some cere-mony to make the moment decent? Should Père Colbert not be led out of the church to say a prayer, sprinkle holy water? But Colbert, even if they could find him, would come among them like John the Baptist with a raging toothache. He would be quite likely to throw someone into the pit – the young engineer, for example.

Lecoeur, with the rain dripping from the brim of his hat, looks at Jean-Baptiste. Jean-Baptiste nods. Lecoeur gives the order to go on, fairly barks it. Without a murmur, the men obey.

After dark, Armand, Lecoeur and Jean-Baptiste are invited by Guillotin to view the preserved women or, rather, to view one of them, for the other has already been investigated by the doctors and is, as a result, less viewable. Lecoeur has a candle, Dr Guillotin a lamp of smokeless whale oil. The coffin is on a trestle table in the canvas workshop. They remove the lid and gaze at her.

'I have named her Charlotte,' says Dr Guillotin, 'after a niece of mine in Lyon who I think in life she might have resembled.'

'She is young,' says Armand, his voice, like the doctor's, subdued almost to a whisper.

'Young and old together,' says the doctor. 'I estimate she died about her twentieth year and was committed to the ground some fifty years ago. Our good sexton claims to have a memory of burying two young women about the time he was first employed here. A pair of local beauties, unwed. The occasion, apparently, of much public lamentation.'

'Then they died virgins,' says Lecoeur, something like reverence in his voice.

'Few local beauties die virgins,' says Armand.

'Perhaps it is true,' says the doctor. 'I have not yet ascertained if Charlotte is *intacta*. But for the other, Dr Thouret and I believe there was some evidence of her having conceived.'

'There was a child in her?' asks Jean-Baptiste.

'I cannot say for certain. The internal organs have taken on the consistency of wood pulp or papier-mâché. There were, however, indications.'

'What will you do with her?' asks Armand. 'Your Charlotte? Cut her up like the other?'

'I think,' says Dr Guillotin, 'I would rather endeavour to preserve her as she is. We might construct a glass cabinet for her. Present her at the academy.'

'And she will keep,' asks Jean-Baptiste, 'now she is in the air again?'

The doctor shrugs, then looks past Jean-Baptiste's shoulder and smiles. 'Were you curious to see her too?' he asks.

The others look round. Jeanne is standing at the entrance of the workshop. With the exception of Dr Guillotin, the men look momentarily uneasy, as if surprised in the strong flow of some improper enthusiasm.

'I wondered if you wished for anything,' she says. She does not step inside, does not approach the box. After a few moments, Guillotin and Lecoeur carefully replace the lid.

10

The new pit offers no more local beauties. As they reach its depths (it is the deepest yet: twenty-two metres at the last drop of the plumb line), the coffins are mostly broken, their occupants muddled with their neighbours, shuffled. All through the middle of the week they stay at it until eight or nine at night, digging and hauling and stacking by the illumination of pitch torches, lamps and bonfires. Then, on Saturday – the serene light of some planet shining in the fading glow of the western sky – they come to the end of it. The men below look up; those above peer down. The engineer gives the order to suspend work. He asks Lecoeur to gather the men by the preaching cross, then goes up the spiral steps with Lecoeur and announces his decision that each time a pit is emptied, each time one is finished, every man will receive a bonus of thirty sous. He did the calculations the previous night, moving figures between carefully blotted columns until he found the money he needed.

'And something else,' he says, feeling for the appropriate

register, a voice that might combine paternal indulgence with something bluff and worldly. 'Tomorrow, the cemetery doors will be open and you will be free to go out until sunset, when the doors will be locked again. As for tonight, the doors may find themselves open for an hour in case any of our friends should wish to visit us.'

Lecoeur claps. He intends, perhaps, the men should join him in a show of appreciation, but there is nothing but some muttered talk, some shifting from boot to boot. Have they understood him? He looks at Lecoeur, but before he can ask his advice, ask him perhaps to put the whole thing into a growl of Flemish, Lisa Saget is beating the saucepan and the men file off to their tents to fetch knives and tins.

'It is very good to let them out,' says Lecoeur, once they have descended the steps. 'Their hearts lifted.'

'You think so?'

'I saw it plainly.'

Jean-Baptiste nods. What *he* has seen plainly is himself on Monday morning without a single miner, or with a ragged half-dozen blind from drinking and fleeced of everything but their shirts. They may be tough as janissaries, these men, but they will be no match for the patter, the quick hands of the locals. Yet if he tries to confine them any longer, he will have a revolt, and one that will not be remedied with clay pipes and tobacco. At Valenciennes – though he did not see it in person – there were stories of the men running amuck, smashing machinery, torching company buildings, even laying siege to the managers' compound until the militia arrived. Most of them are northerners, like himself. Slow to rouse, but when the spirit takes them . . .

An hour after the men have eaten, the women arrive, cautious at first, the face of the boldest peeping round the half-open door from the rue aux Fers; then the door is thrown wide and in they march, calling as they come, cooing, waving their arms.

Lecoeur, Armand, Jeanne, Lisa Saget and Jean-Baptiste watch them from a moat of night-shadow at the foot of the church's western wall. It is not easy to count them. Lecoeur makes it twelve. Armand tells him he has missed one, then names a few – Simone, Marie-Anne, and that skinny one at the back who is called La Pouce. The youngest looks no older than Jeanne, while the oldest – a big, brassy creature with a voice like a colour-sergeant – is almost grandmotherly, and moves over the rough ground with a grim and purposeful hobbling.

The miners wait like the crew of an enchanted vessel. The women wash over them, through them. A party starts in the light of the fire. The men pass round their bottles, their tin mugs primed with brandy. The women drink, grow professionally wild, choose their mates, price themselves. The first couples steer into the darkness, arm in arm, like lovers anywhere. The watchers by the church, who have been standing quietly (and something in the manner of explorers observing the ceremonies of primitives on a beach beneath the Southern Cross), now retreat to the sexton's house. Block and Manetti are sitting either side of the kitchen fire, the sexton asleep, his head against the wing of his chair, Jan Block drowsily awake, flinching a little at the others' arrival and returning the engineer's nod with some awkward deferential movement of his own head.

They sit at the kitchen table. There's brandy here too. (Brandy everywhere, thinks Jean-Baptiste. I shall end up floating the bones to the Porte d'Enfer on a tide of the stuff.) They talk, but their conversation is pierced by the whoops and laughter of the revelry outside. Thoughts are diverted. A carnal magnetism creeps around the edges of the house like wisps of blue fog.

181

'We must have music,' says Lisa Saget, and immediately she starts to sing in a plain but pleasant voice, light, girlish, quite different to her speaking voice. Armand joins her. Lecoeur enthusiastically mistaps the beat on the tabletop. The sexton wakes, looks, in his own house, briefly lost. Jeanne settles him, rubs the wrinkled brown backs of his hands.

Armand reaches for his coat. 'We shall have music after all,' he says. 'We shall raid old Colbert's candle store. You two –' he points to Jean-Baptiste and Lecoeur – 'will man the bellows. The ladies will prettily sit, and I, the director of music, will play for your delight.'

While Jean-Baptiste is searching for some objection to this ridiculous plan (go into the church now? Play music?), the others are buttoning their coats. They look at him: it is hard to resist such looks. He shrugs, stands. If he cannot stop them, he can at least ensure there is no excessive behaviour, though the sudden prospect of it – excess! – wakes in him a kind of lively thirst, and he follows them out of the house willingly enough, eagerly perhaps.

They take the door into the south transept. Armand is at the front, holding high a lantern that throws a feathery light across walls dense with Latin couplets, dates, good works, blazonry. They shuffle, one behind the other. Their whispers fly about their heads. Things lean towards them from the dark, briefly loom. The gilt-flecked wing of an archangel ripples as they pass. A Virgin, her yellow face full of secret amusement, importunes them from a pillar . . .

In one of the chapels, Armand loots candles from an iron box, passes them back. They huddle to light them from each other's flames. As the light grows, Jean-Baptiste sees, lined up on the other side of the chapel, a half-dozen large containers, jars of thick greenish glass in snug wicker baskets, some clear liquor inside them. Around the glass necks, labels hang from twists of wire. He leans with his candle to read one.

Ethanol.

He steps back so rapidly his candle goes out.

'You put these here?' he hisses to Armand.

'These? They came last week. Something for our friends the doctors.'

'It is ethanol! Pure spirit. Put a flame near it and the whole church could burn down.'

'Peace,' says Armand. 'The tops are in tight, see? Sealed with wax. There's nothing to fear. And would it matter if the church burnt down? Would it not save us all a great deal of trouble?'

The engineer ushers them out of the chapel, is easier only once they have crossed the nave and gathered around the organ. On either side of the instrument's keyboards are brass rings in the form of delicate wreaths, and into these go four of the candles. Armand settles himself. Jean-Baptiste and Lecoeur go round to the pump, a metre of priapic oakwood, thick as an oar.

'I shall be glad of the exercise,' whispers Lecoeur, his breath emerging in a silvery gas. 'This place is cold as the moon.'

'Colder,' says Jean-Baptiste.

The women sit thigh to thigh on the nearest pew, holding their candles in front of them like penitents.

'Begin!' calls Armand.

They begin. Down, up. Down, up. Down, up. In its depths on the far side of the panelling, the instrument starts to click and wheeze. For Jean-Baptiste, it feels as if they are having to crank the whole machine into the air, to physically raise it. Or else it is as though they are resuscitating some collapsed leviathan, something like the elephant the minister said so frightened the dogs at Versailles. Then, from the thing's attic, comes a long sigh, the last breath of the world, and upon it, delicate as drops of rain, the music begins. Voix céleste, voix humaine, trompette, cromorne, tierce – the sounds building in layers, breaking in waves. Lecoeur is shouting something to him. Jean-Baptiste grimaces in reply, but he cannot understand him, cannot hear his words. The low notes are feeling out all the architecture of his chest; the high notes are doing something similar to his soul. Sweet Christ! They may as well be inside it. And this pumping! Up, down. Up, down. Beauty, it seems, has hard work at its root, and he begins to imagine a device, an automatic bellows, steam-driven, perfectly doable, and almost has it, the whole mechanism laid out in oiled parts in his head, when the music breaks off, mid-scale.

He lets go of the pump and walks to the front of the organ. In the pews behind Jeanne and Lisa Saget, in the wash of thin light from their candles, a scatter of ghostly figures are sitting, while others are quietly taking their places beside them. The miners and their whores. The whores with their miners. Men and women under a spell.

'You have your audience at last,' says Jean-Baptiste. Armand is watching them in the little mirror he has above the music stand. He turns a page of manuscript, smooths it, orders Jean-Baptiste back to his station.

It begins again: an opening just as delicate as the last (think of seamstresses, watch springs) and then, with no gradation, recklessly huge (think of mail coaches, cannonades), and then . . . then something very like a brawl, a riot. The engineer and Lecoeur abandon their oar. A voice – one Jean-Baptiste has been assaulted with before – is booming from the dark directly above them, and missiles, little black books – missals? – are flying down on their heads, now hitting a miner, now hitting a whore, now – stupendous shot! – slapping the flushed cheek of the organist himself.

Among those gathered in the pews there is a moment of pure panic; then the women, young and old, form up and return fire, the priest's basso damning of them met by a shrill taunting, a mockery, a contempt so well fuelled by historical indignation it is hard to believe the priest will not soon start to shit his own entrails. If they catch hold of him, if they can drag him down from his high place, the night will end with bloodshed. With murder, perhaps.

His arms spread, Jean-Baptiste attempts to herd the women out, but some are fixed like those stout posts sunk into the sides of busy streets for the protection of pedestrians. It is Jeanne who saves the priest's skin. She takes the hand of the biggest whore, their general, and leads her gently away. The others follow her, their shouts unanswered now, or answered only by their own echoes. By the time they are stepping into the air of the cemetery, the mood has become one of general hilarity. The women press around Armand, petting him until Lisa Saget warns them off in terms they all understand.

The party revives: the teasing, the draped arms, the pairing off. The engineer watches for a while, then, trembling with a sudden fatigue (and wondering how many candles have been left burning inside the church, what alarms might be sounded in the middle of the night), he exchanges discreet nods with Lecoeur, peels himself away from the edge of the group and goes quietly towards the door to the rue aux Fers. He is alone – believes he is alone – but on reaching the door sees that Jeanne is walking with him. They stop. He speaks her name. She smiles. His heart sinks.

'You will not be troubled by them?' he asks, gesturing to where, by the fire, the company is growing raucous.

'They would not hurt me,' she says.

'No,' he says. 'I cannot believe anyone would hurt you.'

'I'm not a saint,' she says.

'A saint? Of course not.'

'I wouldn't even tell anyone if you kissed me,' she says, and rests a hand very lightly on the sleeve of his coat. Light as a sparrow.

'I am twice your age,' he says. 'Am I not?'

'No,' she says, 'for you are twenty-eight and I am fourteen.'

'Then I am twice your age exactly.'

'Do you have a girl?' she asks, removing her hand. 'Are you sweet on Ziguette Monnard?'

'Ziguette?'

'She is very pretty.'

'I am not . . . I have no interest in Ziguette Monnard.'

'Good night,' she says.

'Yes,' he says, and she waits as if to see if 'yes' is all there is, if 'yes' might still lead to something.

He looks across the top of her head. The night is colder than it was, clearer. The stars shine blue over blue roofs. In the cemetery, the walls of heaped bones glint like the armour of some old, defeated army.

'Will you ask Lecoeur,' he says, 'to ensure the door is locked when the women leave? They should not stay much longer.'

She says nothing; she walks away from him. He nods at her back, unable at first to stir himself; then he gets the door open and goes onto the street, throws out his legs in long strides as if he hoped to outpace his own embarrassment. Sweet God, would it have killed him to have kissed her? To have dropped his head a little until their lips touched? Armand would have done it in an instant and she would have gone home happy instead of angry and hurt. And what was it stopped him? Some ludicrous attachment to a woman whose favours he could already have purchased for the price of a new hat? Can he not, once and for all, put his life on some proper, rational footing? Tomorrow – tomorrow without fail! – he must draw something up, a scheme, on paper, such as he has often done in the past. A plan of action to guide himself with, a rational scheme drawn out of the best part of himself, the highest. Do this, but not that. This will lead to success, this to the life of an idiot . . . Is he to be nothing but a *body*? A briefly animated example of what they dig up every day at les Innocents? Is that how Voltaire lived? How the great Perronet has spent his years, sitting among models and machines in his office at the Ecole des Ponts, a room – in memory at least – always packed with rich morning light?

By the time he opens the door to the Monnards' house he is starting to feel calmer, more compact, more himself as he can bear himself. On the hall table he fumbles for candle and tinder-box, makes sparks, makes flame. The cat writhes past the kitchen door, follows him up the stairs, seems briefly tempted by Ziguette's room, then follows the engineer into his own. He puts the candle on the table, takes off his coat and boots, wraps himself with the banyan. Is it midnight yet? Later? His watch is in one of his pockets, but he cannot quite be bothered to fish for it. He prepares his medicine – thirty drops or so in a mouthful of sour wine cold as the room – then undresses under the banyan and, when all is ready, blows out the candle, opens the window, peers down.

Have the women gone? He cannot see or hear them. Gone to the tents perhaps to finish their business. At least the church is not ablaze, and the cemetery appears in good order, though a light still shows in the kitchen window of the sexton's house. If he owned a sailor's spyglass, he might be able to see a little way inside, see Jeanne at the table. See her tears? He closes the window, puts the shutters across, worms his way into the bed, feet tucked beside the warmth of the cat. Darkness, darkness and nothing to listen to but the roar of his blood. The drug is working fast. In a minute or two it will sketch the first of the night's grotesques on the backs of his eyes, but before that, before he descends, before sleep and poppy juice atomise him entirely, he sends out his breath in a fading whisper.

'Who are you? I am Jean-Baptiste Baratte. Where are you from? From Bellême in Normandy. What are you? An engineer, trained at the Ecole des Ponts. What do you believe in? What do you . . . What do . . . What . . . you . . . What . . . I . . . I . . . I . . .'

11

When the assault took place, when precisely, no one could ever say with any certainty. Somewhere between very late and very early, some deep, velvet-lined pocket of a winter's night. He was dreaming, pressed under the weight of the drug, and then his eyes were open and there was light in the room, a wavering silver light. Behind the light, the figure of a woman standing by the little writing table, candle in one hand, something else in the other. She was perfectly naked, the light restless over her skin, glistening in her hair, glistening in the tight blond curls over her sex. She did not speak. His own voice was travelling towards him but much too slowly. She stepped to the side of the bed and looked down at him. Her face, tilted over the light of the candle, seemed calm and almost tender, a chiaroscuro angel bent over the bed of some ailing hermit. They may even, for an instant, have smiled at each other. Then her arm swung up, swung down and the whole world broke against his skull in a surge of exterminating pain. Briefly, he was aware of a noise, a sort of gasping, that might have been her or might have been him. Then, mercifully, nothing more.

12

But for Marie and her peeping, he would have bled to death. She had watched him blow out his candle, had got into her own bed, rattled off a Hail Mary, rubbed herself a little between her legs and dozed off for a minute, or for an hour or two, before opening her eyes and seeing a spot of light on the floor. Wide awake in an instant, she lowered herself to the boards, crawled over the cold floor and settled an eye over the hole. What was he doing lighting his candle again in the middle of the night? She was sure it had never happened before. And then – stranger still, *thrillingly* strange – she saw that he was asleep, quite obviously asleep, and the light came from a candle held by someone else, someone she could not yet see. For what felt like an age, though may in truth have been less than half a minute, nothing happened – nothing! – and she was almost beside herself with the frustration of it. What if whoever-it-was simply left and she never knew, never saw them at all? Never saw *her*, for she was convinced the secret watcher – the other secret watcher – was a woman. But

Jesus, Mary and Joseph, what could have prepared her for the shock of seeing Ziguette, dog-naked, step quietly into view! Had there been more than just a mouthful or two of stolen wine in her bladder, she might have puddled the floorboards. Ziguette, with her big, rosy bubs! The big, rosy curve of her arse! In one hand she held a candle, and with the other hand she took something off the lodger's table, something that caught the light and made, knocking against something else on the table, a little chiming sound that he must have heard in his sleep for he started to stir. It was that thing of his, the metal thing for measuring. Was she going to measure him? Measure what? His neck, his feet, his cock-a-doodle-doo?

For the last scene, a very short one, he was, she would swear, awake and looking at Ziguette, though neither of them said even the smallest word. In her imagination, Marie seemed already to be watching what must follow – the covers thrown back, the lovers snugly wrapped in each other's arms, the kissing and cuddling, the oohing and ahing, and she above it all, squirming on the boards. But it didn't happen like that. The metal thing, the ruler, cut through the air and came down on his head and killed him. She must have made some noise herself, a little squeal, for Ziguette suddenly looked up, her face all dark, a dark mask, and at *that*, the sight of that, she had at last lost a few drops of Monnard's wine.

Quiet as a cat, she stole away from the hole, crouched by her bed listening for feet on the stairs. Then, when none came, when there was no creak of the door, no naked mistress with a length of bloody metal in her hand, she wanted to crawl into bed and sleep, thinking that if she did so, she would wake in the morning and none of it would have happened. And this she might have done had she not heard him, his noise, a kind of snoring, a terrible sound, like someone in a nightmare they cannot wake from. She listened and listened. Her fear grew less. If silly Ziguette came in she would just crack her over the head with one of her sabots. That would settle her. Girls from the warrens of Saint-Antoine had no cause to tremble at lily-skinned girls from les Halles.

She pulled on her clothes. Everything was dark but she was perfectly used to dressing in the dark. She felt her way in stock-inged feet down the narrow stairs and onto the landing. Under Ziguette's door a light but no sound of her moving or weeping or whatever a girl does after trying to split a man's head in two. On closer inspection she could see the door was not quite shut and needed only a very gentle push to open it wide enough for her to put her head round. There was her mistress, all tucked up in bed, innocent as a lamb, the ruler on the end of the bed, the candle on the bedside cabinet. She leant in, lifted the candle and crossed to the lodger's room. When she opened the door, Ragoût bolted past her feet and plunged headlong down the stairs. The candle shook in her hand but she did not drop it, not quite. She found her breath again, went on, went in, went right up to the bed and stood over him, as Ziguette had done. And what a mess he was! It reminded her of something seen in childhood, an uncle of hers, a sort of uncle, who had put a lead ball through his temple one boiling Sunday afternoon. Blood, blood, blood. Puddles of it. The lodger, however, unlike her uncle, was still breathing, and not as he had before, noisily, but in shallow gasps, little dips of air like a child after a long cry. To stop a wound from bleeding, bind it with cobwebs. She had picked that up from somewhere. But where would she find cobwebs? Had she herself – good maid that she was – not swept them all away? She went to his trunk, opened it. At the top was the suit of green silk that when she first saw it seemed so funny and so beautiful. She reached below it, dragged out a handful of linen and went back to the bed. She held the candle over his head, touched the gash, its pulpy lips. He moaned, shuddered as if he might be starting a fit. 'I only touched it,' she whispered, then quickly, neatly, pressed a square of folded linen over the wound (some rag for drying himself after washing) and bound it in place with a neckcloth. Then, to be sure of it, she took off one of her own blood-warm stockings, wound it under his chin and knotted it over the already darkening pad of linen. She sat on the bed and looked at him. Now and then his eyes would flicker, but they did not open. She patted his hand, unwilling to give up ownership of this marvellous disaster, but then the thought of announcing to the half-asleep Monnards what their daughter had just done was too tempting, and taking the candle, she went down to their room (one leg bare, one dressed) and told them everything in the plainest speech imaginable, adding at the end – she really could not stop herself – 'Why, madame, I suppose they might even hang her.'

13

In the cemetery of les Innocents, in the pearly light of eight in the morning, the miners have congregated near the door onto the rue aux Fers. Most, perhaps encouraged by their whores, have made some effort to smarten themselves, to look more like regular subjects of Louis XVI and less like men who pull bones, coffins, miraculously preserved girls out of the ground. Jackets have been brushed down, mud kicked off boots. There has even been some washing, some untangling of beards. Three of the younger men – they stand together nearest to the door – have plaited grasses into crowns to wear round the brims of their hats. Others, looked at closely, can be seen to wear items once used to decorate the dead, trinkets picked out of the sticky earth or traded for at night in the privacy of the tents. One fellow, clear-eyed, calm-eyed, his back straighter than the others, sports a pair of memorial rings, *Respice finem* on one hand, *Mens videt astra* on the other, its greenish metal wrapping the hilt of a finger lost at the middle joint.

They have long since eaten their bread and drunk their coffee.

They have piled wood beside the preaching-cross bonfire, which in their absence will be fed by others. They are ready now. They are restless.

Outside the sexton's house, Lecoeur studies his watch, makes faces, mutters under his breath. Of all the mornings Baratte should choose to oversleep, this one is peculiarly inconvenient. Of course, in the comfort of his lodgings, he must find it all too easy to forget them, those who live *below*. The men, however, will take it very amiss if they are kept dawdling. He will take it amiss himself for that matter. Fifty drops of the tincture last night! At least fifty, and heaven knows how much drink to wash it down, but far from procuring a night of restful slumber, it served only to make him an utter stranger to himself. It was – how to express it? – as if he, Lecoeur, was Lecoeur's body only, the ticking flesh, and something, some invasive intelligence, was roosting in him, animating him, directing his actions. Had the *true* Lecoeur made a decision to go outside in the middle of the night? Had he? He did not believe so and yet he went, in nothing but his nightshirt, to the doctors' workshop, and there lifted the lid of the coffin and looked at her, Charlotte, with the light of a glowing stick from the fire that seemed almost to be magically in his hand. A horrible excitement! A great strain on the heart. On the teeth too, for he must, by the pains in his jaws, have been grinding them furiously for hours . . .

Behind him, soft footsteps. He turns, sees Jeanne, a shawl round her shoulders, coming from the house to join him. She smiles at him, prettily as ever, but does not today have quite her usual good colour, her usual *bounce*.

'It is strange he has not come,' she says.

'It might be he took more than was good for him last night,' says Lecoeur.

'I do not think that is right,' she says, smartly.

'No, no,' says Lecoeur. 'Probably he is engaged upon some unexpected business matter. A meeting with that man Lafosse, perhaps. The minister's man.'

She nods. 'Will you go out today also?'

'I believe I will,' says Lecoeur. 'Monsieur Saint-Méard has invited me to join him and a few of his friends on something of an excursion. He did not say exactly what he intended.'

'It will be pleasant, I am sure,' she says. 'You have the key?'

He shows it to her, an old key in his hand.

'I think Monsieur Baratte would wish you to let them go,' she says.

'You think?'

'Do you not?'

'You are probably right.' He looks at the men, bares his teeth a moment, then looks down at the girl. 'Shall we do it together?' he asks.

THIRD

Soon the neighbours wake up and rush to the scene which is no longer of death but of romance.

Cadet de Vaux, *Mémoire Historique et Physique sur le Cimetière des Innocents*

Stone steps, a long flight of them, leading steeply down. The cellar. The knowledge of what is below, what must be.

At first it is too dark to see or understand anything of his surroundings. There is only the descent, the feel of the steps beneath his feet. Then a soft pinkish light, a narrow hall, a table with a tin on it, a little bell. There is a woman sitting behind the table. She keeps her face averted but knows he is there. She rings the bell and though it makes no discernible sound the curtain at the end of the hall is immediately drawn back. A man smiles at him, beckons him with a little gesture of his head . . .

They are in a corridor. On either side of it, swagged drapes conceal what are, presumably, the entrances to rooms. One of these – where the drape has been imperfectly closed – he stops to look into, though perhaps it is not really a room at all. The walls seem to be made of packed black earth. The dimensions are uncertain, so too the number of people in there, the men and women and children sitting, crouching, lying. They look back at him. There is something ardent in their gazes. Ardent, wide-eyed, blank. He turns away. He is afraid that one of them will start to speak, will address him, will know his name . . .

The guide is waiting at the end of the corridor. Another set of curtains. Pretty gestures of invitation. He goes in, the guide close behind him. Whatever is going to happen it is going to happen now and here. They are, it seems, in his room at the Monnards' or something like his room, for there is no window and the walls are bare. Light comes from a single large candle on the table. On the bed is a man. He wears only a shirt, the tails reaching to his knees. His eyes are open, but his lips have been clumsily stitched with black thread.

The guide lifts the candle from the table and steps to the bed. It only takes a moment, he says. We must release the phlogiston. It is the agent of transformation. The destroyer of impurities.

He leans, and as though pouring something precious into the ear of the man on the bed, he touches the candle's wick to his hair. It takes instantly, burns like dried grass. Then flames slide over the man's face, wrap his throat, race over the skin of his chest, his belly. How can a body burn like this? A man should not burn like rolled paper! What has been done? What method is this?

In its wrap of flames the body begins to move. An arm, a leg. The torso lifts – floats! – from the burning sheets. The thread between the lips is sundered. The mouth springs open. Roars, roars . . .

1

'Keep him still,' says Guillotin. He is leaning over the bed. A line of black thread lies over the patient's face like a fine crack. Marie presses down on the kicking legs. She's a good strong girl for the holding-down business. The doctor gets to work.

For the first forty-eight hours there is danger, a very grave danger. If the brain is bleeding, well, something might be done – there's a surgeon on the rue Saint-Honoré with an elegant drill, but could he be fetched in time? The patient is watched continuously. Marie, Jeanne, Lisa Saget, Armand, Lecoeur. Guillotin calls every morning and again in the early evening. He stands over his patient, weighs the odds, then looks out at the church of les Innocents, thinks large thoughts about men, their heads, their hearts, the way of the world. The old world and the world that is, perhaps, coming.

*   *   *

In spite of the succession of watchers, when the engineer finally opens his eyes he would swear that the room is empty. On the bolster, his head is a dead weight, a fist of living gristle sown onto the stump of his neck. The pain is not on the surface but buried in the white depths of his brain. Its rhythm is the rhythm of his blood. At each heartbeat he winces. The door moves. Madame Monnard peeps in. When she sees that his eyes are open, that he is, apparently, looking at her, she flees.

'Who am I?'
    'You? You are the doctor.'
    'And my name?'
    'Guillotin.'
    'Good. And you?'
    'Baratte.'
    'And the name of our king?'
    'Louis.'
    'You remember what happened to you?'
    'Some of it.'
    'Some?'
    'Enough.'

'Monsieur Lafosse has visited us,' says Lecoeur. (How many hours have passed? How many days?) 'I believe Dr Guillotin informed him of your . . . misfortune. He has instructed me to press on with the work. Says it would not do to keep the men idle. That time is money.'

'Ziguette?' murmurs Jean-Baptiste, but too quietly.

'And look,' says Lecoeur, 'Jeanne has sent you a remedy. Herbs of some kind, I think.' He holds out the bottle for inspection. On his hands, there is a stubborn speckling of black stains, black paint.

'Probably a love potion,' says Armand, who is also in the room, though out of the engineer's field of vision.

'What day is it?' asks the patient.

'Day?' says Lecoeur. 'It is Wednesday. Wednesday morning.'

Marie is on a chair by the bed doing something to the fire. He does not wish to move his head to see. Any quick movement of his head sends the world jittering and juddering. 'Ziguette?' he asks.

'Why?' she says. 'Afraid she's going to visit you again?' Then, when he does not answer her, she says, 'It was me what saved you.'

Light is a white sheet at his window, a dull white sheet that is folded each evening and hung out again the next dawn. They no longer watch him all the time. Unwatched, he steals out of bed, sits ten minutes on the chair, clinging to the seat. The following day, he sits for half an hour. Sitting becomes his practice. Sometimes, when swept by squalls of pity – for himself, his bullying father, the haunted lives of strangers, the cold bones in the cemetery – he makes odd shapes with his mouth, a type of dry weeping. Other times he is blank, calm and perfectly blank, until the world's rawness, his own breath, the edges of the air, rouse him again. He studies his hands, looks at the fire, peers quizzically at the picture of the bridge. He lifts his eyes to the window: the clouds are coloured like the sea at Dieppe. Who are you? asked the doctor. He is Adam alone in the garden. He is Lazarus rousted out of his tomb, one life separated from another by a slack of darkness.

Guillotin comes to bleed him; phlebotomy a standard precaution in such cases. First, he carries out his usual examination of the wound. 'You Normans have nice thick skulls,' he says. 'You wouldn't care to leave me your head, would you?'

'What makes you think you will outlive me?'

'Your taste in women,' says the doctor, turning his attention to the engineer's right arm and cutting him close to the elbow. The blood slopes into a tin bowl. 'Don't worry,' he says. 'I won't take much.'

'Where is she?'

'Your assailant?'

'No one will tell me where she is.'

'She was here until two days ago, in the house. Now she is sent away. Elderly relatives in Dauphiné. People of strict religion. I hope you will not object, but I gave the scheme my approval. There can be no more effective cure for a young woman's ardency than a year or two muttering novenas in a cold house in a remote province. I assumed you would have no wish to prosecute her. A man would only make himself ridiculous prosecuting a woman in such circumstances. Had you succumbed, of course, then the matter would have been beyond any purely private solution. You were lovers?'

'No.'

'I shall believe you,' says the doctor, balling a scrap of lint, pressing it over the cut and carefully folding his patient's arm. 'But if it was not love or jealousy or desire, what do you imagine made her walk into your room and try to split your head in two?'

'Les Innocents.'

'The cemetery? To keep you from destroying it? She may be madder than I thought. Let us hope she does not butcher her relatives in Dauphiné. One would feel a certain responsibility.'

'How long has it been?'

'Since the attack? Two weeks. A little over.'

'I must return to the work.'

'A month in the good air of Normandy would be a better prescription.'

'I am well enough.'

'You were struck a very considerable blow to the head. The effects of any such blow are both unpredictable and of long duration. You have noticed anything unusual? Hallucinations? Lapses in memory?'

'Nothing,' says Jean-Baptiste, lying.

The doctor wipes the blade of his lancet. 'In that case,' he says, 'how would it be if we endeavour to get you down to the drawing room tomorrow? The Monnards will no doubt be anxious to afford you every comfort.' He grins. 'In the meantime, you have the Comte de Buffon to keep you company.' He takes the book from the table, drops it onto the bedcovers. 'You are aware, I suppose, that there are another thirty volumes of this?'

When the doctor has gone, Jean-Baptiste looks at the book and, after a moment, opens it. It is not the first time since the assault that he has tried it. He shuts his eyes, opens them, summons himself, the engine of his concentration, which has, in the past, served him so well. He puts a finger on the top left-hand side of the left-hand page. The first four words present no difficulty: 'Now let us consider ...' The next word he cannot read. The next is, he thinks, 'instance'. The next nothing but a shape, meaningless as an ink blot. So too the one after it and the one after that. And it is not just words in books, it is the words in his head that have gone. Names of things, quite ordinary things, objects a child could name. Like   and   .

And if this, this blindness, should become common knowledge? If Lafosse and then the minister discover it, what then? Who in the world would employ such a man even to destroy a cemetery?

He shuts the book, pushes it onto the floor, rolls out of bed, stands experimentally, waits for his blood to arrange itself, then shuffles to the mirror. He has a nightcap on his head, a dressing of some sort beneath it. He looks – what? – foolish and saintly and slightly frightening. He fingers the hair on his chin, touches his skull as though it was a shelled egg and any sharp movement might pierce it, make a hole for the yolk of his brains to run through . . .

He is twenty minutes easing off the nightcap, then the bandage with its damp, pink underside. His hair has been chopped, clumsily tonsured, but however he angles his head, he can see almost nothing of the wound itself except an ugly patch of discoloured skin and, poking from it like a single gross hair, a strand of black thread.

He looks for his clothes, the working suit he was wearing the day before the night Ziguette Monnard came in to murder him. He cannot see it. It has been tidied away or taken away. Spoiled? Splashed with his blood, with blood from the weapon, the thing, the metal thing, the name of which (a spark of panic in his chest) he has also lost? How can a man think at all if he does not have the words to think with? What can guide him if not the words?

He goes to his trunk, lifts the lid. The shock of colour, of light off colour, makes him flinch, but he is relieved to hear 'green' in his head, and 'silk', and even 'pistachio'. He carries the suit to the bed, lays it there, regards it a while, then climbs wearily inside it. Let this be the answer, then. He will simply follow the world. The world, the things of the world, will prompt him. He will do what they suggest. It will not matter if he can name them or not. He will be like a child running after a ball bouncing down steps. Perhaps that is what he always did. He cannot quite remember.

When he is dressed, he looks for the banyan, the tarboosh, the rented wig, the paper they were all wrapped in, wraps them again, a large, clumsy parcel. He puts on his shoes, his riding coat. With teeth clenched he settles his hat on his head as if the wound might be oppressed simply by a shadow. He goes downstairs. No one sees him. The kitchen door is open but the room is empty. He glances at the cellar door, resists the urge to try it, opens the street door, narrows his eyes against the light, stands a full minute with his back against the wall of the house, gathering energy, courage, whatever he will need to go on. He dreads being recognised, stopped, spoken to. He assumes some version of the story is already in circulation, that he is not just the engineer now but the man the Monnard girl attacked, the man who must, in some way, have provoked her. He watches two boys come up the street whipping a toy, a hollow circle of wood. He lets them pass, then shoves off from the wall, launches himself.

At Gaudet's he gets a shave. He is the only customer. When he comes in the barber is sitting in his chair reading the *Mercure de France* and nibbling a fingernail. The shave is simple sensual pleasure. The wound, of course, is not mentioned, though Gaudet has ample time to study it. Instead, the barber speaks of the town, the quarter, the price of things, the recent strikes. None of it requires any comment from Jean-Baptiste. He lets the man chatter, lets him work, is grateful to him.

'I have been ill a while,' he says at last.

'But you are well again now,' says Gaudet, brushing the brown hairs, the little grey ones, from the engineer's shoulders. 'You will be quite your old self again soon.'

'You think?'

The barber grins at him through the medium of the mirror, shrugs elegantly, then folds the sharp thing, the bright thing, into its curved handle.

With the parcel in his arms, the cold air keen over chin and cheeks, he walks up past the Company of the Indies and the rue des Bons-Enfants to the place des Victoires. After being bedridden for two weeks the walk should have done him in; instead it seems to recover him a little. He has no difficulty remembering the address he wants. He shoulders the door. A bell rings. Charvet in his velvet pumps is crossing the polished floor of the shop. He stops, raises his little eyebrows, then tilts from the waist, stiffly.

'Monsieur l'Ingénieur, is it not?'

There is a chair by the door. Jean-Baptiste drops his parcel onto its seat. The parcel starts to unwrap itself as though it contained something living. 'I should like to have my old suit again,' he says. 'The one I wore when I came to you with Saint-Méard.'

Charvet looks at his assistant, then back to the engineer. 'Your old suit? But that was sold, monsieur. To a gentleman in trade, I believe. Is that not so, Cédric?'

The assistant confirms it.

Jean-Baptiste nods, lets his gaze travel slowly round the shop. On one of the wooden mannequins (an adjustable torso on a wooden pillar) is a suit of neatly cut black wool. He goes up to it, handles the cloth, takes in the size. 'This, then. This will do.'

'In *that*,' says Charvet, speaking now as if explaining something to a child, not a good child but a foolish one, 'you will appear like a Geneva parson. It is here only because it is necessary to show a range of styles. A wide range, you understand. But for you, monsieur, it will not . . .'

'And this,' says Jean-Baptiste, unbuttoning his coat to show a line of green silk, 'I have no use for any more.'

Charvet makes a curious bridling movement, lengthens his neck, blinks extravagantly. 'Yet I remember, monsieur, how well you liked it when you first had it.'

'You do?' It is a genuine question.

'You wished to be more *à la mode*.'

'More modern?'

'Exactly. You . . . cannot recollect?'

'I remember being drunk. I remember being flattered.'

'It is still an excellent suit.'

'It is a suit I no longer want. And I have brought the banyan back,' says Jean-Baptiste. 'The rest too. There. On the chair.'

Charvet and the assistant look at the chair, at the parcel, the tongue of red damask lolling from the paper.

They fit him with the black. With a few tucks the fit is surprisingly snug, the colour immediately restful, though it is true that he does indeed look something like a Geneva parson. Charvet leaves the alterations to his assistant. He stands to one side, arms folded. Now and then he glances, with some disgust, at the engineer's battered head.

'This suit,' he says at last, 'may be simple, but it is not inexpensive. And the other has been much worn, has, I see, some stains on the sleeve. Grease stains if I am not mistaken. Grease or something worse. I will be forced to sell it at a discount. A considerable—'

'That old one of mine you had,' says Jean-Baptiste, carefully shrugging himself into his riding coat again and starting to button it, 'the one you sold to a man in trade. It was worth more than the whole of your shop. *That* I recollect perfectly.' He looks at Charvet until Charvet turns away. He goes to the door. The assistant hurries to open it for him. Sheer force of habit.

In the pocket of his coat he has the key to the cemetery, to the door from the rue aux Fers. With his hands in his pockets, he holds the key in a fist and crosses the market. He wonders if he is hungry – he has eaten nothing but some soup for breakfast, a medicinal broth when the day was still half dark. He pauses by the entrance to one of the fish sheds. The market is different to him in some way, strikes him differently, though he cannot say exactly how. It looks the same – same stalls, same red-faced, raw-fingered stall-holders, same hoarse shouts, same muck. He goes inside the fish shed, stands in the dripping shadows among pools of water bright with fish scales, breathes deeply. On the lining of his nose there is a sensation of coolness, of dampness, but nothing that could be called a smell, a stink. So that too has gone! It is at least a symptom he can, without risk of repercussion, confess to Dr Guillotin . . .

And then he is there, the rue aux Fers, where brown smoke coils above the cemetery wall and the black letters – still fresh-looking – are waiting for him: 'FAT KING SLUT QUEEN BEWARE! BECHE IS DIGGING A HOLE BIG ENOUGH TO BURY ALL VERSAILLES!'

Is he reading or remembering? He is not sure. What he does know, does not need to question, is that when he first saw it, *she* was here, almost exactly where he is now, standing with her loaf of bread, a piece of which she offered to him and which he snatched from her like some big, awkward bird, a big, yellow-eyed gull. And then afterwards, in the charnel with Armand, whom he meant to upbraid, to accuse of frivolity, of undermining him, he was himself accused, told he was concerned solely with his professional character, that his politics were the politics of 'undrawn conclusions'.

Had he understood what Armand meant by such a phrase? There had not been much opportunity to think on it. First that business with the men's pipes, then Lecoeur and Armand coming back drunk. That and a hundred other worries. But yes, he had understood well enough. Had felt the justice of it. Had resented it . . .

The door of the cemetery opens. A man – a wiry man with a flow of yellow beard that looks more youthful, more vigorous than the face it hangs from – steps into the street. When he sees the engineer he stops, tenses, stares.

'Block?' says Jean-Baptiste, stepping closer. 'Block?'

Block nods. Under his arm he has two rolled sacks, bread sacks from the dust of flour on them.

'You are sent on an errand?'

Block nods again.

'Jeanne has sent you?'

'Yes.'

'You have your strength back.'

'Yes.'

They look at each other a moment, on their faces some fleeting recognition of shared experience, of dissolution and uncertain reassembly. Then, with a brushing of shoulders, they pass each other by.

Inside the cemetery, the men are gathered about a pit close to the north wall. Pit eight? Nine? A man lifting a clogged, mushroom-brown pelvis onto the bone wall sees him first. He stops, straightens (as far as a miner can). Lecoeur follows the man's gaze, lets out a yelp of delight and hurries over, speaking so rapidly, so confusedly, his words seem to overlie each other. Are those tears in his eyes? From the smoke perhaps. Just the smoke.

The men working the surface gawp. One speaks a word, drops it like a pebble to his fellows below. The engineer greets them. He has no trouble bringing their names to mind. Agast, Everbout, Cloët, Pondt, Jan Biloo, Jacques Hooft, Louis Cent, Elay Wyntère . . . He is glad of them, surprised at how unaffectedly glad he is to see them again. He asks them to go on with their work. They go on.

'We have not,' says Lecoeur, confidentially, 'made all the progress I would have wished for. We finished two this last week –' he gestures to where they have dug – 'and would have finished this had one of the sides not collapsed. It was fortunate the men were on their break. I even feared for the cemetery wall.'

'You were using the . . . the wooden . . . the shapes . . . the shapes that hold the sides?'

'The box-crib? I had hoped it would not be necessary. The weather has been tolerably dry. It was an error, of course. I am sorry for it.'

'It is no great matter. We can shore the wall with the earth. A ramp of earth. Then put the crib in place.'

'Yes,' says Lecoeur. 'That will be best.'

'The men have eaten their midday meal?'

'Some hours ago. It is, I think, past three o'clock.'

'I had not realised.'

'*Tempus fugit*,' says Lecoeur, gleefully. There are little white crusts at the corners of his mouth. His lips, chapped by the wind, look sore. 'You are perfectly recovered?' he asks.

'I am told I have a thick skull,' says Jean-Baptiste. 'And you?'

'Recovered?'

'You are well?'

'Oh, have no unease on my account. We Lecoeurs are a leathery breed.' He laughs. 'I dare say I could wrestle a bear. Were there some need to.'

'Or an elephant?'

'An elephant?'

'I have just thought of it. An elephant. I do not know why. Have we spoken of elephants before?'

'I cannot . . .'

'It is not important.'

214

For almost an hour Jean-Baptiste commands the work from a quarterdeck of winter grass; then, his limbs beginning to finely tremble, he excuses himself and crosses towards the sexton's house.

Jeanne is standing at the table slicing dried sausage, leaning her whole weight over the knife. Armand is in Manetti's chair, a book of music on his lap, big creamy pages, black staves, thousands of dancing notes. He is frowning with concentration, his fingers playing the bones of his knees. He looks up at Jean-Baptiste, grins. 'Well, well,' he says. 'Well, well, well.'

'You must sit,' says Jeanne, putting down her knife and pulling a stool from under the table. Jean-Baptiste sits, heavily, shuts his eyes a moment, then slowly removes his hat.

'You are very pale still,' she says.

'He was always pale,' says Armand.

'You should be at home,' says Jeanne, going quickly to the hearth, where a coffee pot sits on a tile by the fire.

'Home,' says Armand, 'is where they cracked his head open. No doubt he feels safer in a cemetery.'

The coffee is only lukewarm and without its aroma it has no taste, but Jean-Baptiste gulps it and holds out the bowl for more. 'Your grandfather?' he asks.

'He is resting,' says Jeanne, brown eyes flickering shyly over the engineer's grey. He wonders what she is thinking. The last he can remember of her, of any of them, is going into the church for Armand to play the organ. Was that the night he was attacked? The night before? The week before?

'All that work stewing our exhumed friends,' says Armand, 'has quite exhausted the old fellow. It exhausts me just thinking about it.'

'Is this sausage edible?' asks Jean-Baptiste. He takes a piece, puts it in his mouth. Pork and pork fat hard as money.

Armand shuts his book of music. He turns in the chair and watches the engineer, watches him chew and eventually swallow.

'You find me so interesting?' asks Jean-Baptiste.

'Interesting? You know very well I have found you so from the moment you walked into my church. I confess I am intrigued to see what your surgeon has achieved.'

'You mean Guillotin?'

'I mean Ziguette Monnard. I fancy she has finished you off.'

Along the length of Jean-Baptiste's wound the stitches briefly tighten. 'It is what she intended,' he says.

'Ah, but you were in need of something, my friend. You were not quite hatched . . . And is that not a new suit you have? Have you seen it, Jeanne? Black as midnight! Bravo! He has at last revealed himself as the good Calvinist I have always suspected him of being. You know his mother is of that persuasion?'

'My *mother* . . .' begins Jean-Baptiste, speaking to the stone floor between his feet, 'my mother . . .' He falls silent. He is in no mood for Armand's games, in no condition to play them. He finishes the second bowl of coffee, rouses himself and goes upstairs to look in on Manetti, sits a while beside the sleeping man, then, coming down the stairs, suffers an instant of giddiness and only saves himself from tumbling by snatching at the rail.

'You have done enough for now,' says Armand, taking him firmly by the arm and walking him outside. 'The cemetery is yours still. Poor Lecoeur was in a panic without you.'

'I should speak to him . . .' says Jean-Baptiste.

'Tomorrow will be soon enough.'

'I shall come in the morning.'

'I don't doubt it,' says Armand.

'And in my working suit, if I can find it.'

'We shall be ready for you. I will even attempt not to tease you for a day or two.' He smiles.

'When it happened,' says Jean-Baptiste, speaking quickly and quietly and looking over Armand's shoulder at the arches of the south charnel, 'when she struck me . . . afterwards, I mean, there were some moments before I became insensible. Very few, I think, but enough. I wished to . . . hold something. Some idea. I believed I was dying, you see. I wished for something to make the moment possible.'

'And what did you find?'

'Nothing. Nothing at all.'

On the rue aux Fers, grey light, grey stone; the black forms of birds on the steep roofs. To his left, the corner of the rue de la Lingerie, to his right, the rue Saint-Denis. By the fountain, a dog, skinny, pared down, is lapping at a puddle. Sensing itself observed, it looks up, water dripping from its muzzle, then turns, limps into the rue Saint-Denis, pauses a moment as if to see which half of the world beckoned it, and goes north towards the faubourg.

The engineer trails after it, enters the street's stream, stands there clumsily, immediately in everybody's way. He cannot see the animal any more but does not need to. He knows what he will do now, though for a man who has prided himself on possessing a trained and shadowless mind it feels uncomfortably like a descent into ritual magic. He will walk up the rue Saint-Denis. He will circle round to the church of Saint-Eustache. He will follow, as best he is able, the route he took the night he went painting with Armand and his fellow waifs, the night he found himself alone in the mist with Héloïse. He will follow the route and so discover her again and deliver his message – whatever the

217

message is. He has not yet dressed it in words but surely, once she is standing in front of him, it will pour out of his mouth like the Holy Ghost.

He sets off through a cloud of seamstresses, noisy, red-cheeked girls heading towards the river after twelve hours on their benches squinting at needles. On the rue Saint-Denis, it is the fat hour when work is briefly suspended and there is a chance to look up and wring a little pleasure from a scrap of winter's evening. Djeco's wine shop is already full. A pair of porters lounge against the wall outside like Spanish gallants in the Age of Gold. Foundry men, flower-girls, shoe-blacks, stick-sellers, beggars, fiddlers, writers-for-hire – if any among them notice the engineer, the wounded white intensity of his face, and are, for a stride or two, amused or unsettled, they are soon swept past to new distractions. He, certainly, is mostly oblivious to them, would be entirely so were it not for the occasional shoulder-check from some man or woman hurrying in the counterflow. He is looking ahead, as far ahead as he can, looking and trying not to give in to the growing suspicion that all this – what he is doing here – is no more than one of those effects, unpredictable and of long duration, Dr Guillotin warned him of. And then, having walked no more than three hundred metres from the fountain, a movement of red – purple almost in this light – stops him dead, then starts him again at a quicker pace.

Unsettling to have found her so easily! To not have the time to walk off the last of his giddiness, to gather himself. Unsettling to think that magic might work . . .

She is too far ahead to call to, and moving in the same north-ward direction as himself. For a whole minute he loses sight of her, his view obscured by a pair of ambling packhorses; then he spies her again, standing by the window of a shop, her face close to the glass. He knows the place, has passed it a score of times. They sell those things, those – love of Christ, he has one on his own head! – but the ones for women, for women and girls. Ribbons and so on, scoops, coloured feathers . . .

'Héloïse!'

He has called too soon; his voice does not quite carry, though the woman behind him, one of those prematurely aged market crones with a figure like a herring barrel, has heard him clearly enough and mimics him surprisingly well, the plaintive, husky tone: 'Oh HELO-ISE!'

He looks round at her, more confused than angry. Who is she? Does he know her?

'Eh, Queenie!' shouts another woman, sister-creature of the first. 'Can't you see the gentleman wants you?'

But still she has not heard them, still she stares in at the shop window, oblivious of the scene moving up the street towards her.

'She don't want to make her basket-weaver jealous,' says a third. 'Or the old bookseller. Or your old man!'

'My old man so much as looked at her, I'd serve him his balls for dinner.'

Now she turns, watches them, holds her ground as they approach. Whatever she is feeling – anger, fear, astonishment – she is careful to keep all sign of it out of her face. The engineer stops a metre and a half, perhaps two metres from her.

'He's lost his tongue,' says the first woman.

'It's not his tongue he'll want,' says the second, laughing at her own wit.

'It's *him*,' says a man's voice, a shaggy head leaning from the window of an unlit room in the house next to the shop. 'The one digging up les Innocents.'

'You sure?'

''Course I'm bloody sure. Look at him.'

'Expect he wants a bit of what his workers are getting,' says another voice, female, younger than the others.

'I was looking for you,' says Jean-Baptiste to Héloïse. 'I wished . . . to speak with you.' At the mention of speaking, the audience bursts into delighted laughter.

'You got to show her the colour of your money, dear. Bless him. He must be new to it all.'

'And what about the Monnard girl?' asks the younger voice. 'Gone off her, have you?'

Héloïse, who has not once allowed her gaze to be drawn towards anyone other than the engineer, grants him now four or five seconds in which to make everything right. He breathes; he frowns; he opens his mouth. 'Hats,' he says. 'How could I have forgotten hats?'

She makes the slightest of nods; then, very calmly, as if none of it had anything to do with her, as if it was just some nonsense she had happened upon and which now she had lost all interest in, she turns away and continues her progress up the street.

The man in the window leans further out. 'Hats!' he screams. 'Did you hear him? He said, "Hats"! Hats!'

It is only a step or two to the window from where Jean-Baptiste is standing. He goes to it, goes quickly before the man has any chance to react. He takes a fistful of the man's hair, pulls his head down hard against the narrow sill. In his other hand he has the key to the cemetery. He presses the tip against the man's throat, a soft place just below the jaw.

'Who do I look like to you?' he asks, his voice quiet, almost conversational. 'Who do I look like to *you*?'

In the time to come – when there will be cause to speak of such things – the man will say he saw bloody murder in those grey eyes, will insist on it and be listened to. Whatever he sees, it is enough to silence him. Even the women are discomfited. The show is over. They melt away, each to her own small circumstance. Within a minute the engineer stands quite by himself.

2

At his next meeting with Monsieur Lafosse – three days after the events on the rue Saint-Denis – Jean-Baptiste offers his resignation. He is quite clear about it. He no longer wishes to be the director of works at the cemetery of les Innocents. He wants nothing to do with les Innocents. He wishes to go somewhere else, do something different. He is, after all, an engineer: he knows that much. He should attempt to employ himself more appropriately.

Lafosse, who never sits during these encounters in the Monnards' drawing room, waits for the younger man to finish what he has to say, then tells him that resigning is a recourse open to people of some importance in the world and that he, the engineer, is not such a person. He, the engineer, is in fact a type of servant and not even a particularly senior type of servant. A servant who was taken on at the minister's pleasure. A servant who will be released when the minister has no further use for him. Those are the terms. To abuse them would be to destroy utterly any hope of future advancement. It is, perhaps, more pathetic than amusing that the engineer had not understood all this.

'So I must remain here? I have no choice but to remain?'

'Bravo, monsieur. You have grasped the essential fact. And now, if you would permit me to continue with what I have taken the trouble to come here and discuss with you?'

What Lafosse has come to discuss – though between them there is never anything that might be mistaken for a discussion – is the news that the quarry at the Porte d'Enfer is finally ready for its first consignment from the cemetery. His Grace the Bishop has scattered holy water in the vaults and passages where the bones will be stored. The carts will travel at night, accompanied by priests from the seminary at Saint-Louis. Throughout the journey the priests will pray aloud in strong voices. There will be incense, pitch torches, black velvet. Everything is to reflect the concern, the Catholic decency of the minister . . .

'And may I inform the minister,' says Lafosse, 'that your health is now quite recovered? That there will be no repetition of such adventures?'

He makes no comment on the engineer's new black coat, a coat somehow a shade or two blacker than his own.

3

Dinner with the Monnards. A cabbage stuffed with capers. Veal kidneys cooked in wine. Pumpkin tart.

Monsieur and Madame eat in a state of exquisite discomfort. The engineer, for whom all food has now become simply a matter of volume, mass, elasticity, surface texture, degrees of aridity, just eats. Marie is blooming.

4

The night of 9 March, just after eleven by the engineer's watch, a convoy of carts – solid, capacious vehicles built to haul stone – is ready to leave for the Pont Neuf and the quarry. It took more than three hours to load them, though in the cemetery the bone walls look much as they did before. As for the crypts and the attics of bones above the galleries, these they have not even touched.

The horses wait patiently in their traces. Now and then one scrapes a hoof over the cobbles. The priests are pale, rehearsed, young, competitively pious. They grip their flambeaux, glance at their neighbours, glance at the carts with their velvet-draped loads.

'Let us hope these fellows have good boots,' says Armand. 'By the time this is over they will have walked to the moon and back.'

Twenty, thirty onlookers have gathered on the far side of the rue de la Ferronnerie. There has not been much, until now, for people to look at. The smoke of the fires, the weekly appearance of the miners, like sailors on furlough in a foreign port, eyes full of uneasy knowledge. But now there is this, a procession with carts and fire, and priests in their long, brass-buttoned coats. The first undeniable evidence of the end of les Innocents! The first removal. There is – there has been – no protest, no lament. Whatever loyalty people still feel for this patch of foul ground, no one, with the exception of Ziguette Monnard, has bothered to raise a hand to save it.

At the last moment, when everything is ready and the performance is about to commence, Père Colbert appears. He blunders through the cemetery door, shoves his bulk between Armand and Jean-Baptiste, glares at them from behind his tinted glasses, glares at the young priests. From the hands of one of them he snatches a torch, then stamps to the front of the procession and plants himself at its head.

The engineer gives the signal to the carter. The carter whistles to the horses. There is a jangling of tack, the crushing sound of iron rims turning on stone and, from the backs of the carts, a muffled tapping and grating as the bones settle beneath their covers.

The priests begin to chant a psalm – *Miserere Mei, Deus* – but the rhythm of their step, of their singing is confused by the tread of Colbert's boots marching to a rhythm of their own. He leads them towards the river, red face thrust grimly forwards as though on his way to harrow Hell.

5

The pit by the cemetery wall is emptied, filled. Two more are opened. The engineer is refining his methods. He pushes the men harder, adds time to the working day as night slowly retreats before the season. A second miner absconds, returns three days later, silent and hungry. As for the others, who knows? To look at, they seem reconciled to the work, the character of the work, hardened to it. He would like very much to know what they speak of when they are alone. He admires them, their courage, that air of independence they have. Do they not seem less owned than he does? Do they not seem more free? There is one in particular who catches his eye, his imagination. The miner with the clipped finger, the violet eyes, who comes and goes like an apparition. The others, it seems, discreetly defer to him, move about him in some shifting constellation of respect. Lecoeur – a sure source of information on the rest – has little to say about him, only that he attached himself to the party shortly before they left Valenciennes, a replacement for a miner who declared himself unfit to travel. Name of Hoornweder. Probably Hoornweder. Hoornweder or Tant, or perhaps Moemus. They often simply invent names for themselves. Does the engineer have any cause to be dissatisfied with him? No, no, says Jean-Baptiste. There is no cause. It was nothing but his own curiosity.

By the middle of the month they are sending five processions a week to the Porte d'Enfer and for a while these processions – the droning priests, the tapers, the carts with their mournful cargo – are added to the list of the city's entertainments. The *Mercure de France* prints a little guide giving the times of the processions and where they may be seen to best advantage (crossing the river is highly recommended). Young couples, particularly those from the idle classes, allow themselves to be roused by the sight. Moralists, grimly amused, look on with folded arms. Foreign visitors write letters home, strain for metaphor, to see all France in this winding caravan of bones. Then the city offers a collective shrug. It looks around for other ways to amuse itself. The cafés. Politics. Another riot, perhaps.

6

Armand invites himself to the Monnards' house to play Ziguette's pianoforte. He employs, at the Monnards' expense, a man immaculately blind with tools like a tooth-puller, who tut-tuts and grimaces and climbs half inside the instrument, and at last renders it tuneful.

When Armand sits to play, he seems to throw sounds into the keys from the ends of his fingers. At the first big crash of chords, Ragoût cowers under the settle, then comes out and digs his claws frenziedly into the weave of the rug.

'You are killing my organ,' shouts Armand over the sound of himself, 'but you have given me this and so I forgive you.'

'I have not given it to you,' says Jean-Baptiste.

'Ownership,' says Armand, 'will soon be a much more flexible concept.'

Jean-Baptiste suffers with headaches. He will suffer with them for the rest of his life. During the worst of them, the world is covered with a livid purple membrane, as if he looked out of the crack in his own head. He has to sit, perfectly still. The pain builds until it is released through copious vomiting. Other attacks are less severe and can be controlled – it was Guillotin's suggestion – by drinking three or four cups of strong coffee.

Of the lost words some, like pigeons back to their loft, return to him. He writes them down, pen and black ink in the back of his journal:

Razor
Hoop
Ruler
Box-crib
Hat . . .

He still cannot read through a page of Buffon, cannot remember when or why he bought it. He wonders how much of a man's life is the story he tells himself about himself. He wonders how much of his story he has lost. Wonders if it matters.

In the credit column, he is no longer troubled by dreams. He sleeps soundly. The bottle of medicine, the glutinous *lachryma papaveris*, is on the mantelpiece in his room, but he has not touched it since the attack, not even on those nights he lies down thinking of the hundred things he might have said to her, the Austrian, that dusk on the rue Saint-Denis.

At the bottom of the tenth pit, the remains of some thirty or forty children. There really isn't time to arrive at a more exact figure. Guillotin and Thouret age the children at between four and ten years of age at the time of their demise. Manetti, consulted, nods. An epidemic in the orphanage at Plessy – 1740? Perhaps 1741.

230

He couldn't swear. In the pit the children have been laid head to toe, much as they might have slept together in the orphanage. The men are affected; they puff on their pipes, finger their charms. The doctors collect some of the skulls, pile them like cabbages or turnips into one of Jeanne's wicker baskets and take them to the workshop.

The last days of March, there is snowfall. It sticks like melted wax to the black walls of the church, lies crisp and glittering over the piled bones. Then it freezes. Digging is more like scraping. Their tools ring on the earth. To open the eleventh pit, they have to keep a fire burning above it all night. It is winter's last throw.

Through all the next week the ground thaws, turns to mud, molasses. When a coffin is pulled out, a skull, the sound is amphibious, oddly sexual. Coats are unbuttoned, hats pushed back. Even at les Innocents – and even to one whose sense of smell is as withered as the engineer's – the air is altered and has, at unpredictable intervals, an unnerving purity to it that makes them all, men and women, miners and their masters, imagine themselves somewhere else, setting out perhaps on a long walk into the country, a stroll to some river fringed with willows.

Jeanne one morning, just after the engineer has arrived at the cemetery, summons him, her face lit with excitement. She leads him to the northwest corner of the cemetery, close to where they emptied the first of the common pits.

'You see?' she says, pointing to a patch of little yellow flowers, the leaves shaped like mottled green spades, and close by, a clump of taller plants with crimson flowers.

'The seeds were buried,' she says. 'Your digging has brought them to life again.'

He stares at them, the yellow, the crimson flowers. He says nothing. He is utterly disconcerted.

7

He does not see her, does not hear her until she is standing beside him. It is dusk and he is about to enter the Monnards' house. A large wagon – M. Hulot et Fils, Déménageurs à la Noblesse – is rattling down the street towards the rue Saint-Honoré. Startled, he stares at her in a way he imagines must be quite comical.

'You wanted to speak with me?' she says.

'That was weeks ago,' he says.

'So you no longer wish to speak with me?'

'I do. Yes.'

'Yes?'

'Yes. I do.'

'Very well.' She waits, looks directly into his eyes. She is not wearing the red cloak today but has a shawl or scarf of some light stuff covering her hair. Her face is stiff, her lips pressed hard together.

'I have thought of you,' he says, opening his mouth and letting the words come as they will. It is too late for anything circum-spect, for the careful measuring of effects. 'I have thought of you. Often.'

She nods. The gesture does not help him.

'We could go inside,' he says. 'Talk inside.'

'In the Monnards' house?'

'They would not object. They are in no position to object to my wishes.'

'On account of the daughter?'

'Yes.'

'Of what she did?'

'Yes.'

'She was your friend?'

'Not as you mean it.'

'And how do I mean it?'

'You know how you mean it.'

'It would not have mattered.'

'No?'

'Why should it have mattered?'

'No,' he says. 'I don't know.'

They pause, as though the mind of each was briefly dazzled by the sheer strangeness of such a conversation, of it happening at all. It is Héloïse who recovers first. 'And that is what you wished to say? That you have thought of me?'

'It is not everything.'

'And the rest?'

'I wondered if you might . . . come here.'

'Visit you?'

'If you might stay here. Might care to.'

'In the house?'

'Yes.'

'Let us be clear,' she says.

'I thought I was,' he says.

'You wish to take me as your mistress?'

'I want you to stay with me.'

'What is this *stay*? You mean to live with you?'

'Yes.'

Now, he thinks, now she will throw back her head and laugh. She will accuse him, in a voice full of scorn, of not knowing what he is saying. And it is true. He does not. Was this his message? Live with me? Or has he simply said the most extravagant thing he can think of? He readies himself to say some harsh, dismissive thing to her, something to cover his humiliation, but when she speaks again, her voice is quiet, serious. Not unfriendly.

'You have lived with a woman before?' she asks.

'No,' he says. Then, 'Is your question practical? Are you afraid I will not know how to behave?'

'We do not know each other,' she says.

'We do not know each other well,' he says.

'On better acquaintance, you might find me disagreeable. I might find you so.'

'You do not wish to live with me?'

'I have not said that. Only I do not believe you have thought of . . . all that you need to. Not properly.'

'You are wrong,' he says.

'Or you are wrong.'

'I am not wrong.'

'Ha! You do not care to be contradicted.'

She makes a shape with her mouth, forms her lips as she might in the market when dealing with some canny, persistent stall-holder. Then she looks down and slowly grinds the toe of one of her shoes on the cobbles.

'You like me,' she says.

'Yes.'

'Why?'

'*Why?*'

'You must know,' she says.

'Of course,' he says, though in fact it has never occurred to him that he needed a reason for liking her. 'You looked at me,' he says.

'I noticed you?'

'Yes.'

'It is true,' she says. 'I did notice you.'

'You were buying cheese,' he says.

She nods. 'You looked lost.'

'You also.'

'Lost?'

'Out of place.'

'Were I to agree to this,' she says, after another of those pauses in which she seemed carefully to weigh each of his words, 'I must be free to come and go as I choose. I am too old to take orders from you or anyone else.'

'You would be free.'

'And if you ever struck me . . .'

'I would not.'

'I heard you held a knife to a man's throat. That night on Saint-Denis.'

'It was a key, not a knife.'

'A key?'

'Yes.'

'Because he insulted me?'

'Yes.'

'He will not be the last.'

'Then I will fight them.'

'With a key?'

'You could come soon,' he says. 'Do you have many things?'

'Some clothes,' she says. 'Some books.'

'Books?'

'You imagined I could not read?'

'No,' he says. 'I did not think that.'

'I would like more books. The good editions. Not those for fifteen sous that come apart in your hands when you open them.'

'No,' he says. 'Not those.'

'And the theatre,' she says. 'It is a long while since I have been there.'

'The theatre,' he says. 'I would like that too.'

For a while they are quiet together, peaceable. Even the street has entered one of its periods of occasional hush, barely a soul abroad. It is likely, thinks Jean-Baptiste, that from one of these windows they are being watched by someone who knows who they both are. He could not care less.

'Is that you?' she asks, turning to look diagonally across the street to where, on the shutters of the haberdasher's, black paint proclaims another of Monsieur Bêche's threats to the mighty. This one concerns the fate awaiting the governor of the Bastille. It went up a week ago and has still not been painted out.

'You know my name,' he says.

'I know them both,' she says, smiling at him openly for the first time.

8

She will not give him any assurance. She will consider the matter. It is a large matter. She will consider it and send word to him. He, she suggests, would do well in the meantime to consider it too. To wonder if in fact he meant to say what he said. Truly meant to.

For nearly a week he is left in a state of exquisite uncertainty. By the fifth day – the fifth night – he is suddenly sure it will not happen. That is his instinct, his flash of insight. It will not, cannot happen. Most probably she has each week half-a-dozen men asking her to live with them, men who confuse their lust with something more tender, something that has no part to play in the trade she practises. She is hard, she must be: reason insists on such a conclusion. She is hard and hollowed out. Or else she is kind, endlessly kind, and will not come to him for his own good. A man like him, an educated man, a professional man who must naturally seek to rise in the world – for such to ally himself to a woman like her would be to condemn himself to public ridicule, to ignominy. An aristocrat like the Comte de S— might do it, or else someone of small importance, someone who has risen as far as he ever will and can lose very little with the loss of his name. But for him – who is neither grand nor little – it is an impossibility. And she has seen that, has, at the expense of her own comfort, chosen to protect him from his folly.

He longs to speak to someone. He has never felt such a stranger to himself, as if his life was a room in which every familiar object had been replaced with something that merely imitated it. Speak to Armand? But Armand will be too vehement, too furiously for it or against it, too amused. Guillotin? Guillotin would listen, would, with the experience of his years, take a large view of the matter. A medical view? It is not unlikely. It may be the correct view. He is unwell! Unwell and not himself, not as he should be.

He discovers the doctor in the middle of a warm morning seated on a stool in the doctors' workshop, polishing one of the orphans' skulls. At the sight of it, that poor, brightening object on the doctor's palm, all thought of confession instantly departs. Instead, they talk about the bones of the head. Frontal, parietal, occipital. How in infants and young children the various bones are not yet fused and how this is necessary at their birth when the skull is subject to immense pressure on its passage through the birth canal.

'They are perfectly done,' says the doctor, passing the skull to Jean-Baptiste. 'They do not split like melons. They do not shatter like balls of glass.'

He stands to examine Jean-Baptiste's wound, carefully parts the newly grown hair, pronounces himself quite satisfied with the appearance of the scar.

'You still suffer no symptoms,' he asks, 'other than the headaches?'

'I am . . .' begins Jean-Baptiste, then shrugs. 'I am as you see. And I should be pleased if we settled at last on some fee. For what you did. Your kindness in waiting on me. I have never properly thanked you for it.'

The doctor waves the suggestion away. 'Unless, my dear engineer, you have changed your mind about leaving me that famous head of yours?'

He is coming back from the cemetery in the late twilight when a boy, leaning his shadow against the shadow of the cemetery wall, steps out and stands in his path. It is the mute boy, the one who helped carry his trunk the night he moved to the Monnards' house. He has his hand out and for a moment Jean-Baptiste thinks he is asking for something, that he has learnt to beg, but he is offering something, a square of folded paper. There is – by stepping into the middle of the street – just enough light to read the note the paper contains. It is very short. 'I will come if you still wish it.'

He does not have anything to write with. To the boy, he says, 'Can you sign? Can you make yourself understood with signs?'

The boy nods.

'Then go back to the woman who gave you this. Tell her she should come tomorrow. At three in the afternoon. Now show me how you will do it.'

The boy shows him. To Jean-Baptiste it looks perfectly clear. He gives the boy a coin. 'Go,' he says. 'Find her tonight.'

9

For the time it takes to walk back to the house and up the stairs to his room, he imagines himself the happiest man in Paris. He does not light a candle – he sits on the bed in the cool almost-dark as though wrapped in the purple heart of a flower. How simple it all is! And what idiots we are for making such a trial of our lives! As if we *wished* to be unhappy, or feared that the fulfilment of our desires would explode us! Briefly – the old reflex – he wants to examine what he feels, to name its parts, to know what kind of machine it is, this new joy; then he lies back on the bed, laughing softly, and like that comes close to sleep before sitting suddenly bolt upright, everything uncertain again. What exactly did she mean by her message? Was there some ambiguity? Could he have misread it, he for whom words have become such unreliable servants. And then to have sent a mute boy with his reply when, with a little sobriety, a little patience, he could have brought the boy into the house and written something plain and explicit!

He stands, paces the little room, stops by the door, looks into the room – where now all its objects offer only the faintest outlines of themselves – and realises that if she does come tomorrow (and *why* three o'clock?), they cannot possibly be in here, stay in here, live even a single night together in here.

He steals down the stairs, past the door of the dining room, gets a candle lit at the hall table, returns – two steps at a time – to the top of the house. He stands outside Ziguette's room, catches himself listening at the door, rebukes himself in a whisper, opens the door and goes in.

He has not been in here since the night he visited her to see what a melting girl looked like, and found both girl and room in an advanced state of disarray. It is orderly enough now, its atmosphere a little damp from being left to stagnate, but that could quickly be put right. He lifts his candle, takes in the painted wardrobe, the fireplace, the dressing table with its oval mirror (in which his candle flame now sparkles). A bed big enough for two. Does the room still smell of her? He doesn't know; he cannot tell. He crosses to the unshuttered window, gets it open, feels the evening air flow past his fingers. His fit of doubting has passed, but so too the dizziness, those lovely blind minutes of joy. He is hungry. Very hungry. He goes downstairs to join the Monnards at supper. They have almost finished the soup but the tureen is still on the table. It is the moment when he should tell them, Monsieur and Madame, what he intends, who, tomorrow – if a mute boy's signing is understood – will be coming to live in their house. Spooning soup into his mouth, he tries to discover some elegant, decisive way of saying it all, but before he can begin, he starts to laugh. The soup, in a thin, brown stream, comes back past his lips into his bowl. He wipes his lips, clears his throat. Apologises.

*　　*　　*

First light. He dresses in the black suit, goes looking for Marie, finds her in the kitchen. She is bent double by the kitchen table, dangling a piece of cooked meat from her mouth for the cat to reach up and take.

'It's a game,' she says.

He nods, then asks her if she will remove all of Ziguette's clothes, all the china shepherdesses, amateur watercolours, seashells, painted thimbles, painted fans, all of it, out of her room and into his own, where, for now, it may be conveniently stored.

'Why?' she asks.

'I wish to use it.'

'Her room?'

'Yes.'

'For you?'

'For me. Yes. For me and . . . for another. A woman.'

'A woman?'

'She will stay with me.'

'A woman?'

'Yes. A woman. Is it so remarkable?'

'She is your wife?'

'It is . . . an arrangement. Between us. Are the men and women who live together in the faubourg Saint-Antoine always married?'

'No.'

'Then we shall be like them.'

'You will want me to wait on you,' she says. 'And her.'

'I will give you something extra for it. Half again what Monsieur Monnard gives you.'

'When is she coming?'

'Today, I think. Perhaps this afternoon.'

'So you will pay me today?'

242

'I will give you something when the room is made ready. You will have time to spare from your . . . other duties?'

She nods, grins at him slyly, excitedly. All through their conversation the cat has kept its eyes fixed on the maid's mouth.

At two o'clock, having told a series of lies to Lecoeur about having to draw funds at the goldsmith's on the rue Saint-Honoré, Jean-Baptiste returns to the house. When he opens the door to Ziguette's room, he looks with relief at the open and empty wardrobe, the dressing table where not a pin remains, the bare walls. Excellent Marie! He will see she has something handsome for this, enough for a new dress, a good one, something to show herself off in when she visits her home, if she has a home, somewhere one might recognise as a home.

Did she change the linen? He pulls back the bedcover, examines the bolster for blond hairs, then, on impulse, looks under the bed, finds there some small, fine thing, which he pulls out and turns in his hands. Purple satin. A thing of purple satin laced with a purple ribbon. A type of shoe, a soft sort of . . . What does it matter what it's called? There's no time for that now. He folds it, puts it in a pocket, perches on a corner of the bed, then immediately gets up and goes to the window, leans out, scowls at the street, mutters to himself some weak witticism about women and punctuality, goes to the bed again, goes to the mirror, bares and examines his teeth, takes out his watch, sees there is another fifteen minutes before the hour, sits on the bed again, looks at the dirt on his shoes, cemetery dirt, the humus perhaps of dead men and dead women, then finds himself thinking of Guillotin's Charlotte, the preserved girl with her long eyelashes sprouting from grey and sunken lids, lids like old coins. Why must he think of her now? Can he not be free of them, even for an hour or two? Other than for his father he used never to think of them at all . . .

And who the devil is that old face looking at him from the window across the street? So you like to spy, eh? Very well. He stands and stares back, arms folded across his chest, staring, sneering, and is starting to suspect that it is not a face at all but something hanging, perhaps even the soft light of a small mirror, when he hears the sprightly trotting of horses, the rhythm of sprung wheels. Cabs have their own music and this is unmistakably a cab. He jumps to the window, looks down, sees it draw up outside the house, sees an old cabman slither off his box and come round to open the cab door. Sees, a moment later, the top of her head. The crown.

'So this is it,' he says, his voice in the room's new hollowness like an actor's, as false, as strange as an actor's. He runs down the stairs, headlong, shoes clattering on the wood. Madame Monnard comes out of the drawing room, stands on the landing wringing her hands.

'Is the house on fire?' she cries as the engineer runs past her. 'Monsieur! Monsieur!'

10

Their first hours together are so painfully awkward that each is forced to the conclusion that a serious mistake has been made. He talks too much, then for almost half an hour says nothing at all. She sits on a chair by the dressing table, the light coming over her shoulders. He is tormented by the thought that she is suddenly, inexplicably, not as pretty as, on all their encounters in the street, she has seemed to be. She is wearing a white gown embroidered with red and pink flowers. Does it suit her? And high on her breastbone there is a mark, a little blemish, that she has tried to cover with powder. She is – in a way that suggests she pities him – talking about something or other. Polite enquiries about his work. His work! He is little better than a body-snatcher. And should he ask her about *her* work?

The light in the room fades to the colour of laundry water. He is suddenly very angry. He would like to make some sour, idiotic remark about women, about courtesans, prostitutes. Something unforgivable. Instead he says, 'We should eat.'

'Here?'

'Where else?'

'You eat with the Monnards?'

'Of course.'

'Perhaps tonight we might eat in the room?'

'You must meet them sometime. It might as well be now.'

Downstairs in the drawing room, Madame Monnard is sitting alone beside the fire. In the weeks since Ziguette's departure much of the life has gone out of her. There are little tearful episodes, snufflings into a balled handkerchief, sighs, damp looks into the distance, the occasional involuntary mewing sound. She receives no visible comfort from her husband, perhaps from no one at all. At times she gives the impression of being completely unaware of the world turning round her, but she is satisfyingly astonished to see Héloïse Godard walk into the room.

Marie could have warned her, of course; Marie chose not to. The visitor who knocked at the door in the afternoon was, as far as she knew, simply an acquaintance of Monsieur Baratte's, someone from the cemetery, no doubt. Perhaps that rather frightening person, Monsieur Lafosse. And now this. *This!* The sudden, almost dreamlike appearance of a woman whose very name (supposing anybody knew it, her real name) cannot be uttered in polite company.

'Madame Monnard, Mademoiselle Godard. Mademoiselle Godard will be staying in the house now,' says Jean-Baptiste.

'I hope, madame,' says Héloïse, 'that will not trouble you too greatly?'

'I will settle with your husband,' says Jean-Baptiste, 'for the extra rent.'

Madame Monnard nods. She looks from one to the other, twists the ear of a little lavender-stuffed cushion on her lap.

'What a nice room this is,' says Héloïse. 'Elegant and homely. Usually one finds it is one or the other.'

'Oh?' whispers Madame.

'I am no expert,' says Héloïse, spilling onto the older woman the light of a smile so generous, so of the heart, Jean-Baptiste has to look away for fear he will yelp with jealousy. He picks the decanter off the table, pours two glasses, gives one to Héloïse, who passes it to Madame Monnard, who takes it from her as if she had never held a glass before, never seen red wine.

'You embroider, madame?' asks Héloïse pointing to a sampler of indifferent workmanship hung on the wall beside the fireplace.

'embroider?'

'The stitching, madame. I made one such as this as a girl, but it was not near as neat.'

'My daughter did it. My daughter, Ziguette.' It is the first time since the attack she has dared to mention her daughter's name in the engineer's hearing.

'I can see she was well instructed,' says Héloïse.

Madame smiles. Pure gratitude, pure relief. And something heroic gathers in her. Belly to heart to mouth. 'Do you think, mademoiselle,' she says, gripping the cushion more tightly, 'do you think the air was a little warmer today? Warmer than yesterday?'

Héloïse nods. 'I think, madame, perhaps it was.'

A half-hour later – a half-hour that flows past on a little stream of polite feminine chatter – they are joined in the room by Monsieur Monnard, who comes in, as he always does, smelling of some tart, acidic compound employed in the cutlery trade. It is his wife who, almost eagerly, introduces Héloïse – 'A friend of Monsieur Baratte's' – but it is left to Jean-Baptiste to inform him that Mademoiselle Godard will be staying in the house. Living in it. With him.

'Living, monsieur?'

'Yes.'

'*Here?*'

'Yes.'

'In the house?'

'Yes.'

It is the moment Monsieur Monnard might stage his revolt. The moment he might refuse point-blank and at the top of his lungs to have either of them in his house a minute longer, might, conceivably, unhinge himself and fly at the engineer, wrestle with him ... Then the moment is past, swallowed perhaps by the recollection of his daughter lying naked and lamb-innocent in her bed, a length of gored brass by her feet. He brushes something from his sleeve, looks to the window where the fires of les Innocents burn jaggedly in the spring night. 'I see,' he says. 'Indeed.'

They sit at table. Marie, coming in with the tray, serves Héloïse first, already looks to have some crush on her. They start with a radish soup. For the main course, along with some boiled greens and boiled onions, there are tubular sections of a grey meat in a sauce of the same colour.

'Is this eel, madame?' asks Héloïse, and when Madame Monnard confirms that it is, Héloïse manages to say half-a-dozen clever, pertinent things about eels. 'And they are mysterious, madame. I am told no one knows where they raise their young.'

'When I was a child,' says Madame, 'I liked to look at them in their buckets at the market. I used to wonder what would happen if I put my hand in the water. Whether they would eat it.'

'Damn them,' growls Monsieur Monnard.

'Monsieur?' asks Héloïse.

'I do not think I said anything, mademoiselle.'

'My husband,' begins Madame Monnard, 'has a large establishment on the rue Trois Mores. Blades from plain to fancy. Père Poupart of Saint-Eustache cuts his meat with one of my husband's knives.'

'I have seen it, madame. The establishment. Everyone speaks of its excellence.'

'You know Père Poupart?' asks Madame, who seems to have performed in her head the trick of entirely forgetting who she is talking to.

'We have passed in the street, madame.'

'He has a lovely speaking voice. My daughter, I think, delighted in it.'

'One needs a strong voice in so large a church.'

'Oh, one does, mademoiselle. Yes, I think that is very true.'

'*Rogue!*' shouts Monsieur Monnard, springing from his seat. Ragoût, infected by the room's atmosphere of feebly suppressed anarchy, has leapt onto the table and seized a gob of Monsieur Monnard's eel. He escapes with it beneath the pianoforte. Monsieur Monnard, released at last to express himself, hurls his plate at the cat, but too wildly. The plate hits the side of the instrument and disintegrates in a rain of porcelain and grey sauce. In the silence that follows, Jean-Baptiste gets to his feet. A moment later, Héloïse stands too.

'You must be fatigued after your journey, mademoiselle,' says Madame Monnard, airily.

'You are kind to think of it,' says Héloïse, though she has

travelled no more than a length of a half-dozen streets. 'Good night to you, monsieur,' she says.

Monsieur Monnard nods, grunts, but does not – cannot perhaps – lift his gaze from the floor where Ragoût, having bolted his morsel of eel, is carefully cleaning sauce from the larger fragments of plate.

They go up to the room – their room, if that's what it is. The evening, the room, are not particularly cold (a few weeks back, they could have watched their breath leave their mouths), but Jean-Baptiste kneels on the hearth rug and busies himself building a fire. When it takes, he stands back to watch it and, still looking at the fire, tells Héloïse that he must return to the cemetery.

'Now?'

'They will be loading the carts.'

'Will you be long?'

'As long as is necessary.'

'And there is no one else who could do it?'

'That is not the point.'

He leaves, quickly. She looks at the back of the door, hears his feet on the stairs. Shortly, she hears the noise of the street door. For several minutes she stays as she is, her face expressionless. Then she raises a hand, clears her eyes of two tears she does not wish to let fall and goes to the dressing table. She loosens and reties the Madras ribbon in her hair, pushes off her shoes, rubs the outside of her right foot where the shoe pinches, then starts to unhook herself, unlace herself, fiddle with eyelets and bows and pins until she is down to her under-petticoat, shift and stockings. She opens a tapestry bag – one of three large bags in which she has brought all her things – and takes out a quilted bed-gown and a pair of leather mules, a bottle of orange water, a cloth. She cleans her face with the orange water, wipes her throat, wipes under arms and between her breasts. The commode is in the corner of the room. It has a little screen of pleated cotton on a wooden frame. She sits and, when she is done, uses the orange water to clean around the creases of her thighs. She is due to come on in a few days, can feel it building in her, the slight heaviness, slight bloating. She has known men who were disgusted by a woman's bleeding, others who – more troublingly – were attracted to it. The engineer, she suspects, will be among that mass of men who take care not to think of it at all.

She buttons the gown, stirs the fire with the poker, starts to examine the room. It is, very obviously, not the room he is used to occupying, for there are none of his things here. The wardrobe is empty (she will not, just yet, put up her dresses). There is no manly clutter. She would like to have had a look at that suit she once spied him in, that thing the colour of wild lettuce, but there is nothing, not even a shirt. So whose room was it, if not his? She could guess – guess correctly in all likelihood – but tomorrow she will get that odd little maid to tell her things. The maid will know everything.

At least the window looks over the street rather than the cemetery. And she had no clients on the rue de la Lingerie, no one she need be embarrassed to walk into. Not that she intends to be *embarrassed* by anything. She has left her old life – old by a day or two – but will not lower herself to the indignity of pretending. She has lived publicly, has been a public woman almost four years, has lived out in the full light of public regard that career her parents, by their actions if not their words, apprenticed her to at the inn on the Paris–Orléans road. But four years is long enough. The point is made. Grief and rage have made their passage; she has pulled them like a thorn-bush through her own entrails, and they have scoured her, have left a thousand little scars, but have not killed her. And now this. A new life. A new life with an awkward, grey-eyed stranger who, nonetheless, she seems to know rather well. A stranger who wants her – she has no serious doubt of that – and not just on the first Tuesday of the month like old Ysbeau . . .

At the thought of the bookseller, she goes back to her tapestry bag and takes out two books, carries them to the dressing table, sits and draws the candle close. What will it be? Cazotte's *Le Diable Amoureux*? Or Algarotti's *Newtonism for Ladies*? Tonight, perhaps, she should stay with Algarotti and Newton. Then, when he comes back, she can calm him by asking him to explain things to her. (He will like that; they all like it.) She settles herself, finds her page, and is about to begin a chapter on optics when she hears, low on the door, the sound of scratching.

He does not go to the cemetery, never intended to. He goes in the opposite direction, towards the Palais Royal. He needs to walk, to think, to stop thinking. Is he getting one of his head-aches? Surprisingly, he is not.

How bitterly she must regret her arrival! That supper! Grotesque! And worst of all, his own behaviour – the dullness, the rudeness of it. As if he resented her! She who he has longed for all winter! Why can nothing ever be simply wanted, simply desired, with no contradiction, no inexplicable 'no' in some unex-amined fold of the heart? And now he has run away when he should be doing what any proper man would be doing in the company of a woman like Héloïse Godard. Armand would be on the second go by now. The windows would be spilling out of their frames. A nasty thought, of course, Armand with Héloïse. If he ever lays a finger on her . . .

At the Palais, the night air shimmers with superfluous light. Flambeaux, chandeliers, strings of Chinese lanterns. If he could illuminate the cemetery like this they could dig all night. Another thirty men, one gang sleeping, one digging, then a change of shift at dawn and dusk. At Valenciennes, there were seams worked like that, men and women, pumps and horses, working round the clock. God knows he will need to think of something, some innovation if they are not still to be digging up the dead when the new century arrives.

He fights his way forward, his black coat brushing against green and reds, silvers and golds. Faces swim out of the crush. A man, heavily powdered, pokes out the tip of his tongue at the engineer. Two women, who may or may not be courtesans with apartments on the first floor, glance up at him from their game of teasing a monkey, the creature tethered by a length of silver chain to a spike . . .

Outside the Café Correzza, a young man with yellow hair stands precariously on a chair making a speech. What is it? The usual stuff. The hearts of men, the requirements of Nature, the promise of philosophy, the destiny of mankind, indomitable justice, virtue . . . And did he mention Bêche? Bêche the Avenger? Impossible to hear over the din the others are making, the gossip, the laughter, the broken marching of harlots and gentry, the half-dozen little bands playing in the courtyard.

He goes into l'Italien, gets a seat near the porcelain stove, orders brandy. He is, he fancies, served more quickly these days. It is the black coat? A black severity that makes him appear half priest, half functionary, the wielder of ambiguous powers? Or is it something Ziguette Monnard unearthed? A newfound willingness to press a key to a man's throat? Violence is respected; he has learnt that much about the world. It may even be one of those virtues the young man on the chair was preaching about. Gentlemen with blood up to their shoe buckles, bowing and making to each other *un beau geste*. Virtuous violence. The virtuous necessity of it. Violence as a duty. It is, very likely, the coming thing.

When he reaches into his pocket to pay for the brandy, he pulls out Ziguette's satin shoe-thing. The waiter treats him to a waiter's almost invisible grin. Outside, he steps through a family of female mandolin players, abandons the satin thing on the windowsill of Salon No. 7 and regains the dark, the sudden hush of the streets behind the Bourse. A little brandy has sobered him up. He knows what he's about now. When he reaches the buttresses of Saint-Eustache, he starts to run.

Coming in, he is momentarily disappointed to find her looking less unhappy than he had imagined she would. In fact, she does not really look unhappy at all. She smiles at him, calmly, holds out her book above the head of Ragoût, who has curled his bulk tidily on her lap. She points to a word halfway down the page.

'I cannot see it,' he says.

'You are not looking at it,' she says.

'You cannot read it?' he asks.

'"Refraction",' she says.

'Oh,' he says, laughing. 'Yes. I know it. Refraction. To use a lens to change the angle of the light.'

He carries the cat onto the passage (set down, it shivers with disgust), then comes back into the room, takes off his boots, coat, waistcoat. They sit side by side on the bed. She wets two fingertips, puts out the candle. There is light enough from the fire. They lie down. They kiss. Their mouths at first feel cool to each other, then warm. She is, unsurprisingly, good at buttons. He

254

struggles out of his breeches, presses his face into her breasts, clings to her. Gently, she disentangles herself, works her shift up until it is rucked about her hips. When he dares to look, he sees flame-light on the skin of her thighs. Under his shirt, he's hard as a bottle, too hard. Almost as soon as she touches him, he convulses, lets out the sort of strangled half-shout he might have made the night Ziguette Monnard brought the ruler down on his head.

It is another week before, in an unexpected mid-afternoon encounter, neither of them much undressed, he finally enters her. Once he is inside her, he lowers his brow, lets their skulls press lightly against each other. With her thumb she traces the line of his scar, the ridge of nerveless skin. From that moment on, in his own heart, he considers her to be his wife.

11

At les Innocents, there is a sharp increase in the number of rats. Rats visible. Guillotin is of the opinion they are leaving. The men acquire cats. Each tent has at least one, though not even Lecoeur seems to know where they have got them from. From their Saturday-night women perhaps, their moppets. Sometimes the engineer thinks he sees Ragoût among them, patrolling in the dusk, but at a distance one cat can seem much like another. At night, they fight epic battles. A cat is killed, but so too many of the rats, their bodies, whole or sundered, found in the lengthening grass or left as trophies on the steps of the charnels.

A new pit – pit fourteen – is opened in the vicinity of the south charnel. In addition to this, the engineer decides to broach the first of the private crypts. He gathers a small team – Slabbart, Biloo, Block, Everbout – and walks them to the west charnel under the windows of the rue de la Lingerie. They will start with the Flaselle family, the tomb sealed in 1610. With chisel and mallet they break the mortar, loosen the top-stone, then drive in their long, wedge-tipped steel bar and haul down until the stone shifts. They lower a ladder; it only just reaches. The crypt, it seems, has aristocratic dimensions. Jan Biloo is the first man down. As he descends, his light begins to flicker. Somewhere near the bottom of the ladder, it goes out. They call; he does not answer. Jean-Baptiste and Jan Block go down to get him. They hold their breath like scallop divers. They find him with their groping hands, drag his dead weight up the ladder until Everbout and Slabbart can take hold of him. He comes to almost immediately, but he and the engineer and Jan Block are some minutes together crouched on the grass outside the charnel, spitting, sucking in air.

Later, in the sexton's kitchen, Jean-Baptiste sketches designs for breathing equipment, masks with filters of treated lamb's wool or powdered charcoal. Or something more complete, a closed hood with an air-pipe and some manner of clapper valve to allow exhaled air to be expelled. He tries to interest Lecoeur in his ideas, but Lecoeur's mind is elsewhere.

'Monsieur Lecoeur is exhausted,' says Jeanne, perhaps more sharply than she intended. 'Everyone is exhausted.'

He nods. She knows about Héloïse Godard, of course; the whole quarter knows, though only Armand will speak to him about it. He folds the sketch, pockets it.

Lecoeur smiles at them both, dreamily. 'We Lecoeurs,' he begins, 'we Lecoeurs . . .' Then he shrugs and turns away and gazes out of the window again.

12

Each morning, in the liquid half-light of spring dawns, he wakes from blank sleep beside Héloïse. Some mornings he wakes to find her watching him, wakes into her smile. And some mornings *he* is the first and lies very still, studying the lovely imperfections of her face, the privacy and mystery of her shut eyes. Then, when she opens them, her gaze, its roots deep in sleep and dreams, often has some taint of sadness to it, though it is a sadness she denies if he ever asks her about it. With dry mouths they lie a while talking of intimate, unimportant things. With dry lips they kiss a little. And this is medicine to him, this gift of mornings, the doggish warmth under the covers, the birdsong on the neighbours' roofs, the new heartbeat in the bolster. He hardly notices how much he has ceased to notice, how much of the world beyond this room he has ceased to properly attend to.

When Marie remembers to bring them anything, they breakfast together in the room. On the mornings she forgets, Héloïse stays

in bed and he eats at the cemetery with Jeanne and Manetti and
Lecoeur. As to how she spends her days when he is gone, it is a
source of continual fascination to him. No detail is too trivial. It is
not enough that she informs him Madame Monnard cheats at
backgammon; he wants to know exactly how she does it. The dice?
The counters? And when the two women spend an afternoon
sitting by the window embroidering, he wants to be told what, and
what patterns they stitched. Rosebuds? Zigzags? Peacock tails?

'What do you talk about?'

'You, of course.'

'Me?'

'No. Never you.'

'Ziguette?'

'Sometimes.'

'And Monsieur Monnard?'

'Sometimes of him too. And the price of bread, the probability
of rain, whether senna or buckthorn is best for a constipation.'

'You have made her happy again.'

'No, Jean. I have not. You know I have not.'

A month after Héloïse arrived at the house on the rue de la
Lingerie, she sits up in the bed drinking a little dish of coffee
from a bowl painted with roses, and says that she wishes to visit
the theatre. Did he not promise her? He nods. He goes to see
Armand. Armand will know about theatres.

'The Odéon,' says Armand, as they stand together in a green
lozenge of sunlight beside the preaching cross. 'They are perform-
ing a play by Beaumarchais. Beaumarchais is of the party.'

'The party of the future?'

'Of course. And I shall come with you. Lisa too. You will not
know how to behave otherwise.'

'I don't object to your company.'

'Mademoiselle Godard is not well enough acquainted with you. She has not studied you as I have.'

'Tell me this, Armand. You think Héloïse belongs to the party of the future?'

'Héloïse? She and Lisa will be among its queens.'

'And my own membership?'

'Ah, you will be informed, dear savage.'

'Informed? By whom?'

'By circumstances. By what you will and will not do. We shall all be found out in time.'

'When you speak like this you remind me of the pastor. My mother's pastor.'

'And what does he say?'

'Desolation alone is left in the city and the gate is broken into pieces. If a man runs from the rattle of the snake he will fall into the pit. If he climbs out of the pit he will be caught in the trap . . .'

Four days later, Jean-Baptiste and Héloïse dress for an evening at the theatre. He has nothing brighter than black. She teases him. Where is that coat of his the colour of pea soup? Pistachio, he says, peeled pistachio. And back where it came from. Good, she says. Green was not your colour.

They cross the river in a cab. Armand and Lisa have their backs to the horses; Jean-Baptiste and Héloïse are facing. The two women, having met for the first time in the hall of the Monnards' house, having observed each other carefully among the woody shadows of that place, have, apparently, decided to like each other, a great relief to Jean-Baptiste, who has developed a powerful faith in the rightness of Lisa Saget's judgements.

The cab's two windows are hard down. The evening sun is on the river. On the Pont Neuf, the crowd flows through itself, slowly. Each time the cab is forced to stop, strangers peer in for a moment. A girl in a straw hat climbs onto the cab step and reaches in with posies. Armand insists Jean-Baptiste purchase the two largest, the two prettiest. The cemetery is a thousand miles away, its pits, its walls of bone, like things imagined, some old trouble they are finally getting free of. And could they not keep going like this? A bare week and they would be in Provence letting the sun's heat scour them. Or cross the Alps to Venice! The four of them in a gondolier sliding under the Rialto Bridge . . .

The cab sways to a halt by the theatre steps. The two couples join the throng filtering between the white pillars. Jean-Baptiste has never been to the Odéon (it has only been completed four years). Nor has he been to the Comédie-Française or any other grand theatre. The last time he saw a play it was one of those rough affairs put on twice a year in Bellême by companies of travelling actors who arrive noisily (bellowing, blowing hunting horns) and leave quietly (with stolen chickens, scrumped apples, the honour of certain local girls).

This, well, it is more like Versailles, though of course less theatrical. They are shown to their box by a flunky in a tight lavender coat who, though graceless and offensively casual, will not leave without his tip. Their box is cramped and does not have a good view of the stage. The chamberpot at the back of the box has not been emptied. The candle wicks are untrimmed and one of the chairs looks as if, during a recent performance, it was briefly on fire. None of it matters; their mood is impregnable. The flunky is made happy with the size of his tip, then sent to fetch wine and . . .

'What do you have?' asks Armand.

'What do you wish for? Oranges? Roast chicken? Oysters?'

'Yes,' says Armand, 'we'll have those.'

The place is filling up. It starts to roar. People call across to each other, signal with their hats and fans. Some of the women shriek like peacocks. A scuffle breaks out by the spikes at the front of the stage. 'Author's friends,' says Armand, knowledgeably. 'Author's enemies.'

The lavender coats move in. A man is carried out, arms and legs waving like a beetle on its back.

'The minister is here,' says Jean-Baptiste quietly. 'Box opposite the stage.'

'The one with a face like an axe?' asks Armand.

'That's him,' says Jean-Baptiste. 'But do not stare. I do not wish to be sent for.'

'You've as much right to be here as he does,' says Héloïse.

'Even so,' says Jean-Baptiste. 'I do not want him in my head tonight.'

They sit back in their seats. Behind the curtain, the musicians are tuning their instruments. The engineer does not mention the other man in the minister's box, the young man in the shimmering coat. The name of Louis Horatio Boyer-Duboisson would mean nothing to them.

First, there is a short, frantic mime, then a lengthy interval, then, finally, the play. The audience sits in the light of five hundred candles, charmed, restless, a little bored. The engineer, Armand, Héloïse and Lisa Saget suck oranges, chew on the bones of high-flavoured chicken, drop the bones under their seats. Jean-Baptiste finds the play elusive, sometimes baffling. Who exactly is Marceline? Why can Suzanne *not* marry Figaro? And who is hiding in that closet? Héloïse, her lips beside his ear, patiently explains. He nods. He watches the audience, watches them watching. Dead, stripped of their feathers and fans, their swords, canes, ribbons, jewels, stripped bare and piled like bacon, could he not fit them all into a single pit? He has the thought; feels the disturbance of it; lets it go.

Another chicken is delivered, and more wine, and almonds tasting like scented sawdust. The engineer is tipsy. He kneels to piss in the pot at the back of the box, pisses into another's cold piss and returns to his chair to discover that Suzanne will, after all, marry Figaro.

'So they will have what they wished for?' he asks, though his question is lost in the noise of applause and renewed skirmishing. Cautiously, he leans forward to see how the minister has liked the play. The minister is standing. Next to him, Boyer-Duboisson is whispering in his ear. The minister laughs. Boyer-Duboisson steps away from him, also laughing. Below them, the theatre-goers are fighting their way through the doors like scummed water draining out of a sink. The minister, still laughing, rests a hand on his chest as if to settle himself, and glances over, casually, to the box where Jean-Baptiste is watching. Does he see the engineer? His engineer? Would he even remember his face? And still he cannot stop laughing. It is as if nothing short of death could bring such a flow of amusement to an end.

Impossible once they get outside to find a cab. They trail through the little streets, almost careless of where they are headed, find themselves (just as the women's shoes are starting to pain them) on the Ile de la Cité, eat bowls of tripe from a night-stall beneath the walls of the Conciergerie, then hire a skiff and are rowed along the black scarf of the river to the steps under the Pont Neuf.

They stumble up the treacherous steps, and on the rue Saint-Honoré, with embraces and promises of doing it all again – soon! soon! – they finally part.

At the house, Jean-Baptiste lights a candle, and with Héloïse behind him, both of them yawning extravagantly, they start up the stairs to bed. As they pass the drawing room the door swings open. Marie comes out. 'A girl called for you,' she says.

'A girl?' asks Jean-Baptiste. 'What girl?'

'Well, it wasn't Ziguette,' says Marie. She lets out a squeak of laughter. In the candle-shadow her face looks like a mask she has put on in a hurry.

'It might be best,' says Jean-Baptiste, 'not to let Monsieur Monnard know you've been at his wine. Though God knows how you managed to get drunk on it.'

'You're a fine one,' she says. She turns to Héloïse. 'Before you came, he used to talk to himself all night. Mutter, mutter, mutter. Drove poor Ziguette right out her brains.' She sniffs.

Héloïse steps closer and takes one of the maid's hands.

'But who was the girl?' she asks. 'The one who called here?'

'Oh, I sent her away,' says Marie. 'He's got you now, hasn't he.'

'Yes,' says Héloïse softly. 'Yes.'

He had intended – had planned as much as they skimmed over the river – to spend the night, or a good part of it, diligently plundering his Héloïse, but within a few minutes of climbing into bed (he is lying on his side watching her disrobe and listening to her speculate about the identity of his mysterious caller) he has fallen asleep, and for the first time since the attack he starts to dream.

He is back in the theatre, walking on the frayed red carpeting in the corridor behind the boxes. He is looking for the minister's box. He has a message for him, an important message, one that he must deliver in person, but the little polished doors to the boxes have no numbers on them and there is no one to ask. And then, in the sudden way of dreams, there is someone, a lanky figure lounging against the wall under a branch of candles . . . *Renard?* Renard the foundling? There is no mistaking him. Scrawny neck wrapped in a collar of greasy fur, a tight little grin on his face. He bows to Jean-Baptiste, points to the door opposite him, turns and hurries away down the empty corridor. Quietly – no knocking or scratching – Jean-Baptiste opens the door and slips inside. The only light is a dull, red pulsing, as if from some conflagration in the stalls below, but it is enough to show him the minister and Boyer-Duboisson, their chairs side by side at the front of the box. Have they really not heard him? Are they so engrossed? From his pocket he takes out the message. A message with weight, a point, an edge. He steps behind the minister's chair, puts a hand gently but firmly across the minister's eyes, feels the fluttering of his eyelids. No nerves now. No more uneasiness. He is a boy from the country; he has seen this sort of thing often enough; has sat with his brother watching the pigman come over the winter fields with his ropes, his canvas roll of blades. As he sets to work, the minister's feet kick like an excited child's . . .

Waking, coming to the surface of himself as though flung into a place more confusing even than the dream, he is already trying to explain, to excuse. He stares at his hands, at the sheets, but they are perfectly clean, freakishly normal. Héloïse is pressing his shoulders. He blinks up at her, still babbling, but she is not listening to him. She is trying to tell him something of her own, her own dream perhaps.

'Hush,' she says. 'Hush and come now, Jean. Come. They are waiting for you.'

He sits up. Marie is in the doorway with a candle. She is, apparently, fully dressed. From behind her a draught of cold, sluggish air flows in from the landing.

Héloïse gives him his breeches. Obediently, he puts them on. Odd how he cannot properly wake up. Is he ill? Is that it? A tainted oyster at the theatre? The chicken? No. He does not feel ill.

Kneeling, she buttons the legs of his breeches. He buttons his waistcoat. His watch is on the floor by the bed. He leans for it, flicks up the lid.

'It's half past four in the morning,' he says, a remark that should occasion some sort of explanation but doesn't.

'Very well.' He stands, wipes a hand across his face, accepts his hat from Héloïse, then follows Marie onto the landing. He does not ask her any questions. He knows her well enough now to know she is quite likely simply to invent something.

On the floor below, Monsieur Monnard, nightcap askew, is standing outside his bedroom door. 'Are we to have no peace?' he asks huskily, tearfully perhaps. 'My wife, monsieur, my wife is very—'

'Go back to your bed,' says Jean-Baptiste.

In the hallway, a tall, gaunt figure is restless in the dark. Jean-Baptiste takes the candle from Marie, holds it up.

'He doesn't speak any French,' says Marie.

'Of course he does,' says Jean-Baptiste, but when Jan Block starts, at great speed, to try and explain what he is doing there at half past four in the morning, it is only with the greatest difficulty, and by drawing on his small though slowly growing reserves of Flemish, that the engineer is able to follow him. There has been an accident in the cemetery. Yes. An accident or an incident of some sort. Jeanne has been hurt. Monsieur Lecoeur is looking after her . . . or no. Monsieur Lecoeur is *not* looking after her. Monsieur Lecoeur has in fact – what? Run away?

'Enough,' says Jean-Baptiste, putting the candle on the hall table and stepping towards the street door. 'I will see it for myself.'

Outside, a milky pre-dawn vapour hangs in the street, something like the shed skin of a cloud, damp, miasmic, coating their faces with droplets of moisture. Block is already at the corner of the street. He looks back, silently urging the engineer on. 'I'm damned if I'm going to run,' says Jean-Baptiste, though more to himself than to Block. He is trying to imagine what manner of accident could possibly have befallen Jeanne in the middle of the night. As for Lecoeur, why the devil should he disappear? Or did Block mean he had gone to fetch help? Perhaps even to find Guillotin or Thouret. That would make some sense of the story, though even as he thinks it, he knows the truth's something quite different.

The cemetery door, when they reach it, stands wide, but once they are inside the walls, everything looks normal enough. The fire by the preaching cross burns as it has for weeks. The church is the same mad shadow as always. Then he sees, over by the south charnel, the movement of torches, hears the rumbling of men's voices.

Block runs towards them. Jean-Baptiste, cursing under his breath, jogs after him. The miners are gathered on the ground between the charnel and the sexton's house. Block calls to them and they fall silent, look at him, look past him to the engineer; then the talking resumes, louder now, more urgent. Some of them point to the charnel, wave their hands at it, their fists. He has not known them like this before. Block he has lost sight of. He sees Jacques Everbout, asks him where Jeanne is.

'The house,' says Everbout.

The house. Naturally. Where else would she be? He nods to Everbout, issues a perfectly unnecessary order for the men to remain where they are, then sets off towards the house. He has only gone four or five strides when he is suddenly falling, arms flailing, onto the black grass. He gets up, looks to see what has tripped him, reaches to feel it with his hand. A lime sack some fool has left carelessly in the grass? Then he touches hair, the rough parchment of skin. He snatches back his hand. A corpse! Though not, thank God, a fresh one. One of the preserved girls? Guillotin's Charlotte? Why *here*?

Another ten strides and he is in the sexton's house. There is a lamp in the kitchen and around it a little of the mist is glittering in a blue nimbus. Jeanne – though it is not at first obvious that it *is* Jeanne – is lying on the kitchen table. She has a blanket over her. Her eyes are shut. Her grandfather is beside her, stroking her brow. He is making a low but terrible noise, a keening such as one might hear in the throat of some beast whose progeny the farmer has just led away towards a reeking shed. At the sound of movement behind him, he blinks his muddied eyes, bares the stumps of his teeth.

'It's me,' says Jean-Baptiste. 'The engineer.'

The sexton gesticulates. A mime, a dumb-show. He is far beyond words. Jean-Baptiste approaches the table. A quarter of the girl's face is disappearing into the swelling above her left eye. Her mouth . . . her mouth must have been struck repeatedly. Fist? Boot? Some implement? What other wounds she has – and he is certain they exist – are hidden under the blanket. He is glad of it.

He leans over her, whispers her name. The eye by the wound

will not open, but the other does. It opens and stares at him, without expression. He touches her shoulder; her whole body flinches. He takes back his hand.

'Lecoeur?' he asks.

The eye tells him it was so.

'He has . . . attacked you?'

And the eye tells him it was so.

'I will bring the doctor to you,' he says. 'I will bring some women to you. I will send for Lisa.'

The eye shuts. He walks outside. It seems noticeably lighter, but the mist is lingering, thick skeins of it tangled in the bars of the charnel arches. By the door of the house, a spade with a heart-shaped blade is leaning against the wall. He takes it – the haft worn smooth – and walks towards the men. The first he meets is the tall one, the one with the missing half-finger. He asks him if Monsieur Lecoeur is in the charnel.

'He is,' says the miner, quietly. Then, as Jean-Baptiste is stepping away from him, the miner touches his arm, stops him. 'He has a pistol,' he says.

'I remember it,' says Jean-Baptiste. For an instant he is tempted to ask the miner to come with him, is desirous of having the other's calmness and strength beside him. Then he goes on his own, down past the doctors' workshop to the charnel's first open archway. He steps inside, into the frigid stillness of its air, stops, turns his head to listen. Outside, the men have ceased their noise. They too are listening.

He moves forward: impossible, with no light but what is offered by the thinning darkness, to move soundlessly over such a surface. Too much debris. Pieces of stone, pieces of bone. Who knows what else besides. There is no hope of surprising Lecoeur, of stealing up on him. He decides to announce himself.

269

'*Lecoeur!*'

An echo but no reply.

'Lecoeur! It is Baratte!'

Nothing.

He goes on, trusting as much to his memory of the place as to his eyes. To his right, the archways stand out a faintly luminous blue against the speckled blackness of the gallery. One way or another it is light that will bring this thing to an end. Light will make a target of him. Light will leave Lecoeur nowhere to hide. And then? When Lecoeur *is* able to see him? The only reason he can imagine Lecoeur will not shoot him is that he would not then have time to reload his pistol before the miners reached him.

He looks back, counts off the archways. He will soon be up by the door onto the rue de la Ferronnerie, the door through which they load the carts. Is that why Lecoeur came in here? To make his way more secretly to the door? There would have been a key in the sexton's house. He might have pocketed it before attacking Jeanne, the escape planned before the crime was committed.

Gripping the spade in one hand, he feels for the wall with the other, his fingers trailing over lettering, then rough stone, then, unmistakably, the shaped edge of a hinge. He fumbles for the iron ring of the doorhandle, turns it, pulls, pulls again more sharply. The door is locked. Either Lecoeur had the coolness, the presence of mind, to lock it after him, or he is still here, in the cemetery, in the charnel.

He is poised to call out again – his nerves have had quite enough of this game of hide and seek – when he is aware of movement in the gallery behind him. Someone, something, is coming towards him, coming fast, sure-footed, recklessly fast. His first thought is not of Lecoeur at all but of the thing the minister spoke of, the dog-wolf. Would this not be its moment? A man alone at night, deep in its secret lair? Whatever it is, he has no hope of avoiding it. The thing's energy, its intention, is already upon him. He swings the spade, arcs it blindly through the black air while in the same instant a voice roars at him, '*Violator!*'

The force of the contact comes near to throwing him off his feet. He skitters backwards until his shoulders collide with the wall; then, bracing himself against the stones, he jabs three or four times, furiously, at the dark, but there is no second assault. He waits, heart thundering behind his ribs, then creeps forwards, spade held out like a pike. Beneath his left shoe the snap of breaking glass. He stretches down, touches a curl of wire, a shard of smooth glass. Spectacles! He takes another step, sees beside one of the pillars of the nearest archway, the shape of a man's head. He goes closer, lowers the edge of the spade against the man's chest, feels it swell and fall.

'Who was it?'

The engineer spins about, spade at the ready.

'Who have you struck?'

'*Lecoeur?* Where are you? I cannot see you.'

'Do not worry about that. I can see you well enough. My eyes have grown quite used to the dark.'

'It was the priest.'

'Colbert?'

'Yes.'

'Is he killed?'

'No.'

'And what did you strike him with? What is that you have in your hands?'

'A spade.'

'Ha! He mistook you for me, perhaps? Or there again, perhaps not.'

From his voice it is evident that Lecoeur is no more than four or five metres away, yet somehow he seems to be speaking from within the wall.

'You have hurt Jeanne, Lecoeur.'

'I have?'

'You know it.'

'And you?'

'What of me?'

'Have you not also hurt her? Abused her willing nature? Made her your creature. Forced her to assist in the destruction of her little paradise?'

He has it now. Lecoeur must be sitting or crouching on one of the flights of steps leading up to the bone attics. A good place to choose. Easy to defend. Dark even in the middle of the day. 'I have not raped her,' he says.

'So I am a little worse than you. Bravo. It is all a matter of degree, Baratte. And I can assure you she was no saint. I lived in the house with her. I knew her.'

'If the men catch hold of you . . .'

'The men? What do you know about the men? You know nothing of them.'

'I do not think they will hurt you if I am with you.'

'You will be my protector? And then what? A trial? Or shall I be sent to join that mad girl who broke your head? Where was it she went?'

'Dauphiné.'

'Why did you bring me here, Baratte? Could you not have left me to rot in Valenciennes? Do you imagine you have *helped* me?'

'Then let me help you now.'

'Idiot! You cannot even help yourself. Look at you, standing in a stinking cemetery with your spade, wondering if you can get close enough to batter me with it. When you came to the mines, you were gentle. Shy as a girl. When I first saw you, I thought . . . I thought, here at last is a man I can open my heart to.'

'There is no time for this, Lecoeur.'

'We were friends.'

'I have not forgotten it.'

'Was there nothing to value in such a friendship?'

'The light is coming up. This cannot last much longer.'

'The light! Ah, yes. The light. Tell me, then. She will live?'

'Yes. I think so.'

'I had some good in me once,' says Lecoeur decisively. 'Do not let them say otherwise.'

There is a pause – a dense, seashell hush, several seconds long – then the clear, mechanical articulation of a pistol being cocked. The engineer does not move. He waits, outlined against the growing light. The shot, when it comes, is both loud and muffled, a noise as though, in one of the crypts, a great stone-headed hammer had been launched against the slabs above. Echo, reverberation, silence.

He steps forward. 'Lecoeur?' he calls. 'Lecoeur?' He does not expect an answer.

13

Between eight and nine in the morning, a relentless downpour reduces the preaching-cross fire to a heap of smouldering black beams like the doused wreck of a small cottage. The men keep to their tents. There is bread to eat but nothing more, nothing hot until, in the late morning, Jean-Baptiste and Armand brew two large cans of coffee, lace them heavily with brandy and carry them over the wet grass.

A strange somnolence has settled over the cemetery. No one imagines any work can be done. Not today, not tomorrow either perhaps. And the day after? The day after that?

Guillotin (who, to the high amusement of his colleagues, has dubbed himself 'physician to the cemetery of les Innocents') examines Jeanne in the upstairs room where she has been made as comfortable as possible in her grandfather's bed. When he comes down – his feet heavy and unhurried on the bare wood of the steps – he tells them that the only immediate danger comes from the operating of her own mind, from the morbidity that is the inevitable consequence of such an ordeal. Grief, terror. The loss of maidenhood in such doleful circumstances. And so on. The wounds to her flesh are survivable. A probable fracture of her left cheekbone, some lacerating of the soft tissues of her mouth – lips, tongue, gums, etc. Bruising – extensive – on both arms and much of the torso . . .

'She is young; she is hardy. You, my dear engineer, might convincingly empathise with her, though, I think, not yet. It may be a while before she finds the company of men agreeable again. Madame Saget can remain with her?'

'She will wish to,' says Armand.

'Good. As to whether there will be any issue, any . . . Well, let us hope it is not so.' He smiles in kindly fashion at the sexton, who sits by the unlit grate and who may or may not have taken in much of what he has said. 'A little time, monsieur. Time will put things right. You have not lost your Jeanne.'

The engineer accompanies Guillotin to the doctors' workshop. Lecoeur is on the trestle table nearest to the entrance.

'He was not unlikeable,' says Guillotin, bending his knees a little to squint into Lecoeur's head. 'And at least he had the decency to put out his own light.'

'I mistook him,' says Jean-Baptiste.

'Mistook? Perhaps. Yet a man may be one thing and then another. He was not some drooling degenerate from the Salpêtrière. He was diligent, well read. Courteous.'

'If I had been less distracted. Or had been with him more. Outside of here, I mean.'

'Ah, so you think the cemetery is the culprit? That he was too much among lugubrious scenes?'

'It is possible, is it not?'

'Poisoned by them?'

'Yes.'

'And thus was uncovered some criminal weakness.'

'Yes.'

'He told me you once planned together an imaginary city. A utopia.'

'When we worked at the mines.'

'And what was it called? Your city?'

'Valenciana.'

'After Valenciennes?'

'It was . . . a game,' says Jean-Baptiste.

'You were idealists. Dreamers.'

'We were young.'

'Of course. And clever young men like to play such games. You are free of the vice now, I suppose?' He looks up, grins, then goes to the other trestle table, lifts the lid of the casket. 'Poor Charlotte,' he says. 'These post-mortem adventures have not improved her. You say you carried her back yourself?'

'Yes.'

'One presumes he attacked Jeanne upon realising Charlotte could not serve his purpose.' He settles the lid, taps it thoughtfully. 'And the priest? There is any news of him?'

'None.'

'He has vanished?'

'It was still dark and there was much confusion. My guess is that he is inside the church.'

'Gone to ground, eh? And you do not much feel like looking for him? Not, at least, without a shovel to protect yourself with. You have had quite a morning. None of it could have been easy. But no doubt the minister saw that you were a man who might be trusted to manage in such a circumstance.'

For some seconds the pair of them gaze down at the corpse on the table. The eyes are part open and give to the shattered face the air of someone intent upon remembering. Then they look away from him, turn away, as if he had passed beyond all relevance.

14

Héloïse comes to the cemetery. Jean-Baptiste has not sent for her; she comes on the authority of her own misgivings. She raps on the door. One of the men – Joos Slabbart – opens the door to her. Though she has often looked down at the cemetery from the windows of the house it is the first time she has been inside the walls of les Innocents. She pauses a moment to take it in – the cross, the stone lanterns, the charnels, the bone walls, the tents – then Slabbart escorts her to the sexton's house. When she hears what has passed she rests a hand on the sexton's arm, then takes down Jeanne's apron from its peg by the stairs. She reminds Jean-Baptiste that she grew up in an inn, and that whatever the failings of her parents (not seeming to care for her much being one), they knew their business and made sure she knew it too. She hikes her skirts, crouches by the empty grate. 'This first,' she says, long fingers picking quickly among the kindling.

The next to arrive is Monsieur Lafosse, to whose office in Saint-Germain the engineer sent a runner with a letter as soon as he was able to put his thoughts in order. The letter, written at the kitchen table, was intended to be a dry, almost technical relation of the night's events, though when he read it through before sealing it, it struck him as more like one of those disturbing dramas full of blind mortals and intractable gods he sometimes flicked through in the library of the Comte de S—, those days when it was too wet to work on the 'decoration'.

He takes Lafosse to see Lecoeur's corpse, though not, of course, to see Jeanne, who could hardly be soothed by the sight of a man like Death's steward at the end of her bed.

When they come out of the workshop, Lafosse dabs with a handkerchief at the bloodless tip of his nose. 'And the girl will live?' he asks.

'Jeanne? It is what he asked. Lecoeur.'

'And you answered?'

'Yes. She will live.'

'Then I do not see there is any difficulty.'

'I should be pleased if you told me how to proceed.'

'We are in a cemetery, are we not?'

'We are.'

'And how many have you taken out of the ground?'

'I cannot say exactly. Many thousands, I think.'

'Then putting one in should be a matter of no great consequence. The balance will still be in your favour.'

'Bury him? In les Innocents?'

'Bury him, bury his effects. Remove his name from all documents, all records. Never mention him again.'

'Those are the minister's instructions?'

'Those are your instructions.'

They cross to the cemetery door together. The rain has moved through, replaced by a strange damp warmth, febrile.

'One less mouth to feed,' says Lafosse. 'One less wage to pay. It should enable you to make a saving. The country is bankrupt, Baratte. The minister pays for all this from his own purse.' He scans the cemetery, in his face a slow flowering of disgust. 'How do you tolerate it here?' he asks.

The engineer pulls open the door for him. 'I did not think I had any choice.'

'You do not. But even so . . .'

'You get used to it,' says Jean-Baptiste.

At dusk – an early moon skitting between clouds – he walks Héloïse back to the rue de la Lingerie. She has cooked and cleaned. She has laboured all day. He thanks her.

'Tomorrow I will do the same,' she says. 'I will do everything Jeanne did. I will go to the market.'

He wants to object – is this what he had in mind for her, a cemetery housewife? – but he knows he will find no one more competent, more to be counted on.

'I will pay you,' he says.

'Yes, you will,' she says. They smile into the gloom ahead of them. First smile of the day.

They reach their room without encountering either of the Monnards or Marie. She lights a candle; he lights the fire.

'You are going back there,' she says.

He nods. 'Some matters . . . outstanding.'

'Of course.' She looks at the candle, strokes the flame. 'I am half afraid to let you go,' she says.

'And I,' he answers, 'am half afraid that if I do not go now I will never set foot in the place again.'

15

He has already settled on pit fourteen. Newly emptied, scraped, its earth at the side of it, and far enough from the tents for there to be some hope of secrecy, pit fourteen is the obvious place.

In the sexton's house the kitchen is deserted. The old man must be upstairs with Jeanne. Lisa, presumably, will have gone home for the night to her own people. There is no one to be curious, to ask questions. He stands in the doorway of the records office, blocked for a moment from entering it, intimidated by some spectral afterglow of the life that so recently inhabited it; then he barges in, lifts Lecoeur's bag onto the bed and starts quickly filling it with those few objects he troubled to unpack. A pair of square-toed shoes. A horsehair bob-wig. A shirt left draped across the desk. The knitted waistcoat. Two books: Rousseau's *Les Rêveries du Promeneur Solitaire*, and La Mettrie's *L'Homme Machine*. The empty bottle of tincture. An inexpensive watch. The ribbon-bound parcel of Valenciana papers.

He consults his own watch. It is too early for what he has in mind. He takes *L'Homme Machine* out of the bag and sits with it at the kitchen table. He has not read the book. La Mettrie is not remembered kindly. A provincial like himself, a clever rogue, a man who died from eating an excess of pâté. After a moment, he opens the book, survives almost half a page before he loses the first word. He looks away, looks back, sharpens his focus. Nothing gets any clearer. He flushes: that old schoolroom shame he has become reacquainted with these last months. Then shame is swept away by something more urgent. A spasm in the guts, deep in the lower-left quadrant, the soft coils. It fades, but only to return more sharply, sharp enough to make him groan. He stuffs the book into a pocket, stands up from the bench, gets outside and runs, an awkward, lopsided, wounded-animal run, round the back of the church to the slit canvas wall of the latrines. Unwise to come in here at night without a light! He grips one of the poles, feels with his toe for the hole, one of the holes. Here? Here will do: he cannot wait longer. He gets his breeches down (loses a button in his haste) and lets the muck fly out of him, hears it slap the surface of the muck already in the hole. A pause: the body seems to be listening to itself; then another burst, almost burning him as it passes. He clings to the pole, his forehead against the planed wood, panting, waiting for the next convulsion. They will name squares after us, said Lecoeur that morning in Valenciennes, the snow brushing the window. The men who purified Paris!

One dead now with a ball in his head. One hanging from a pole above a pool of his own sewage.

When it is done, he tears pages out of *L'Homme Machine*, cleans himself as best he can, drops the pages and then the book into the hole, draws up his breeches.

In the sexton's house, he scrubs his hands with vinegar. The fire is burning low. He prods it, lays on more wood. He looks for brandy but for once cannot find any. Overhead, the boards creak, but no one comes down. He goes outside again, peers towards the tents, then goes back into the kitchen, lights a lantern and carries it to the doctors' workshop. He puts the lantern on Charlotte's coffin, then takes hold of the lapels of Lecoeur's coat, tries to raise him to a sitting posture, but Lecoeur, dead some eighteen hours, is stiff as a clay pipe. He stands back and tries to think it through as a *problem*, then goes to Lecoeur's feet (where one stocking has unravelled to a cold white ankle), swings the feet out and lets the body cantilever against the edge of the table. It works, more or less. Lecoeur rises, though he seems not so much a clay pipe any more as a rolled carpet, a heavy rolled carpet, sodden. There is a thud onto the earth between them. The pistol? He will come back for it later. In three movements, he turns the body about, clasps it under the arms, adjusts his grip and is shuffling backwards to the workshop entrance when he hears the canvas flap being drawn.

'You might have trusted me to help you,' says Armand. 'Or did you think I was squeamish?'

'Get the lantern,' says Jean-Baptiste. 'And the pistol. It's on the ground.'

'There's moon enough for us to see our way,' says Armand, coming round to take hold of Lecoeur's feet. 'And he will not miss his pistol.'

They go without speaking, carry the body side-on to the edge of the pit, set it down beside the pulley. The engineer returns to the house for Lecoeur's bag. Manetti is in the kitchen now, sitting in his chair.

'I am taking some of his things,' says Jean-Baptiste.

The sexton nods, solemnly. Who knows what he understands.

Out of the door, Jean-Baptiste reaches again for the convenient spade. At the pit, he drops the bag to the bottom. It lands discreetly enough. They lift Lecoeur into the sling, the cradle. Armand wraps a loop of chain round his waist, leans back his weight, takes up the slack, while Jean-Baptiste pushes both sling and body out over the pit. Then the pair of them play out the chain, the pulley wheel complaining like a mechanical goose.

'How deep is this damned pit?' hisses Armand.

'Sixteen metres,' says Jean-Baptiste. Then, 'He's there!'

'You wish me to come down?' asks Armand.

'I would prefer to know there is somebody above. Someone I can trust.'

He drops the spade into the pit, goes to the ladder, swings himself onto it. Armand was right: now the clouds have scattered, there's moon enough for what they need. Darkness enough too. He looks over to the rue de la Lingerie, the backs of the houses, the windows, sees in one high window – conceivably his own former room – a light move from left to right as though signalling. He climbs down to the ledge, goes cautiously to the second ladder and reaches the bottom of the pit. It takes a long minute to find the spade (a minute in which all manner of lunacy threatens to erupt in his head); then he goes to the sling, pulls Lecoeur free of it and hauls him towards a pool of moonlight in a corner of the pit. He starts to dig there, the spade's edge sinking easily enough into the spring-softened earth. The men, perhaps, would find it instructive to see him labouring like this, the engineer, the chief-of-works, hatless and bent to his task, starting to sweat.

He digs long enough for the moon-pool to shift a little, then steps back. It's hard to see what exactly he's done – moonlight is not a true light – but suddenly he cannot bear to continue with it.

He leans the spade, stoops, takes hold of Lecoeur, lies him beside the hole and rolls him in. The bag goes by his feet. Neither bag nor body is deeply laid, but neither needs to be. Tomorrow, he will have the whole pit filled with earth and lime. Sixteen metres of it: deep enough for anyone. He kneels a moment by the hole, catches his breath, and in a gesture secret almost from himself he reaches down to touch the dead man's shoulder. Then he stands, takes up the spade again and begins quickly to cover him. The legs first, then the body. Finally the face.

FOURTH

Nothing is lost, nothing is created, everything is transformed.

Antoine Lavoisier

1

They dig – dig and fill like men who lack the invention to do anything else. Pit fourteen gets its sixteen metres of earth and lime. In the next pit, the very centre of the cemetery, the bones are piled so thickly they can be handed up like bundles of brushwood. The dead are no longer surprised to see us, thinks the engineer, standing at the edge of the pit in spring drizzle. Where once even the barest bones seemed affronted, cowed, like some man or woman pushed naked into the street, now they lie passive as brides waiting for the hands of the miners to lift them into the Paris light. The Last Trump! The gone-ahead, the passed-over, reassembled by bearded angels smoking clay pipes. It is enough – nearly enough – to make him grin. Poor, credulous skulls imagining their wait in the dark is over!

By the end of the month they have nineteen pits – almost half those Jeanne identified the previous autumn. Pit twenty is begun in the first week of May, and it is while they are at work on this, eight metres down on a warm morning (a pair of blackbirds picking worms from the soil beside the pit), that Jeanne comes out of the house, her first outing since the assault. She has an arm looped through one of Lisa Saget's. She looks half blinded by the sunshine. A few steps behind them is Héloïse, apron on, meat cleaver in one hand, the other raised to shade her eyes. The men on the surface stop work. Jan Block at his post by the bone wall looks moonstruck, and for the first time it occurs to Jean-Baptiste that the miner is in love, truly in love. And would he, given all that has passed, be the worst match Jeanne could make? He would need no explanations, knows all he needs to know. Does she like him? Or is the thought of any man touching her again repellent, impossible? The engineer lifts a hand to salute her. She waves back, wearily.

On the streets, in the little squares, among the stalls in the market packed tight as the combs in a bee skep, rumours about what happened that night in March are still plentiful and freely traded. Some of the miners, despite express orders to the contrary, must have been talking to their whores, for within a week of Lecoeur's death everyone knew of it, knew he had been shot, knew beyond a shadow of doubt that the grey-eyed engineer – an example of whose rages some of them had witnessed that evening on the rue Saint-Denis – must have been the one who pulled the trigger. It stood to reason; they were not fools. *Why* he had done it, that was less certain. The miners, it seems, had kept their lips more tightly pressed when it came to mentioning Jeanne's name. As a result, the favoured explanation was that the engineer shot the overseer in an argument about the engineer's woman, the Austrian. The overseer had perhaps called her what she was and paid for it with his life. It was monstrous, of course, savage, and yet the women of the quarter – whose judgement would be the final one – were not entirely opposed to one man killing another in such an affair. Everywhere women were insulted with impunity, insulted by men. If a few of them suffered for their insolence as the overseer had, it might be no more than they deserved.

As for the Monnards, though they were not immune to rumour and would have observed the unusual comings and goings at the cemetery, their imaginations were, perhaps, less excitable, less succulent, than those of their neighbours, and they were distracted still by the memory of a different, earlier night, a disaster much closer to their hearts. Thus, they had not demanded to know why they were woken that night by one of the cemetery labourers beating at the door, or what was the meaning of the noise just before daylight, a noise like a tree snapping in a gale. The only moment of awkwardness was the dinner the week after Easter Sunday, when Madame Monnard – apparently in all innocence and sincerity – enquired if that charming Monsieur Lecoeur would care to visit the house again. Jean-Baptiste had been unable to do anything but stare dumbly at the dregs in his soup plate. It was left to Héloïse to say that Monsieur Lecoeur had been called home. Home? Yes, madame, quite unexpectedly. On family business? Urgent family business, madame.

Throughout the first weeks of May, with the new leaves unfurling, the first butterflies out of winter hibernation, small flowers pressing stubbornly through cracks in smoke-blackened walls, Jean-Baptiste is aware of himself waiting. He does not know what he is waiting for. The arrival of Lecoeur's sister, perhaps, angry, frightened, confused. Or the sudden appearance of some implacable state official, someone not even the minister could shield him from. He has to remind himself, surprisingly often, that he did not kill Lecoeur, that Lecoeur killed himself. This is the truth. Should it not feel more convincing, more reassuring?

On the 22nd, 23rd and 24th of the month, he suffers a violent headache, the worst he has had since his head was cut. He lies in Ziguette's old room, Ziguette's old bed, a cloth folded over his eyes, clenching and unclenching his fists. On his chest, sixteen metres of earth and lime are crushing him. Then the pain resolves in the usual fit of vomiting. He rinses his mouth, drinks a little, finds his hat, reels from the room.

The city is hot now. Its stones give off a steady pulse of heat for an hour or more after sunset. In the cemetery, the men want more water with their brandy, need it. They work in their shirts. By the middle of the morning the cloth is stuck to the skin of their backs. Work slows down. Swifts and martins play in the blue above the charnels. All winter it seems they held on to something, some resolution the heat now leaches out of them. The engineer feels it as much as anyone, more so. A longing to let go, to have done with it all. To mask it, he goads the men on, restlessly paces the edge of the pits, talks more, shouts more. When the man on the pulley struggles with a cradleful of bones, the engineer lends his own weight to the rope. When they need to fit a box-crib, he clambers to the bottom of the pit to direct the operation. At night, he watches over the loading of each cart, shuttles between the street and the cemetery, speaks to the carters, even to the young priests who still look nervously at the door waiting for Colbert to appear, though Colbert has not been seen by anyone in weeks.

On what he calls to himself an impulse but which is perhaps a desire to confess *something*, he tells Héloïse about his word blindness. It is a Sunday afternoon, the pair of them kneeling on the bed, a little raw about the loins, the gleam of his seed on her belly, their bodies in shadow from the two-thirds-shut shutters.

292

t is, anyway, hard to keep hiding it from her, from everybody, hard and wearying, so he explains to her how he cannot get through a page of print without stumbling, that he still finds himself suddenly dumb in the face of the most ordinary objects. He tells her about his notebook with its list of recaptured words.

She kisses his brow, drops her shift over her head, adjusts the shutters and fetches a book. It is a book by an English writer with a French name. *The Life and Most Surprising Adventures of Robinson Crusoe of York, Mariner*. Holding the book in front of them both, he reads a page aloud, slowly. The next page is his, the third hers again. After an hour, he asks, 'Is this true?'

She laughs. 'You like it?'

He nods. He does. The castaway. His loneliness and ingenuity. It speaks to him.

'As payment,' he says, 'I shall build you a bookshelf. It could go by the wall there.'

She thanks him, then adds, 'Not so big we cannot get it out of the door.'

'The door?'

'We will not be here always,' she says. 'Will we?'

An extra grog ration, a few extra coins in the men's hands. (He has what he would have given Lecoeur to spread around.) It will not do. It cannot. It is not enough. And Guillotin warns him that digging in the heat is unhealthy, decidedly so. Vapours, contagion. The place's sour breath excited by the sun's heat. Already four of the men – occupants of the same tent – have been struck by some low fever that has left them listless, weak, drooping like cut flowers. The doctor recommends the work be carried on entirely at night, or better still, suspended until the cooler weather in the autumn.

'Suspended!'

'Might it not be the wisest course?'

'And come the autumn,' says Jean-Baptiste, 'I would be working here on my own.'

'You think they would not return?'

'Are you not amazed they have stayed at all?'

They are walking together in the late afternoon while the men are being fed. Having reached the cemetery's western limit, they turn and start back, walking by the shadow-line of the wall.

'What about the church?' asks the engineer.

'Mmm?'

'We can work in there. It will be cool.'

'Begin the destruction of the church?'

'I would need more men. Specialists. Not many.'

'It looks,' says Guillotin, pausing to regard it, the streaked black cliff of the church's west face, 'horribly solid.'

'Buildings are mostly air,' says the engineer, quoting the great Perronet. 'Air and empty space. And there is nothing in the world that cannot be reduced to its parts. With enough men you could turn the Palace of Versailles into rubble inside of a week.'

The more he thinks of it, the more convinced he is he has been thinking of it for a long time. He tries the idea on Armand.

'Oh, my beautiful church,' wails Armand, grinning broadly.

'It will mean the organ too,' says Jean-Baptiste.

'Naturally.'

'You don't object?'

'It is what I said to you before. The night we went painting. One does not resent the future or its agents.'

'And the future is good whatever it brings?'

'Yes,' says Armand, without a moment's hesitation.

'I do not believe that,' says Jean-Baptiste.

'Think of the light,' says Armand.

'The light?'

'The church of les Innocents has been hoarding shadows for five hundred years. You will free them. You will let in light and air. You will let in the sky. *That* is the future!'

'That,' says Jean-Baptiste, 'is a metaphor.'

'A metaphor? Where did you go to school?'

'Nogent-le-Rotrou.'

Dawn: he lies in bed frowning into the indeterminate space above him, trying to work out the best way to destroy a church. What exactly *did* Maître Perronet say on the subject? Did they cover demolition while Jean-Baptiste was at home in Bellême, helping to care for his father? If it stood out in a field somewhere, he would simply blow it up. God knows he could make enough black powder from all the potassium in the soil of the cemetery. But a church halfway up the rue Saint-Denis? In theory, of course, a building could be *imploded*: mined and brought down upon itself in a tidy cloud of dust and tumbling stone. In practice – well, he has never heard of a single successful instance. There was that case in Rome five, six years ago, some old basilica they wanted rid of in a hurry. Filled the crypts with barrels of gunpowder, laid the fuses, lit them, obliterated the basilica and most of the neighbouring tenement. Two hundred men, women and children blown to rags. Shook the windows of the Vatican. He cannot remember what became of the engineer. Does he work still? Did they hang him?

For les Innocents, he will need a more methodical, a more prosaic approach. Get the lead off, the tiles, cut rafters, purlins, drop them in. Make the church disappear like a slow forgetting.

Are the pillars solid or cored with rubble? And the foundations? This close to the river, the whole thing could be floating on mud.

He will need to speak to Manetti. And Jeanne. If the church is coming down, so is the house. And if the house is coming down, then he must, as he once promised, find them something new. The lead and tiles, carefully traded, should raise more than enough to provide for an old man and his granddaughter, provide for years.

And how is she, this girl whose rapist he put into her house to live with her? Guillotin tells him she has lost some of the sight in her left eye but is otherwise healing well. For himself, though it is almost two months now, he has been careful not to be alone with her. He remembers how she shrank from his touch the night she lay on the kitchen table. And he wants to leave it long enough so that when they are alone, Lecoeur will not sit bloody and leering at the side of them. Leave it much longer, however, and there may be another subject, equally difficult to ignore. Lisa Saget says Jeanne is with child, has said as much to Héloïse. It is not yet certain. There are some technical proofs to be established, and Jeanne herself has offered no confidences. Hard to think, however, that a woman like Lisa Saget could be mistaken. Does a child have any sense of the circumstances of its conception? There are plenty who think so.

He tilts his head to look at Héloïse, her softly piled hair on the bolster. At some hour of the night, she made little noises, uttered a dozen half-words out of a dream, a hurt, reproachful tone to them, but now she is in that pure last sleep before waking, her breathing no louder than if someone brushed a fingertip, to and fro, slowly on the linen.

Are the pillars solid or cored with rubble? And the foundations? Does the whole thing float on mud?

*　　*　　*

With Armand he walks down the rue de la Verrerie, the evening sun between their shoulder blades, their shadows rippling over the stones in front of them. From Verrerie onto Roi de Sicile, then Saint-Antoine, then five minutes walking towards the Bastille, a royal flag on one of the turrets, hanging limp. Down the narrow rue de Fourcy, past the walls of the convent and right again into the rue de Jardin . . . This is the district of Saint-Paul. There are stonemasons here: a blind man would know it. Armand and the engineer stop outside the open door of a workshop. Stone dust simmers in the warm air by the door. After the light of the streets, the inside of the workshop is ink-dark. Armand enters first, stumbles over a pallet, curses loudly. The sound of hammering stops. A heavyset man in an apron and white cap walks out of the ink to look at them. Every crease and bearing surface of his face has its dusting of stone.

'You are?' he asks.

'Baratte,' says Jean-Baptiste. 'Engineer at les Innocents. I am here for Master Sagnac. I sent word.'

'And I am the organist,' says Armand, making a little bow.

'From the cemetery, eh?'

'Yes.'

'I am Sagnac. Your letter said you were demolishing the church. That you needed masons.'

'A master. Four or five senior apprentices.'

'And labour?'

'I have labour.'

'Used to heights?'

'They are miners. Or were.'

Sagnac laughs. 'Then I'll bring some of my own,' he says. 'At least until yours find their wings.'

'As you wish.'

'I've heard the king himself is behind the project.'

'My orders come from the minister,' says Jean-Baptiste.

Sagnac nods. 'We all work for them one way or another, eh? You want me to get the green wood for the scaffolding? My contacts will be better than yours.'

'But everything at a good price,' says Armand, quickly. 'My friend here may have a country accent, but I am Paris and learnt my tricks at the Hôpital des Enfants-Trouvés.'

'You'll find me true enough,' says Sagnac. 'I will not cheat any poor foundlings.'

One of the mason's apprentices, a gangling boy dusted like his master, puts three stools outside the door and the three men sit and drink white wine and barter.

'I almost trust him,' says Armand as he and the engineer walk back to the cemetery together.

'He will know his work,' says Jean-Baptiste. 'And we will not pay him for what he does not do.'

'You're shaping up nicely,' says Armand.

'Thank you.'

'And you have heard the latest about Jeanne?'

On Monday morning, half past six, 10 June, Sagnac arrives with four senior apprentices: Poulet, Jullien, Boilly and Barass. There are also a dozen labouring men in jackets and little hats, some with tools in their belts. The engineer walks Sagnac around the site. They tap the walls, prod the earth, confer, prod and tap some more. They meet the sexton and Jeanne. One of the apprentices makes careful sketches of the church. The others look at the charnels, the bone walls, shake their heads. Look at the miners too – that ragged band of saints – with no attempt to hide their distaste.

'Well?' asks Jean-Baptiste.

'We'll put the scaffolding up this south wall to start with,' says Sagnac. 'What's that there?'

'The doctors' workshop.'

'The what?'

'It can go.'

'Right.'

'When does the wood arrive?'

'You can have the first of it tomorrow. And if your men know how to hammer in a nail, I can use them.'

Spars of green wood. A simple, repetitive geometry of squares and triangles spreading up the side of the church. It climbs fast. Each day the engineer climbs with it, soon climbs above the charnels, looks over the rue de la Ferronnerie, sees into the rue des Lombards, sees into first, second, then third-storey windows.

The miners are not as agile as the mason's men; they do not skip from beam to beam or lean back insouciantly into the summer air, one hand casually gripping a strut, but they betray no fear of heights. They lift, tie, hammer, outdo the others in strength of limb, in sheer doggedness, in the calm efficiency of their labouring. At eating times, the two groups keep themselves apart. The mason's men eat on the scaffolding, carry their food up there, look past their dangling boots at the miners, who, gathered below in their accustomed place, make a point of never looking up.

A week of shouting and the rattle of hammers and they reach the roof of the church. Jean-Baptiste climbs to join Sagnac.

'The air's a little better up here, eh?' says Sagnac, his broad backside perched on the parapet at the edge of the roof.

'If you say so,' says Jean-Baptiste. He can see the river. The roof of the Louvre. The flour mills on Montmartre.

'I suggest we break through in that gully,' says the mason, indicating. 'See what we've got.'

'Very well.'

'You want to keep the tiles?'

'As many as possible.'

'You'll need hoists, then.

'We have rope, chain, wheels.'

Sagnac nods. 'Your men work well enough for foreigners.'

'They're not all foreigners,' says Jean-Baptiste. 'But yes, they're good workers.'

'A hell of a job all the same,' says Sagnac, eyeing the young engineer, studying him as though, in the rareness of the air, he is seeing him for the first time.

In the church, the air is like standing water. Chill, stagnant. Having descended the scaffolding, the engineer goes inside with Armand and four of the miners. The mason is somewhere above the south transept. From the floor of the church nothing of the roof can be seen at all; everything must be imagined. They crane their necks, wait, rub their necks and look up again. A muffled thump brings a sudden creaking of invisible wings. The first blow is followed by a long series of them, two-second intervals.

'This should wake up Colbert,' says Armand.

'If he's here,' says Jean-Baptiste.

'Oh, he's here, all right.'

'What does he live on?'

'Wax. Liturgy. His own thumbs.'

A miner steps back, brushing something from his face. 'Dust coming down,' says Jean-Baptiste. 'Stand away a little.'

The thumping is less muffled now. There's a pause; then it

begins again, a double beat, harder to place. 'Are they right over us?' asks Armand.

'No, no. By that edge there. They'll try to come in between the rafters near the bottom of the gully.'

Something hits the flagstones. Not dust any more. More of it comes down, comes down with each strike of the hammers. Flakes of stone plaster, of rubble. Then something big, crashing down seven, eight metres ahead of them, smashing into fragments. The double beat shifts to a triple. Ba-ba-bang, ba-ba-bang, ba-ba-bang. Then half a minute of silence; then two strikes, very aimed and deliberate, as if they had discovered some unguarded place on the dragon's head, something yielding. Another large piece comes down. The party below retreat. In the black, the stared-at black above, something winks. A small white eye, small and almost too bright to gaze at.

'They're through!' says Armand. A flurry of strikes and the eye widens. A beam of swirling light cuts at a slant from roof to floor and breaks not on some gilded angel or plaster saint, but on the boot of a miner, who hops backwards as if it had burnt him.

Shyly they reach for it, the light, turn their hands in it. Another dozen blows from above and they can bathe their chests, then their whole bodies. Héloïse must see this, thinks the engineer. Héloïse, Jeanne . . . they must all see it.

'Below there!' shouts a voice. Sagnac. His head small as a coin.

The engineer steps into the light, peers up. 'We are here,' he calls. It is an odd sort of conversation. It is perhaps how Adam spoke to Jehovah. 'Any trouble?'

'Like breaking snail shells,' says Sagnac. ('Snail shells . . .' sings the echo.) 'Beams are rotten to the heart. Another twenty years it would have come down on its own!' The head disappears.

'I'm going to play,' says Armand, lacing his fingers and cracking the knuckles. ' A pair of these lads can pump for me.'

'Is this a time for *playing*?' asks Jean-Baptiste. Then, 'You are right. You have never been more so.'

A half-hour later, while Armand improvises on the organ, the engineer conducts a tour of the light. Héloïse squeezes his elbow. The sexton looks up, blinks his eyes like a prisoner trapped fifty years in some oubliette, some dank *cachot* like those said to exist in the fortress of the Bastille. Lisa wets her lips, opens her face like a flower.

Guillotin says softly, 'But this is philosophy.'

Jeanne begins to cry silently. She will not at first touch the light. Jean-Baptiste – it is the moment's permission – takes her hand. She does not flinch. He lifts it, and when the light strikes it, her skin – the skin of both their hands – seems surrounded with a fragile blue fire.

Over the following days a score of holes are punched in a line along the south wall. The air thickens with dust, but at night the dust settles or escapes. Beams of light spread out until separate shafts become a jagged fringe moving slowly north towards the rue aux Fers. By the end of the month light laps at the edge of the nave, streaks the choir, pools by the foot of the altar. How filthy everything below now appears! How much the place depended on its darkness! The pews – most so beetle-ridden they would be dangerous to sit upon – are heaped together in a great pile under the crossing. Now that the light is here, it's obvious that anything of value – monetary value – has been taken out already, officially or otherwise. With Armand, the engineer spends an hour searching for les Innocents' most celebrated relic, the stylite's toe bone in its box of iron, but there is no sign of it and something, some pantomime quality in his friend's searching, prompts Jean-Baptiste to ask him if he has, in fact, stolen it.

Armand agrees that he has. 'It was to raise funds for the hospital,' he says.

'Is that true?' asks Jean-Baptiste.

Armand shrugs.

A shout from above means something big is coming down – a sprocket, a wind-brace, an oaken hammer-beam spearing into the debris below. Or stone, something dislodged, then shattering on the flags like ordinance.

Half the miners work inside the church, wrecking. They have sledgehammers and picks and iron bars and bring, it seems, a certain sectarian relish to the business. The others work on the roof or man the hoists that lower parcels of salvaged tiles and folded lead. Jean-Baptiste starts to feel like an engineer again. Stone and dust and rotten wood are more than bearable after black earth and bones. And isn't there something addictive about destruction? Does it not satisfy some shadowy appetite, some boyish urge to swing a blunt tool at what is silently, stupidly there?

He writes to his mother: 'I am destroying a church!' He encloses the usual money, suggests – only half playfully – she might want to use it to visit Paris to see him, her son, sleeves rolled, face caked with dust, bringing a stone elephant to its knees. And perhaps the pastor would care to accompany her?

He scores out that last thought. Scores it out carefully.

Working in one of the side chapels, one of those made plain and secular by lightfall, he finishes the bookshelf. A free-standing structure of five shelves built with wood from the church, the backs and seats of pews mostly (those few the beetles had not visited), though at the top he fits a carved panel cut from the reredos behind the altar, little figures, apostles perhaps, or just examples of those bystanders who must always be standing at the fringes of miraculous or terrible events. Guests at the wedding in Canna, villagers watching the arrival of Herod's soldiers. Héloïse fills three of the shelves with books she already owns. An afternoon with Ysbeau down by the river – the pair of them genteel, forgetful – fills most of the fourth, the new books all good editions, not those for fifteen sous that fall apart in your hands.

About the city, these days of high summer, black paint and fresh graffiti.

Next to the church of Sainte-Marie on the rue Saint-Antoine: 'BECHE WILL EAT A BISHOP AND SPIT OUT HIS BONES. A CARDINAL FOR DESSERT.'

On the quai de l'Horloge, below the Conciergerie. Painted from a boat? 'M. BECHE WILL DROWN THE RICH IN THE SWEAT OF THE POOR!'

On a wall opposite the Company of the Indies: 'BECHE HAS SEEN YOUR CRIMES! THE BILL IS ON ITS WAY.'

On the parapet – left side going south – of the Pont au Change: 'BLOOD-SUCKING LORDS! M. BECHE WILL ORPHAN YOUR CHILDREN!'

Spying graffiti, spying it before the authorities do, authorities now much keener to efface such sentiments, becomes a type of sport. People exchange new sightings with each other, casually, good-humouredly, though also with a certain questioning seriousness. For what if he exists, this Bêche? What if one day he does what is promised?

Jean-Baptiste, informed by Armand (who continues to deny all involvement), or Dr Guillotin, or Héloïse (who has not entirely given up her old free habit of threading the city's thoroughfares), or on one occasion by Marie, of the existence of these scrawlings, nods and shrugs. What are they to him? And yet he cannot deny a creeping interest in this Bêche, even sometimes falls into the fantasy that there is indeed, in some fetid *bâtiment* in the faubourg Saint-Antoine, a man with thoughts like knife blades, a philosopher assassin, the people's murderer. Would he oppose such a man? Betray him? Or would he follow him? Become, like him, implacable. Bloody and implacable . . . Then he wakes from the fantasy and turns back to his business. Stones and sweat and calling orders across the mazed air. What the world is doing, what it is readying itself for, he will attend to later. History must wait a little on les Innocents.

A vantage point, a good one, from which to view the progress at the church, is his old room at the back of the Monnards' house. He goes in there most days when he can, stands between the bed and the table looking out of the window. The air in the room is stifling. Heaven knows what it is like in Marie's room above. Across the bed, Ziguette's dresses lie slack as weed raked out of a river. Little golden moths, the type that crushed between thumb and finger, leave a smudge of gold on the skin, skip and flutter among the fabrics. Ragoût, remembering perhaps their old intimacy in the room, those winter nights he lay by the man's feet, sometimes joins the engineer, makes himself comfortable on the dresses, has the habit of climbing half inside them – a cat becoming a girl, a girl a cat.

One Sunday evening at the end of July, the two of them are there in the room, Ragoût nuzzling a muslin frill, Jean-Baptiste propped drowsily against the table, gazing out to the church. It has a pleasingly stricken look. A quarter of the roof is still to come down – they will need scaffolding on the rue aux Fers next week – and they have still not dug a trench deep enough to examine the foundations, but the progress is acceptable, more than acceptable, so much so that even Monsieur Lafosse on his last visit could not entirely conceal his approval, and stood a full minute at the drawing-room window before turning to say (a voice oiled with suspicion) that the minister would not be displeased to learn that his project at last went ahead as it should.

If the miners can be kept at it just a little longer! The miners, Sagnac. And himself, of course, himself particularly. He has at least managed to find somewhere for Jeanne and her grandfather. Four decent, well-lit rooms on the ground floor of a house on the rue Aubri Boucher, opposite the church of Saint-Josse, a few minutes' walk from the market. Convenient for a mother-to-be – convenient for a mother – for there is no longer any question but that Jeanne is with child. She has visibly thickened about the waist; her breasts are swelling. She looks younger. Young, shy, dreamy. Not unhappy. She smiles at them, speaks little, looks both ruined and saved, as perhaps Christ's mother once did. And always nearby, always contriving somehow to stand at the end of her shadow, that booted, bearded, carved peg of a man, Jan Block . . .

His face breaks in a yawn. He rubs the heels of his palms over his eyes, feels the body's steady, monotonous instruction, his heartbeat's heartbeat: this, this, this, this . . . When he opens his eyes, he finds himself looking not at the church but at the picture on the wall, the etching of the Rialto Bridge in Venice, its single high arch high enough to let shipping through whatever the tide, its twenty-four narrow houses with their lead roofs. The picture dangles from its nail just as it has since the night he first came to this house, but it is months since he last considered it, months since he considered those old ambitions it once stood as emblem for. Bridges and roads? Yes. Bridges and roads crossing France, leaping her rivers, stringing towns and villages like pearls along a thread, and then the whole enterprise, dependable, sweetly cambered, laid like a gift at the walls of some shining city. Himself on a horse, gangs of men behind. Men, horses, carts, stone. Clouds of dust. And he could do it now. It is perfectly credible. He does not doubt himself, does not feel any more he must, through some anxious exercise of the will, hold all the pieces of himself together or cease to exist. But are his ambitions what they were? Are they, for example, less ambitious? And if so, what has replaced them? Nothing heroic, it seems. Nothing to brag of. A desire to start again, more honestly. To test each idea in the light of experience. To stand as firmly as he can in the world's fabulous dirt; live among uncertainty, mess, beauty. Live bravely if possible. Bravery will be necessary, he has no doubt of that. The courage to act. The courage to refuse.

On the bed, the cat is watching him, placidly, out of the depths of its own mystery. He grins at it. 'You think, old friend, they'd have me back on the farm?' And then his gaze is drawn to the window again, to the church, where a black smoke is spiralling up through the broken roof. It rises, dips, swirls round the scaffolding, dips as low as the cemetery walls, then climbs again, circles in the clear air, circles, circles, circles, then swoops away towards the east. He shouts for Héloïse. She runs across the landing.

'They're going!' he cries. 'The flying . . . . Damn! Like flying mice.'

'What? Bats?'

'Yes, yes. Hundreds of them! Thousands!'

She looks to where he is pointing, squints, but there is nothing now above the church but night itself.

2

Mid-August; sunrise is twenty past six. Already the days are noticeably shorter. He folds back the shutters, studies the shadowed houses opposite, wonders if he is looked back at, cannot tell. In the bed behind him, Héloïse stirs. He asks if she wants a candle, if he should light one. There is no need, she says. She can see enough. Is there some water? He finds some for her, puts the glass into her hands, listens to her drink.

He is dressed only in the shirt he has slept in. He pulls on his breeches, tucks the shirt around his thighs, finds his stockings, sits on the end of the bed to draw them on. Héloïse is fetching down her peignoir from where it hangs overnight from an edge of the screen.

'A clear sky,' she says.

'Yes.'

'No rain for weeks.'

'No.'

'I should welcome a storm,' she says. 'Something to wash the streets.'

Their speaking is barely above a whisper. He is buttoning his breeches; she is about her business behind the screen. Across the street, the tops of the chimneypots show a thin, gold line of sunlight. Pink gold, orange gold.

'What if we went away?' he says.

'Away?'

'Two weeks.'

'You could do that?'

'I could ask Sagnac to take care of things here. The work is mostly his anyway.'

'And where would we go?'

'To Normandy. Bellême. It will be fresher there. Much fresher. And is it not time you met my mother?'

'Your mother?'

'Yes.'

'But what if something happened here?' asks Héloïse, coming out from behind the screen, dabbing her face with the orange water. 'What if your men would not work for Sagnac?'

'Why would they not work for him?'

'Perhaps they do not like him.'

'They do not need to like him. I do not know if they like me. And it would only be for a fortnight. Less, if you wished. Do you not want to meet my mother?'

'I do,' says Héloïse. 'But it scares me a little, that is all. We live . . . irregularly.'

He goes closer to her. He loves to see her face in the morning. 'She is kind,' he says, taking hold of her water-cold fingers.

'Kind?'

'Yes.'

She starts to laugh. He joins her, a soft, hissing sort of laughter stopped short by an improbably loud sneeze from the room below, the first eruption followed by a rapid series of others.

'Monsieur Monnard,' says Héloïse, 'has caught Marie's cold.'

'I had wondered,' says Jean-Baptiste, 'if Monnard . . . If he and Marie . . . Is that possible?'

'Last Saturday afternoon,' says Héloïse, 'I swear I heard the oddest noises coming from the attic.'

'Noises?'

'Like someone birching a child.'

'And now they have caught colds together,' says Jean-Baptiste.

'Poor Madame,' says Héloïse.

'She should go to Dauphiné,' says Jean-Baptiste. 'I do not know why she does not.'

'Or *she* could come back here.'

'What? Ziguette? You could sleep soundly with a murderer in the house?'

'She is not a murderer, Jean. But no, I could not be in the house with her. We would need to find somewhere else. For example, Lisa says there is a nice apartment near to her own on the rue des Ecouffes. A notary and his wife have been renting it, but they are to move in September.'

'That for example, eh?'

'A place of our own,' she says.

'We would have Armand for a neighbour.'

'We could survive that,' she says. 'Will you think on it, Jean?'

'I will,' he says.

'You promise?'

'I promise.'

They separate, go on with their dressing. He buttons his waist-coat by the window, looks down on the swaying canvas roof of a cart going by, one he knows well enough, M. Hulot et Fils, Déménageurs à la Noblesse.

And what was it prompted his sudden talk of going away? Light on a chimneypot? Was that it? Half the time, it seems, one does not know what one is thinking, what one wants. Yet the idea is not so impossible. Sagnac would likely be agreeable, at a price. As for the miners, why should they object so long as they receive what is due to them? He tries to imagine it, he and Héloïse carefree in the verdant country, walking in the woods, pillowing their backs against hayricks, spotting trout in the stream, his mother's blessing on their heads . . . It is not as easy to imagine as he would wish. Easier to see himself fretting the whole while about the cemetery, then finding some excuse to hurry back.

'I will buy oxtails today,' she says. 'Butcher Sanson has promised them to me. The men will like it. I will cook them with onions and garlic and tomatoes and thyme and a great deal of red wine, and perhaps some pig's trotters. A trotter is an excellent thing in such a stew. The sauce is much the richer for it. Did your mother cook trotters for you, Jean? Is it not a common food in Normandy? Jean . . . what are you doing?'

He has moved from the window to the dressing table, is sitting there gazing into the blue sheen of the mirror.

'Are you getting one of your headaches?' she asks, going to him and laying her hands gently either side of his head.

'No,' he says. 'Not at all.'

'I should not have mentioned Ziguette.'

'It does not matter.'

'But you are frowning.'

'I have just noticed,' he says, 'that I am starting to resemble old Dudo.'

'Dudo? Who is Dudo?'

He finds her eyes in the mirror, grins at her. 'One of our Baratte peasants,' he says. 'The purest.'

There is already a deal of heat in the sun. It pours down the rue aux Fers, pours into the bones of his head. At the far end of the street, he sees the dark forms of the laundry women beside the Italian fountain, the water flickering about them like bees. He opens the door of the cemetery: it is not locked and has not been so since the night with Lecoeur. A locked door did not serve him then, serve any of them. Certainly it did not serve Jeanne. As for those who might steal a little wood, let them have it. They are, anyway, he suspects, the type of people who disdain the use of doors.

On the roof of the church the masons and labour are already in place, though from the noise they are making it seems there is more banter than actual work going on up there. He scans the scaffolding, the parapets, but cannot see Sagnac. Perhaps he is not come yet and his apprentices are making the most of their freedom.

A dozen of the miners are seated in a circle on the ledge round the base of the preaching cross, boots in the long grass. Some are smoking their pipes, some chewing still on bread from their breakfasts. The engineer bids them a good morning, goes past them to the sexton's house. The kitchen in the house is bare now, stripped of all but what is necessary for feeding the men. In Lecoeur's old room, the cemetery's mouldering records have been crated, though what should be done with them, where they should be sent, who would want them, is far from clear. The big bed upstairs will be dismantled tomorrow or the next day, its parts carried to the rue Aubri Boucher. All cooking will be done in a new shelter at the western end of the cemetery. It will be too dangerous soon for anyone to be in the house. A toppled stone from the church would pierce the roof like a cannonball.

At the far end of the kitchen table, a shadow moves, becomes substantial. The sexton is there, his silver hair brushed and neatly tied but no coat or waistcoat, just an old, greyish shirt of unbleached lined unbuttoned to the middle of his chest. He has a hen's egg in his fingers and is carefully shelling it.

'You are nearly done here,' says the engineer.

Manetti nods, does not look up from his peeling.

'I suppose you will miss it? Something of it?'

'The garden,' says the sexton. 'We will not have a garden any more.'

'A garden? No.' From the kitchen window Jean-Baptiste can see the thin crescent of poppies down by the Flaselle tomb. And there are spikes of willow herb by the western charnel, and sorrel, whose leaves the men like to chew on. 'Is it true,' he asks, 'they once cut the grass for hay here? That they grazed animals?'

'It is true.'

'Jeanne told me that. When I first came. She had learnt all your old stories, monsieur.'

'There are some stories,' says the sexton, fixing Jean-Baptiste with a steady and not entirely friendly regard, 'you cannot tell to a child.'

The silence between them is broken by the doctor leaning in at the door. 'Glorious morning,' he says. 'A very good day to you both.' He beams at them. To Jean-Baptiste he says, 'You are coming to the church? And where is that beautiful woman you have unaccountably persuaded to live with you?'

'She will be here by and by,' says Jean-Baptiste.

Outside, walking together, the doctor says quietly, 'I fear that his mind is beginning to wander.'

'Manetti? He seemed clear enough to me.'

'Really?'

'And what of Jeanne?' asks Jean-Baptiste.

'My professional opinion?'

'Yes.'

'For her,' says the doctor, 'the only reality is the child. That above everything. When her time comes, I have offered myself as her accoucheur. No fee. I have designated myself a type of uncle.'

'You have a niece in Lyon, do you not?'

'My darling Charlotte. Yes.'

'And the other?'

'What?'

'The other Charlotte. What did you do with her?'

'Ah. She we had to burn, poor girl. She would not keep.'

They have walked round to the west door. It is not safe any more to enter into the south transept. Jean-Baptiste asks the doctor if there is something he wants from the church.

'Now that you mention it,' says Guillotin, 'there are a pair of small paintings in one of the chapels. You know the sort of thing. Hazy landscapes with something inoffensively religious in the distance. Cleaned up, I think they would look well on the wall of my consulting room. You don't object, do you?'

'You are very welcome to them. They would only end up on a fire.'

'A fire! My dear engineer, you have something of the Hun in you. Incinerating art indeed!'

Once inside the church, they go in single file. The sun has risen above the roof line and where the roof is gone, the light breaks in a shallow angle on the facing wall, picks out, with a kind of unnecessary perfection, the fluting of a pillar, the bevelled edge of an arch, a stone face staring goggle-eyed at some wonder in the middle air. Sagnac's labourers and apprentices continue to twitter like birds. Something falls, flickers through light into shadow and hits the piled pews with a noise of thunder.

The north aisle is vaulted still, sheltered, dark as the edge of a wood. When they come close, they can see Armand is there, Armand and two of the miners, Slabbart and Block, all three bent beside the organ, working at it with tools. When Armand stands and looks at Jean-Baptiste, there are tears on his cheeks.

'This wretched provincial,' he says to the doctor, jabbing a finger a coin's breadth from Jean-Baptiste's waistcoat, 'is making me butcher my own instrument.'

'Oh, monsieur,' says Guillotin sweetly, 'monsieur, monsieur! I have already accused him of being a Hun. And I am sure he will find some nice thing for you. Some recompense.'

'What are you doing to it?' asks Jean-Baptiste.

'Getting the keyboards out. If I have the keyboards, I can still practise.'

'You want the stops too?'

'You can get them?'

'Of course,' says Jean-Baptiste, reaching to touch the shaped end of the closest. He has learnt their names now, some of them. Cromorne, trompette, voix céleste, voix humaine. 'I would have kept it all if I could.'

'And done what with it?' asks Armand, whose fit of grief seems already to be passing. 'The thing has had its day. Had thousands of them. It dies with the church.'

'Then come and play at the house tonight,' says Jean-Baptiste. 'Bring Lisa. And we may persuade Jeanne and her grandfather to come. You are welcome too, Doctor.'

'A little concert?' asks Armand.

'If we like. I am sure the Monnards will have no objection.'

'The Monnards?' says Armand, giving the engineer his chisel.

'No. I am sure they will not. The Monnards will never object, eh? By the way, isn't it time you considered leaving them alone? They've had their punishment. Listen to Héloïse.'

For half an hour in the dusty cool of the north aisle, Jean-Baptiste works with Slabbart, loosening the keyboards, then starting on the panelling around the stops. The miner has a neat way with the tools and it's pleasant to work with him, but once it is clear Slabbart can finish the job perfectly well on his own, Jean-Baptiste skirts the walls to the west door and steps outside again. Ahead of him, above the charnels, the sun is full on the backs of the houses of the rue de la Lingerie, every window blind with light. Was it really about *punishing* the Monnards? Punishing them for having a mad daughter? He had not, knowingly, thought of it like that. On the contrary, his behaviour towards them – treating them with the barest possible civility, keeping Ziguette in her exile, doing exactly as he wished in their house, living there with Héloïse – all this had seemed entirely reasonable. Just and reasonable. Now it strikes him he has behaved towards them much as Lafosse has behaved towards him, much, perhaps, as the minister behaves towards Lafosse. He has set them at nought. He has humiliated them.

From the roof, more whoops and skirls. He steps away from the church's shadow, squints up at the scaffolding, decides he must go up there soon, talk to Sagnac. First, though, he will set the men to work shifting the bones for tonight's convoy. After that, they can begin the business of forcing out the iron grilles from the fronts of the bone attics. He has already examined most of them, seen (perched on a ladder) how weathered the stone is about the bars, how rusted the bars themselves are. Remove the grilles and they can simply rake the bones from the attics, a task immeasurably less arduous than carrying them, armful by armful, down the narrow, black stairways to the charnel archways. Rake them onto big tarpaulins, bundle them up, drag them to the door. An ass might be useful. A pair of them even more so. Would Louis Horatio Boyer-Duboisson deal in such humble creatures? Hard to believe he would not.

He gathers the men to him. They come at their own steady pace, shirtsleeves rolled, collars open. Brown necks, brown arms. Looking more like farmers now than miners. He starts – in his usual gnarled mix of French and Flemish – to give them their orders, starts to explain his thinking about the attics and the grilles. Out of the corner of his eye he sees Héloïse arriving from the market, two big straw bags in her hands. One of the men, Elay Wyntère, hurries to help her.

'Our dinner,' says the engineer. He smiles at them, then looks round at the church. A flurry of shouting has been followed by a strange silence. No one is hammering or sawing now. The labourers on the roof, those who can be seen from the ground, seem simply to be standing there, staring down into the church. The day ticks. Light falls, admirably and unchangingly. It is the miners who understand it first. What have the works at Valenciennes failed to teach them of such things? Disaster felt as a gentle vibration through the boots, the hush that follows. They run past the engineer, brush past him, run towards the church. After a moment of confusion, he runs behind them.

'What is it?' calls Héloïse. Then, 'Don't go in, Jean!'

He shouts back to her, 'Wait!'

'Jean-Baptiste!'

'*Wait!*'

Inside the church, the miners are already circling a spot midway between two pillars, south side of the nave. Jean-Baptiste has to pull hard at the arm of one, push the shoulder of another, raise his voice, bully his way through. And there on the ground in the midst of them is a sprawled man, a length of sawn beam on the stones nearby. Already there is a jagged halo of blood around his head, though the wound is not immediately obvious. Is it coming from his mouth? Is the wound on his face? One of the miners is crouching beside the stricken man. Jean-Baptiste kneels on the other side.

'Slabbart,' says the miner.

'Find Guillotin,' says Jean-Baptiste. 'Fetch him here.' The miner stands; the others open a passage for him. There is an urgency to their movements still, though it is nothing but the moment's vile excitement. Slabbart is quite obviously dead, must have died instantly, died mid-stride, perhaps starting to look up in answer to a warning, the wood striking him, spinning him.

'Who is it?' asks Armand, shoving through.

'Slabbart,' says Jean-Baptiste, then looks to the roof and the faces staring down from its edges. He gets to his feet. The cloth at the knees of his breeches, black with blood, sticks to his skin. He goes outside. He has gone slightly deaf. He sees Héloïse, but he does not clearly hear what she says to him. He starts to climb the scaffolding, uses ladders where he sees them, clambers the structure itself when he can find nothing else. Ascending, climbing with reckless haste, he receives oddly gimballed views of the streets beyond the cemetery walls – a big dray turning into the rue Troufoevache, a young woman in a straw hat strolling with an older woman, an open doorway on the rue des Lombards . . . When he reaches the upper walkway, the sky rears. It is as if he had climbed out of les Innocents' deepest pit, climbed panting to its surface. Ahead of him, shocked, scared-looking faces. Bodies braced. And over there, on the cat ladder above the nave, two faces stiff with the horror of what has happened, stiff with fear, stiff – to the engineer's mind – with guilt. He pulls himself onto the parapet and runs for them. They have perhaps never seen a man run like that on the top of a narrow wall fifty metres above the ground. His deafness has passed now. He can hear them all shouting. A clamour, like seabirds. The two on the roof begin to look demented. They slither along the tiles, closer and closer to the edge, the drop. Then Sagnac's voice rises above the others. 'Baratte! Baratte! You'll kill them! You'll fucking kill them!'

It's probably true. They will fall; someone will fall. Fall or be thrown. Is that what he intends? He pauses, looks back. Sagnac is making his way, clumsily, along the deep gutter between the roof and the parapet. The mason holds out his hands, palms up, that posture – placatory, defensive – one adopts when dealing with a person whose behaviour is entirely unpredictable. 'Just an accident,' he says. 'No one meant to do any harm. But I'll see they're punished for it. Their carelessness. You have my word on it. They'll learn their lesson.' He watches the engineer, watches him intently, then lowers his voice. 'For pity's sake, Baratte. One of them is my son-in-law.'

Now that things are stiller, Jean-Baptiste is aware of the heat of the sun. It's fierce up here, a heat redoubled by being reflected off the unstripped tiles. He cannot quite see down into the church where the others are, where Slabbart is. The son-in-law and his friend are pressed together like terrified children. He has no more interest in them. On the ground, the distant, shining ground, Héloïse and Jeanne stand, two slight figures, on the grass by the preaching cross. He nods to them, makes a little movement with his arm, a kind of wave, then steps into the gutter.

*   *   *

She is waiting for him near the bottom of the scaffolding and the first thing she does is hit him, a curious female punch with the underside of her fist against his shoulder. She does not say anything. She walks away from him, arms crossed tightly over her breasts. He goes back into the church. Guillotin has arrived. Slabbart has been turned onto his back. The wound – an oozing gash as long as a man's ring finger – is almost exactly where, on Jean-Baptiste's head, Ziguette cut him with the ruler, but the wood has gone deeper than the brass, has touched not just the bone but the tenderness below it, pierced it. Guillotin is careful to keep the toes of his shoes out of the blood. He looks at Jean-Baptiste, makes an almost imperceptible movement with his shoulders.

'Get a blanket,' says Jean-Baptiste to the miner beside him. 'Wrap his body. Carry it to the far chapel.' He gestures to the northwest corner, beyond the organ, then moves forward as if to crouch or kneel again next to the dead man, but hands are stopping him, turning him away, pressing him, ushering him out of the circle. Guillotin comes next, the same respectful strength. After him, Armand. The circle closes.

For a few seconds the expelled men, masters until a moment ago, stand awkwardly, silently, behind the miners' backs; then together they quit the church, step out into the harsh morning light.

'They have a faith?' asks Guillotin.

Jean-Baptiste shakes his head. His mouth is bone-dry, his heart still thudding from his climb. 'There was a church at the mines, but none of them went near it. Among the managers it was thought they believed in nothing.'

'There isn't a man in the world who does not believe in something,' says Guillotin.

'I need a drink,' says Armand.

'I will join you gladly,' says Guillotin. 'And you, my dear engineer, should certainly take a glass. Two or three might be best.'

'If I tell Lafosse of this,' says Jean-Baptiste, 'he'll order me to bury him here.'

'Like our old friend,' says Armand softly.

'Ah, you refer to Monsieur Lecoeur?' asks Guillotin, peering at them over the hook of his nose. 'I had wondered if he was here. Does Jeanne know of it?'

The engineer shakes his head, looks up at the church roof. What are they doing up there? Sitting? Talking? Waiting?

'The dead man could go to the cemetery at Clamart,' says Guillotin. 'It is where most of those who would have come to les Innocents are now sent. A perfectly decent place. Or there's the Protestant yard at Charenton. If that is more suitable.'

'I shall ask them,' says Jean-Baptiste. 'I will do as they wish.'

'I wept for my organ,' says Armand, 'but my eyes are dry now. I cannot think what sort of man that makes me.'

'There is no grief in the abstract,' says the doctor. 'What was he to you? To any of us? Ah, here come the women.' He rubs his hands, smiles at the approaching forms of Jeanne, Héloïse and Lisa Saget. 'They will know what to do,' he says. 'They will have *insights*.'

The women's insight – Lisa Saget's at least – is to prepare the food. Stewed oxtails. Twenty loaves of bread stale enough to soak up the gravy. Wine cooled in the charnels.

By one o'clock, when Lisa beats the saucepan, Sagnac has taken his men away, spirited them out quietly by the door to the rue de la Ferronnerie. The miners file from the church tamely enough. Nothing in their demeanours, the voices they use to each other, suggests anything is much amiss. They collect their tins, their utensils, queue up by the kitchen annexe, carry their food to the preaching cross, sit and eat.

'I am sorry, Jean,' says Héloïse to Jean-Baptiste, the pair of them standing privately in the shade of the sexton's house. 'But you frightened me so. I do not even think Ragoût would run along a wall like that.'

'Then I am sorry too,' he says. 'But to lose a man in such a manner . . .'

'It was an accident?'

'We shall never prove otherwise.'

'And what will you do with him?'

'Slabbart? He can stay in the church tonight, but we must do something tomorrow. In this heat . . .'

'He had family? A wife, perhaps? Children?'

'I don't know. I shall find out.'

'They could be given some money.'

'Money!'

'Money would help them, Jean. You have nothing else to give them.'

The long summer's afternoon. A great stillness over the cemetery, over the whole quarter. The sky high and pale, a few puffs of cloud, then the sun slipping towards the rue de la Lingerie, and as soon as it has dipped behind the ridges of the roofs, a stealthy, rousing coolness. A moon rises, fat and orange. The carts come from the quarry. The men, who have spent the greater part of the afternoon beside the openings of their tents, set to with no resentment, no undercurrent of complaints, though Jean-Baptiste halts the work as soon as he judges there are bones enough for the overseer at the Porte d'Enfer not to make sour remarks about idlers at the cemetery. The priests begin to march; the hems of their soutanes are white with dust. The singing is ragged, unenthused. Left to their own devices, they might tip every bone into the Seine. August in Paris is not a pious month.

It is close on eleven before Héloïse, Armand, Lisa and Jean-Baptiste leave the cemetery. Guillotin is long since gone, and Jeanne and her grandfather have not been invited to join them: it is late, and there can, of course, be no concert now, no jollity. Armand suggests they go to the Palais Royal, find some corner they can settle into, drink like soldiers. Héloïse protests. The Palais, its unrelenting gaiety, will embarrass them. They can drink in the house. The Monnards, in all likelihood, will have retired for the night, and there is brandy in the kitchen, a bottle of eau de vie upstairs. And wine, of course, Monsieur Monnard's wine. Should that not be enough?

They go to the house. In the hallway, the air is thick as felt, the whole house dark and quiet. The Monnards have indeed retired. Marie too, though she seems to have taken the brandy to bed with her, perhaps for her cold. Héloïse fetches the eau de vie. In the drawing room, Armand pours four glasses half-full of wine, then tops them up with the spirit. 'It might taste like wine now,' he says. 'Here's to Slabbart.' They raise their glasses, sip.

'What was his first name?' asks Héloïse.

'Joos,' says Jean-Baptiste.

'Joos,' repeats Héloïse softly.

'Play for us, Armand,' says Lisa.

Armand shakes his head. 'Music will add new emotions. We should stay with those we have.'

'But play anyway,' she says, touching his hand, stroking the ginger hairs on his fingers.

He shrugs, sits on the stool, shuffles through the music on the stand – those pieces Signor Bancolari tried to teach to Ziguette Monnard – then drops the music onto the floor and begins something slow from memory.

'It's out of tune already,' he says. 'Everything's at least a semi-tone flat.'

'It's perfect,' says Héloïse. 'Please don't stop.'

Jean-Baptiste has crossed to the window. He stands there, arms folded, looking out. As they only have a pair of candles in the room, both of them on the piano, he can see out without much difficulty. The moon is high now, almost directly overhead, smaller, no longer orange. Armand plays for several minutes, a piece more beautiful than sad but only just.

When it's over, Jean-Baptiste says, 'They've gone into the church.'

'The miners?' asks Héloïse.

'Yes.'

'A vigil,' says Armand.

'Forget about them a moment,' says Lisa. 'Let them be.'

Jean-Baptiste nods, joins the others by the piano.

Armand starts a new and livelier piece. 'You remember the play we saw?' he says. 'The servants and masters thing? This is the opera.'

He plays the overture, two or three of the arias. As he warned them, new emotions are being added. The atmosphere is shifting, becoming – in a troubled, melancholy, drink-inspired way – almost merry. When he pauses, the women applaud. He bows to them.

'They are still there,' says Jean-Baptiste, who, during the playing of the last aria, was unable to keep himself from drifting back to the window. 'They have light. Fire.'

Armand gets off the stool, joins him by the shutters. 'You cannot expect them to stand around in the dark,' he says.

'What do you know about them?' asks Jean-Baptiste quietly.

'The miners?'

'Yes.'

'As much and as little as you. They are mysterious as eels.'

'I want to see,' says Jean-Baptiste.

'See? See what?'

'He wants to see what they are doing,' says Héloïse. 'Are you worried, Jean?'

'But what harm *can* they be doing,' asks Lisa, 'in a ruined church in the middle of the night?'

'I have no idea,' says Jean-Baptiste, collecting his hat off the table. 'I shall not stay long.'

'Go with him,' says Lisa to Armand.

'As you wish, my dove,' says Armand, rolling his eyes. He does not have a hat. He follows the engineer out of the room. The women look at each other.

'What are we now?' asks Armand as they stop in the shadow of the cemetery door. 'Spies?'

'Hush,' says Jean-Baptiste. 'Hush.'

They move over the grass towards the church. A wash of light ripples on the panes of the window above the west door. Under the preaching cross, they pause again, watching and listening. Are those voices they can hear, voices rising past the beams of the roof?

'If we are going in,' whispers Armand, 'then for God's sake let's go.'

The west door, open all day, is shut now. Jean-Baptiste raises the latch, pushes the studded wood. Four steps take them the length of the vestibule. Then a second door, flaps of tattered leather over its hinges. It opens quietly enough, but immediately

326

there is the sense – the certainty – that whatever was happening inside the church has been suspended. A dozen points of light mark out where the miners are gathered around the pile of pews in the nave. The first man the engineer recognises is Jacques Everbout. Behind him – who's that? – Rave? Then Dagua on his left, Jorix, Agast. None of them move. All of them are watching, intensely watching, the new arrivals.

'Can you smell it?' whispers Armand.

'What?'

'Liquor. The place reeks of it.'

'It's ethanol,' says Jean-Baptiste. He nods to two of the big wicker-wrapped jars, their seals broken, that have been placed, side by side, next to the pews.

A movement . . . A man steps forward, emerges in almost leisurely fashion from behind the others. A figure in white. White shirt, white trousers, white cloth at his neck. He walks to within parlaying distance. His shadow, thrown forward by the taper of the man behind him, spills over the stone floor to the engineer's feet. It is the miner with the missing half-finger. The miner with the violet eyes. The only one Lecoeur did not know. Hoornweder? Lampsins? Whatever his name, there is no question but that he is the master here.

'It was not our intention,' begins Jean-Baptiste, finding his voice with difficulty, 'to disturb you. We saw lights. I was—'

'Is that Slabbart?' asks Armand. He points to a bundled form laid on a pew at the top of the heap.

The miner in white nods. 'Our brother was killed today,' he says. 'Tonight we will part with him.'

'Part?' asks Jean-Baptiste. 'Where will you take him?'

'He is where he needs to be,' says the miner. 'We will part with him here.' He looks at the engineer, waits patiently for him to

understand, to piece together the elements – the night, the ethanol, the wrapped corpse . . .

'You mean to burn him? Here?'

'This place killed him,' says the miner. 'Our brother. We have
done with it.'

'But if you burn him here, you will burn down the church!'
says Jean-Baptiste. 'You could burn down the whole quarter!'

'It is the church that will burn,' says the miner. 'We will guard
the rest.'

'Once the church is on fire, it will be beyond anyone's
control . . .'

'We know about fire,' says the other. 'It is a thing we understand well.'

'And what of Jeanne, and her grandfather?'

'I will fetch them out,' says another voice, a voice the engineer
immediately recognises. Jan Block.

'Listen to me,' says Jean-Baptiste, wildly seeking a new tone,
something better than mere incredulity. 'Your brother who died
today. I am sorry for it. Truly sorry. The mason has promised
that those whose carelessness caused the accident will be
punished. He has given me his word. There may even be . . . some
compensation.'

'What the mason does,' says the miner, 'is for the mason to
decide. It does not concern us.'

'By why this? Why risk everything?'

'You too take risks. You took a risk the night you went into the
charnel after Monsieur Lecoeur, did you not? Coming here
tonight, you have taken another.'

'Let them do it,' whispers Armand excitedly. 'You have no
authority here now. They will not listen to you. All that's over.'

The miner has turned away from them. He is issuing orders.

He is in his own tongue now. He does not raise his voice. More of the ethanol is brought from the chapel where the jars were stored. They break the seals, splash the liquid over the wood. For the final act, two of the miners scale the wood and spill the last half-jar over the wrapped body. When they come down, the miner in white gestures to them all to move further back. He speaks – a prayer or some ceremonial farewell – then takes a taper from the man at his side, steps towards the pews, stops, glances to the engineer, takes hold of a second taper and walks to him.

'Together,' he says.

'What?'

'Together.'

'Burn the church? Be party to this?'

'Take the damn taper,' says Armand, body poised as though ready – eager – to take it himself. 'Take it before he puts us up there along with poor Slabbart.'

It is not, in the end, so hard to do. He looks into the miner's eyes, the cool violet depths of them, sees no threat, no menace. Sees what, then? Reason? Philosophy? Madness? Or just himself, his own eyes, his own gaze reflected? He reaches for the taper. The moment he has it, the moment he closes it in his fist, every-thing assumes the character of a ritual, something rehearsed, something with its own irresistible progress. They walk together to the pyre, stand there with the wood rising over them to the height of six or seven men. The miner swings his taper first, lands it two-thirds of the way up the pile. Jean-Baptiste, after a brief and final hesitation, casts his to fall a little below it. For a while the tapers burn quietly, look almost as if they will gutter out, then a swirl of night air descending through the roof rouses them and blue flames spring from their tips, race up to gather round Slabbart's blanket, race down again, following the trails of ethanol, down to the stone floor, to the jars themselves, which fill on the instant with roiling blue flames.

What have I done? thinks Jean-Baptiste. *What have I done!* Yet he feels like laughing, feels he has set alight not just this hateful church but everything that ever oppressed him, grossly or subtly. Lafosse, the minister, the sneering Comte de S—. His own father. His own weakness and confusion . . .

They stand; they watch. The wood, baked for weeks in the summer sun, begins to snap and to flare. At moments, the air itself seems to burn. Then a small explosion – one of the jars? – and the miners are leaving, getting out quickly, quietly. No hullabaloo yet. The fire must be kept a secret until its hold is unbreakable. It will not be long.

Armand grips Jean-Baptiste's arm, jolts him out of his dreaming. 'Colbert,' he says.

'Colbert? We don't even know if he's here!'

'There are rooms,' says Armand. 'Behind the altar.'

They circle the burning pews, jump little streams of flickering ethanol, pass through the choir, pass the altar. On the right, two doors. The first opens into darkness: a small room quickly searched. The second door is locked. They beat at it, call the priest's name. They try shouldering it, kicking it.

'Use this!' shouts Armand, starting to topple a wooden statue, one of those pieces no one would trouble to steal, a clumsily shaped Joan of Arc, the saint in wooden armour, a cross held in front of her like a posy. At the second swing, she cracks the door. At the third, the door flies open.

'He's in here all right,' says Armand, recoiling. 'Stinks like a fox hole.'

The glow from the fire guides them, that and their groping hands. At the rear of the room is another door, also locked, leading out to the street. It's Jean-Baptiste who finds the priest, discerns a blur of curled white on a bed at the side of the room. The skin is clammy – some dew of fever or starvation on it – but it is not the skin of a dead man. They pick him up between them, carry him like a sack of oats. Out of the room, they can see he is entirely naked. His eyelids flutter, spring open. His expression is that of a man who has woken to find himself in the grip of devils hurrying him into a furnace.

Another explosion. The pews and beams of Slabbart's pyre are beginning to squirm in the heat. Slabbart himself is hidden behind walls of flame whose tops fling themselves closer and closer to the open sky. And parts of the choir have caught, the flames threading themselves through the narrow wooden arches. Twice, with the priest swinging between them, Armand and Jean-Baptiste jump broad lines of snaking fire. Heaven help them if the miners have barred the doors! But the doors are not barred, the way is free. Outside, they stagger as far as the tents. There is no one there. They drop Colbert in the grass, wipe their hands on the grass, rake the smoke out of their throats. Has the alarm been raised? The flames are clearly visible through the west window and must by now be equally so through the windows on the rue Saint-Denis.

Jean-Baptiste looks for the miner in white, but it's Block he sees first, Jan Block hurrying Jeanne and Manetti away from the house. He runs to them, pulling the house key from his pocket, thrusts the key into Block's hand. 'Take them to the rue de la Lingerie. Tell the others there to wait. You wait there too. If the fire comes close, lead them down to the river. You understand?'

Block nods.

Jeanne says, 'You must come too!'

'I will come soon,' says Jean-Baptiste. 'Go now.'

She holds out her fingers to him. For a second he clutches them. 'Forgive me,' he mutters, though he is not certain she has heard him. He watches them leave, the miner, the old man, the pregnant girl, watches their departing backs, the fragility of their diminishing forms. It is, he thinks, like the beginning and end of every story ever told.

How long since they threw the tapers? Ten minutes? Half an hour? Already the fire gives off an unearthly noise, groaning and thrumming and hissing. What fuels has it discovered in that place? What incendiary atmospheres were pooled in the crypts, waiting for a spark? Phlogiston! Each object's secret fire woken and released! In the west window, the diamond panes begin to shatter. Single shots at first, then a fusillade.

And at last a bell! The urgent, irregular tolling of a bell. From Saint-Josse? Saint-Merri? He runs to the door onto the rue aux Fers, out onto the street. Plenty of people here who needed no bell to warn them. They churn about in their bedclothes, some of them shouting, some grimacing in silence at the church, some apparently happy, as if at a carnival. He jostles in the crowd, rocks in it. Useful now to be a little taller than he is, but he can see the miner in white, see him standing on the rim of the Italian fountain, one hand on the head of a stone triton, the other gesturing, directing his fellows, his brothers. They look to him occasionally – musicians to the capellmeister – but seem to know already what they must do. They press back the crowd, ease them away from the walls, establish a cordon. Some of them carry tools, home-fashioned billhooks ready to haul down burning debris. Nothing haphazard about these preparations. Nothing slack in their discipline. *We know about fire*, the miner had said. *It is a thing we understand well.* Is this the first, the second, the third church they have burned? And what besides? A factory? A chateau?

Lit from below, the smoke pours in a dirty orange torrent through the church roof. He follows it upwards, sees how, as it rises, it bows towards the west ... An east wind! Not strong but strong enough perhaps. A wind from the west and the flames would skip the rue Saint-Denis with ease. Like this – if the wind stays true – the fire has only the cemetery in front of it. The cemetery, the charnels. The rue de la Lingerie too, of course, though surely it will not reach as far as that. And if it does? Can he trust Block to do what is necessary? He has greater faith in Héloïse and Lisa, cannot imagine what emergency would be beyond such women.

He looks round for Armand, but the man beside him in the crowd is not Armand. He is pointing into the sky, where sparks sized like doves are soaring past the tiles. Sparks that *are* doves – doves or pigeons or whatever blind things had clung to their roosts and now, frantic and ablaze, make pitiful attempts to escape. 'Human souls!' shouts the man. 'Human souls!' and he grips Jean-Baptiste's arm in a kind of ecstasy. The engineer scuffles free of him, elbows his way to the front, forces a passage between two of the miners (Rave and Rape, for whom he has, perhaps, not lost all authority, all prestige). He runs past the open cemetery door. He shouts for Armand, runs, shouts again more hoarsely, and at last receives an answer from somewhere near the sexton's house. They must have set a fire there too. The tiles are already smoking and a flame-light shivers behind one of the upstairs windows. Armand is jogging away from the house. There is light in his red hair. In his hands he is holding out some trophy. A glittering green bottle.

'I knew there was one left in there,' he says, pausing to hack the smoke from his lungs. 'Though if it had taken me much longer to find ...'

He tugs out the cork, takes a deep, amorous pull at the bottle. 'The party of the future,' he says. He wipes his lips, passes the bottle to Jean-Baptiste. The engineer takes it, drinks, then points over Armand's shoulder with the neck of the bottle. 'The grass is on fire,' he says.

It's true. Hundreds of burning tips of grass between the church and the preaching cross, each tip a delicate flower blooming only for a second or two. It is unexpectedly beautiful. Hard to look away from.

Behind them, in the fire's shadow, the old priest, nude as a worm, begins to howl.

3

A man – a man neither young nor old – sits in an anteroom in a wing of the Palace of Versailles. Other than for his own black shape in the furred green of the mirrors, he is alone. There is no elegant stranger this time on the narrow armchair opposite him. But it is October again, and there is symmetry enough in that.

At the end of the room the door to the minister's office is shut (symmetry in that too). In a while, if no yellow-eyed servant comes out to admit him, he will go and knock on it or scratch on it and deliver his report, the thirty neat, ribbon-bound pages he has on his lap detailing – with many necessary omissions – the destruction of the church and cemetery of les Saints-Innocents.

He smooths the cover of the report with the edge of his hand, brushes from it some imagined imperfection, a dust of ashes perhaps. Instructive how much can be enclosed in a document as cool, as innocuous-seeming as a folded napkin! A year of bones, grave-dirt, relentless work. Of mummified corpses and chanting priests. A year unlike any other he has lived. Will ever live? A year of rape, suicide, sudden death. Of friendship too. Of desire. Of love . . .

As for the fire that brought it to an end, that was matter for the report's last five pages and not, when he came to it, as hard to write as he had feared. A scatter of lies about how and when he discovered the fire, some spurious suppositions as to how it might have started. After that, a brief description of the fire itself, how it burned until daylight the following day, how it destroyed the church in the most complete way imaginable, destroyed the sexton's house, burnt down the charnels (with the exception of the west charnel), damaged two houses on the rue Saint-Denis and one on the rue de la Ferronnerie, though none of these beyond repair. There was – for what could it matter to the minister? – no need to recount how the grass the next day was like stems of black glass, shattering under their boots, how the preaching cross stretched like a blackened arm out of the wreckage, how the smoke hung over the quarter for two days before a great burst of rain dispersed it, or how the old priest was certified insane by Dr Guillotin and taken in a cab by the doctor himself to the Salpêtrière asylum.

About the miners, it was sufficient to record that their vigilance and courage had saved many properties from the flames, and that after the fire they worked admirably to clear the ground. Five weeks of knocking down what still stubbornly stood, of separating, where it was possible, bones from the tangle of burnt things that resembled them . . . Another nineteen convoys were sent to the quarry before he, the chief-of-works, declared that what was left could stay and become part of the hardcore under the new cobbles Mason Sagnac would be laying, the mason having been given formal charge of the site for its final transformation into the Marché des Innocents . . .

For that was what had been decided, decreed. A new market on the old man-eating earth of the cemetery! The hustle of small trade, the crying of wares where once there was only the priest's bell, the thud of the sexton's spade. And Jeanne will have a stall there. She has said she wishes to. Flowers, dried flowers and herbs, though first she must be delivered of what she carries in that big neat swelling that lifts her skirts from the ground. Guillotin still promises to be her accoucheur. He visits her often and recounts witty, fond stories of the domestic life at the apartment on the rue Aubri Boucher, the dreaming girl, the old gravedigger, the miner. In his last instalment he told them – Jean-Baptiste, Héloïse, Armand, Lisa – of the crib Jan Block had built, a little bed on half-moon rockers, the whole thing, according to the doctor, exquisitely done, a rose carved at the foot end, a little bird like a sparrow at the other.

Of the rest of them – Block's brethren – they have been gone some two weeks now, though where is uncertain. There was a last interview between Jean-Baptiste and the violet-eyed miner in the gardens behind Saint-Sepulcre, where the men had re-established their camp after the fire. It was dusk, a fine mist over the last of the summer flowers, the dahlias and geraniums. Jean-Baptiste had come with the men's money. The money was accepted – the pouch briefly weighed in the palm of the miner's hand – and then, with a slight softening of his habitual formality, the miner informed the engineer that they would be gone by the following morning.

To Valenciennes?

Not there.

But you will remain together?

We will.

Then I wish you . . . I am grateful to you. To you all.

337

A nod.

You are Hoornweder?

Lampsins.

Lampsins, then.

Moemus.

Moemus?

Sack, Tant, Oste, Slabbart . . .

The next morning, the gardens were empty. Nothing but some flattened grass to say anyone had been there at all. An odd, unsettling feeling not to have them there any more, there or anywhere. Héloïse accuses him of missing them, and though he laughs at her – how can one miss such people! – there is truth in what she says. He depended on them, depended heavily. Without their specific mix of steadiness and riot, would les Innocents not still be throwing its shadow over the rue Saint-Denis?

And who did he *not* depend upon? Who did he not burden in that way? The very report could not have been written without Héloïse sitting beside him, page by page, at the table in his old room. When a word he needed was a word still lost, she found it for him and, if necessary, wrote it out for him to copy (her hand taught to her by a lascivious cleric, his thrashed into him by the brothers of the Oratorian Order). Three days it took them, late September heat rolling through the open window, dry thunder over the city. Then, when it was done, they separated and packed their possessions. His own took a bare hour to put into his trunk. Héloïse, with her books and hats, her pins, slippers and ribbons, took an hour longer, though she might have done it more quickly if Marie had not been sitting on the bed in tears and needing every quarter-hour to be soothed with the prospect of Ziguette's return.

He does not intend to see Ziguette Monnard, not if it can be avoided. Unlikely, of course, she will want to see him – what could they possibly say to each other? – but she is not expected at the house until the end of the month and by then he will be with Héloïse in Bellême, and after that at their new apartment on the rue des Ecouffes.

And after that? What? The cemetery has stolen something out of him, some vitality he will need to restore before he is ready to go on. He should imitate the dead a while; or better still those seeds that lay so long asleep and undisturbed in the earth of the cemetery. Then, when he is ready – and when those ministerial livres and golden louis he has tucked away run dry – he might visit his old teacher, Perronet, ask for something decent, something small, something that does not place him at the disposal of men he does not respect, who do not respect him . . .

He looks at the door of the minister's office. Odd thing how all shut doors are not alike, how in their way they are expressive as human backs. This one tells him that were he to sit there until the end of time, it will not be opened, not unless he does it himself. He gets to his feet, pushes a lock of hair behind an ear, puts his hat under one arm, the report under the other, goes to the door, knocks twice, listens, then reaches for the cold, curved brass of the handles. The room is empty. Of course it is empty. The desk is there, the great desk, but there are no papers on it, no macaroon crumbs, no minister. Has anyone been here in weeks? Months? He lays the report, tidily, at the centre of the desk, shuts the door, goes through the anteroom into the corridor, turns, goes down a flight of stairs, walks the length of a second corridor, descends more stairs, and is stepping into the mouth of yet another broad, door-lined and feebly lit passage when he realises he is following the exact route he took the previous autumn, that he has retraced all his former confusions, has in some manner remembered how to be lost in precisely the same way. Behind *this* door the Polish gentlemen were playing at cards. Through *this* he saw the woman carried as if she were a type of boat. And here are the tightly winding service stairs down to where, a year ago, he found soldiers and laundry girls and boys in blue uniforms. Today, apart from a pair of small dogs asleep on a bench, he is alone.

He opens the door to the hall of lemon trees. The trees too are somewhere else. A few empty terracotta pots (each big enough for a man to hide in), some rolled lagging, a row of rakes and hoes and spades dangling from pegs along one wall . . . He crosses to the window, forces the damp frame, climbs onto the sill, onto the water barrel, drops down.

No clocks chime in the palace behind him – it is not quite the hour – but the path offers itself just as it did a year before, leads him to the arbour, the bench, the stone cupid above it. He sits. Why not? The afternoon is nearly warm and he does not expect to be a frequent visitor to the Palace of Versailles. The cupid's shadow falls across his knees. He closes his eyes, breathes, is briefly touched by a sense – utterly convincing – of the moment's eternity. Is he asleep? Small birds come to wake him. They gather round his feet, but he has nothing to give them. They come closer and closer, seem as if they might hop onto his hands; then, at the thud of heavy boots running on the path, they scatter into the air. A man appears, pauses by the arbour, regards Jean-Baptiste over the top of the scarf wrapped round his nose and mouth, speaks a few muffled, incomprehensible words and runs on. Some seconds later, another man is there, also masked, also running. Then a third, this one in the kind of leather hood with pointed snout house-searchers used to wear in times of plague. After a fourth has run by, Jean-Baptiste gets up to follow them. It s like following bees to their hive. Every time he comes to a fork in the path and is unsure which direction to choose, he has only to wait a moment for another man to run past him. For twenty minutes he plays this game, moves stop-start through a maze of high hedges until he comes to a gate in a brick wall and beyond it to a sanded courtyard. On the far side of the yard is a large stone shed, the sort of building one might imagine being used to house carriages of the better sort, the sort there are a great many of in Versailles.

He stands with his back to the bricks, watching. It is through the shed's open double doors that the masked men are disappearing. Some of them reappear, run out of the doors and lean panting against a wall before trudging back inside. One, a boy in blue, staggers to a horse trough, tears down his mask and vomits.

Clearly, it is the moment to leave. Clearly too, it will be impossible to leave without knowing what is in the shed. He goes closer, makes a circling, sidling approach to the doors, then passes into the gloom beyond them. In the centre of the shed, the shadowy tumult at its centre, masked men are hauling on ropes. Four gangs of men, four thick ropes. And attached to the end of the ropes something grey and vast and lonely. Each time the men pull and the grey mass is rocked, there is a chiming like the playing of a hundred small bells. Overseeing it all, this hauling, is a man on an upturned pail. He does not notice Jean-Baptiste, not until the engineer has crept close enough to finally understand what it is the men are trying to shift, the great death-swollen bulk of it in its nest of empty wine bottles, one dull eye big as a soup plate, the delicate veined edge of an ear, a curving yellow tusk . . . Then the overseer is raging at him, his breath puffing out the cloth over his mouth. He points to the dangling end of the nearest rope. He flails his arms: despair as fury. For several seconds Jean-Baptiste looks up at him, feels for him a terrible brotherly pity, a terrible brotherly disgust. Then he turns away from him, wipes the flies from his face and hurries back to that soft line at the edge of the shed where the light begins.

Author's Note

This is a work of the imagination, a work that combines the actual with the invented, though the church and cemetery of les Innocents certainly existed, much as they are described in the story. Today, of course, there is nothing to be seen of the cemetery except for a small square surrounded by restaurants and fast-food outlets near the underground shopping complex of les Halles. The old fountain, the Italian fountain, was moved in the nineteenth century to the middle of the square, where it serves as a meeting place, a place for weary shoppers to sit and rest. The bones from les Innocents may be viewed in the Catacombs of Paris, where later they were joined by the bones from other cemeteries: countless human remains arranged along thousands of metres of dripping walkways deep below the city traffic. Victims of the Terror that followed the destruction of les Innocents by a few years are also said to be hidden in the old workings of the quarry. Above the entrance to the catacombs, a carved inscription reads, '*Arrête! C'est ici l'Empire de la Mort.*'

The market established on the site of the cemetery, the Marché des Innocents, was closed for the last time in 1858.